Further Praise for *Between Us* by Batj

"Ultimately, [Batja] Mesquita's [*Between Us*] presents a powerful and stirring argument for viewing emotions and emotional episodes holistically. It's a call to action that will make our schools, businesses, and justice systems more equitable. Empathy, that much-lauded concept, is not enough. Mesquita argues that we must move past empathy, which entails imagining that we can project our own experiences onto someone else, and instead learn to compassionately ask questions and understand what a person's emotional response means to them based on their cultural background."
—Emily Cataneo, *Undark*

"The book contributes much to the discussion of the origins of emotions, presenting a dazzling array of cross-cultural studies interspersed with personal anecdotes about immigrants' struggles to reconcile diverse emotional and social worlds."
—Asifa Majid, *Science*

"The bounty of case studies captivates and makes a strong argument that social conditions have the power to dictate how one expresses and experiences emotions. The result is a bracing and bold appraisal of how feelings develop."
—*Publishers Weekly*, starred review

"An astute psychological study of emotions around the world."
—*Kirkus Reviews*

"Batja Mesquita's work on culture and emotion is highly original and highly important and has been influential in shaping the science of emotion. It's no surprise that *Between Us* is a groundbreaking book."
—Carol Dweck, author of *Mindset: The New Psychology of Success*

"With globalization increasing, time and again we face the unsettling realization that emotions unfurl so differently across cultural lines. Why is that? Now, from the world's leading expert on the science of culture and emotion, you'll find answers to this increasingly consequential question. Beyond an informative read, Batja Mesquita's *Between Us* is a fun read. Stemming from more than three decades of scientific study and immigrant experiences, *Between Us* presents engaging stories and evidence-based insights that both satisfy and fascinate. You'll come away understanding how and why emotion scientists got answers to the culture question so wrong for so long, as well as how Batja Mesquita and others ventured to get it right. *Between Us* is a must-read."

—Barbara L. Fredrickson, PhD, author of *Love 2.0:*
Creating Happiness and Health in Moments of Connection

"*Between Us* takes you on a grand tour of the world and the mind, led by one of the world's leading experts on emotion and culture. The journey is a joy, full of puzzles, insights, and empathy, and by the end you'll understand yourself, your culture, and our common yet variable humanity better."

—Jonathan Haidt, author of *The Righteous Mind:*
Why Good People Are Divided by Politics and Religion and
coauthor of *The Coddling of the American Mind:*
How Good Intentions and Bad Ideas Are Setting Up a Generation for Failure

"Emotions are cultural tools for surviving, thriving in, and even shaping the world we live in. *Between Us* is a vibrant tour de force from the preeminent scholar on cultural variation in emotions. Prepare to be astounded."

—Lisa Feldman Barrett, author of *How Emotions Are Made:*
The Secret Life of the Brain

"If you want to understand how the patterns of your emotional life emerge from the sociocultural context of your life, there is no better book to read than *Between Us*. It's a profound book. Yet, at its core, it is also a powerful humility, a humility that is an actual methodology for understanding and navigating cultural differences in emotion. It should be read by everyone from kindergarten teachers to corporate CEOs. And blessedly, it's a great read—accessible, delightful, and inspiring."

—Claude M. Steele, author of *Whistling Vivaldi:*
How Stereotypes Affect Us and What We Can Do

"In *Between Us*, acclaimed affective scientist Batja Mesquita compellingly shows that understanding people across cultural and racial divides requires immersing yourself in their diverse emotional realities. The book is a must-read for everyone working toward justice and inclusion—from law enforcement to schools to the workplace."

—Jennifer Eberhardt, Morris M. Doyle Centennial Professor of
Public Policy and professor of psychology at Stanford University, and
author of *Biased: Uncovering the Hidden Prejudice*
That Shapes What We See, Think, and Do

BETWEEN US

. . . .

HOW
CULTURES
CREATE
EMOTIONS

. . . .

BATJA MESQUITA

W. W. NORTON & COMPANY
Independent Publishers Since 1923

To Oliver and Zoë Zajonc

Copyright © 2022 by Batja Mesquita

All rights reserved
Printed in the United States of America
First published as a Norton paperback 2024

For information about permission to reproduce selections from this book, write to Permissions, W. W. Norton & Company, Inc., 500 Fifth Avenue, New York, NY 10110

For information about special discounts for bulk purchases, please contact W. W. Norton Special Sales at specialsales@wwnorton.com or 800-233-4830

Manufacturing by Lakeside Book Company
Book design by Lovedog Studio
Production manager: Devon Zahn

Library of Congress Cataloging-in-Publication Data

Names: Mesquita, Batja, author.
Title: Between us : how cultures create emotions / Batja Mesquita.
Description: First edition. | New York, NY : W. W. Norton & Company, [2022] | Includes bibliographical references and index.
Identifiers: LCCN 2022008952 | ISBN 9781324002444 (cloth) | ISBN 9781324002475 (epub)
Subjects: LCSH: Emotions—Cross-cultural studies. | Ethnopsychology.
Classification: LCC BF511 .M47 2022 | DDC 155.8—dc23/eng/20220513
LC record available at https://lccn.loc.gov/2022008952

ISBN 978-1-324-07473-1 pbk.

W. W. Norton & Company, Inc., 500 Fifth Avenue, New York, N.Y. 10110
www.wwnorton.com

W. W. Norton & Company Ltd., 15 Carlisle Street, London W1D 3BS

1 2 3 4 5 6 7 8 9 0

CONTENTS

PREFACE

I BECAME A PSYCHOLOGIST BECAUSE I WAS INTRIGUED BY what people felt. I wanted to understand their inner lives, what made them tick. Though it is hard to reconstruct my interest in emotions, it may have had something to do with my background. I am from a Dutch Jewish family and my parents survived the Holocaust in hiding. I was a "psychologically minded" child, always trying to figure out how my parents felt. Many of my parents' emotions were not rooted in the circumstances that I saw right in front of my eyes, but rather in events long (or perhaps not so long) past. Desperation was around the corner, and lurking under the surface was the hurt of rejection and discrimination. A small defiance on my side could meet with my parents' hurt feelings or desolation; my adolescent rebellion against the culture and religion was taken by my dad as disrespect, or worse, lack of love.

My coming to the topic of emotions was my sense that people keep deep inside themselves these emotions that can erupt. It was easy for me to see emotions as a property of the individual, because many of the ones I observed were stronger than warranted by the current situations or relationships. It was my childhood aspiration to become a psychiatrist or a clinical psychologist who could help individuals whose emotions made them suffer. And I imagined that I could change these emotions by changing the person from the inside.

My view of emotions as part of our deep inner lives was helped by a broader cultural focus on feelings. In Western, Educated, Industrialized, Rich, and Democratic (WEIRD) cultures, the 1960s and '70s were the time of emancipation of feelings. Authenticity and freedom of choice reigned supreme, and so it was important to know what you really felt and really wanted. What moved you inside should determine how you lived. Soul- and emotion-searching were utterly important, because they would help you to make better choices. The focus was inward. My generation in WEIRD cultures questioned institutional rules, and put personal feelings and preferences center stage. I have done my share of soul-searching, and in my younger years I focused inward to find my emotions.

During my thirty years as an emotion researcher, and through my encounters with different cultures, I have come to realize that many of the answers about emotions are not to be found in our insides, but importantly, in our social contexts. I started my studies at the University of Amsterdam with Professor Nico H. Frijda, who, right around the time we met, was finishing his book *The Emotions*, for which he became world-renowned. The book was a milestone in the psychology of emotions, and covered everything from neuroscience to philosophy. However, it did not cover culture very well. My graduate work under his supervision, which started in 1987, was meant to fill this gap. I surveyed the psychological, anthropological, sociological, and philosophical research on culture and emotions, and in 1992 published a synthesis (coauthored with Nico Frijda) that was one of the turning points for the study of culture and emotion in psychology. It helped to shift psychological research from an almost exclusive focus on universality to one also including cultural differences. It launched me as a cultural psychologist of emotions: I became interested in how culture and emotion "make each other up."

My research turned my focus outward, but so did my personal experience as a sojourner and an immigrant. In the early '90s, I left my comfort zone, and started living and working outside of the Netherlands. I lived in Italy for two years, worked as a psychological consultant for UNICEF in war-struck Bosnia for six months altogether, and ultimately moved to the United States. As a postdoctoral researcher,

I joined the Culture and Cognition Program, a hub of the emerging interdisciplinary field of cultural psychology at the University of Michigan, and later I became an assistant professor at Wake Forest University, in North Carolina. Roughly twenty years later, in 2007, I returned to Belgium, which from across the Atlantic may seem close to the Netherlands, but is culturally different enough. Exchanging my familiar Amsterdam for other places brought home in a more personal way that emotions are tied to culture. Being out of sync with my environment made apparent, time and again, that my emotions were not the universal default, as I had (implicitly) assumed until then. My emotions were created by my culture. They were good currency for interactions in my native context, they were beneficial to the kinds of relationships valued there, and they positioned me well in my Dutch culture, but they weren't as useful in these other environments. These experiences, too, turned my focus inside out: they led me to follow the trail from my emotions outward, to the values, goals, and practices of my social and cultural environment.

I also started to look outward for answers on emotions, because this is closer to how people from many other cultures think about emotions. I conducted research in Japan, Korea, Turkey, and Mexico, and among immigrants from these countries to the United States, the Netherlands, and Belgium. Many of these individuals talk about emotional events as taking place *between* people, while de-emphasizing inner feelings—another reason to follow emotion's tracks outwards.

IN *BETWEEN US*, I WILL introduce you to this radically different way of thinking about our emotions: one that ties them to our position in the world, our relationships with others, and to the sociocultural contexts in which we participate. I will show how your emotions engage you with, and make you part of, the communities in which you live. I will reveal how emotions are OURS as much as they are MINE.

Adopting this perspective on emotions will enrich your emotional life, adding to your understanding of your own and other people's emotions. It will make transparent the many ways in which our feelings make us social and connect us to others. An OURS perspective on emotions does not so much replace as supplement the MINE model of emotion.

Perhaps most important is that an OURS model of emotions provides us with tools to understand and navigate the differences in emotions across cultures, genders, generations, ethnic and racial groups, socioeconomic groups, and even between individuals with different personal histories (as was the case for my parents and me). This understanding may have never been more important than it is today. As our societies grow increasingly multicultural, our business organizations, schools, courtrooms, and health institutions are meeting points for different groups and cultures. Emotions are the currency of many of these intercultural encounters, yet we do not all use the same currency. Understanding how the emotions of each of us are tied to our respective social and cultural contexts will allow us to respectfully communicate about, and even resonate with, differences in emotions.

Between Us helps to resolve differences—even clashes—between individuals from different groups and cultures. Undeniably, my motivation to write this book was strengthened by growing nationalism, xenophobia, white supremacy, racism, and religious intolerance in the United States, Western Europe, and beyond. But more of an incentive still has been that people with the best intentions—people who *want* to be inclusive—believe that to say that people from other groups or cultures have different emotions is equivalent to denying their humanity. If you are one of these people, I hope to convince you of the opposite.

IN *BETWEEN US*, I'LL TAKE you on the journey that my research took me. I make you part of the discoveries that I made during my research on emotions in different cultures, sharing my findings and surprises, but also recounting my blind spots. Chapter 1 introduces me as a researcher and an immigrant, and situates my work in the field of emotion research. In chapter 2, I will delve into the differences between MINE and OURS emotions, contrasting contemporary Western constructions of emotions to the globally more common OURS model of emotions. I will show MINE and OURS constructions as "real": not just ways of talking about emotions, but ways of "doing emotions" (or "experiencing" them, if you will).

The next four chapters follow emotions outwards to their social and cultural context. In chapter 3, I will show how emotion socialization turns children into members of their specific cultures. Caregivers, helped by the wider social environment, teach their children from a very early age onwards to do their emotions in the right ways—that is, the ways that bring the shared goals and values. In chapters 4 and 5, I will illustrate how emotions run very different courses, depending on the specifics of the interactions, relationship, and cultures in which they play out. In contrast to popular belief, emotions such as *anger*, *shame*, *love*, or *happiness* do not have universal signatures. Instead, the experience and expression, the associated physiological and neural response patterns, and the moral connotations and social consequences are different across instances, individuals, interactions, relationships, and of course, cultures. Chapter 6 takes on emotion words. These words allow us to communicate about the reality shared by others in our group, community, or culture, but they may be less obvious tools for communicating across the boundaries of different social groups. Using an emotion word means to tie a specific instance to the collective experiences of the speakers of your language. It is another way in which your emotions make you part of your culture.

Once we understand how our emotions connect us to our communities, it becomes obvious why emotions may be a roadblock for interactions between people who were raised in different communities. Knowing others' realities takes more than merely translating a word. In chapter 7, I will introduce you to the research on learning a new culture's emotions. The good news is: It is possible. The potentially bad news is: It takes immigrant groups more than a generation to be indistinguishable from nonimmigrants. In the last chapter, I'll show how taking an OURS perspective can be a first step to communicating across dividing lines and finding common ground. While emotions may be a liability when we interact across cultures (or positions, class, religion, and so on), an OURS model makes sense of the *differences* in emotions, and provides a wonderful window on other cultures' values and priorities. Communicating about different ways of understanding and acting in the world—about our emotions—will humanize each of us, as it shows how we each are part and parcel of our social connections.

BETWEEN US

Chapter 1

. . . .

LOST IN
TRANSLATION

DO ALL HUMAN BEINGS HAVE EMOTIONS, JUST LIKE WE ALL
have noses or hands? Our noses have different shapes and sizes but
when all is said and done they help us breathe, and let us sniff and
smell the world around us. Our hands can be big or small, strong
or weak, but regardless they help us touch, grasp, hold, and carry.
Does the same hold for emotions? Is it true that emotions can *look*
different but, in the end, we all have the same emotions—that deep
inside, everybody is like yourself? It would mean that once you take
the time to get to know somebody, you will recognize and comprehend
the feelings of people who have different backgrounds, speak different
languages, come from other communities or cultures. But are other
people angry, happy, and scared, *just like you*? And are your feelings
just like theirs? I do not think so.

The first time I became aware that my emotions were not like those
of people from another culture was when I moved to the United States.
I was raised in the Netherlands, and, save some short ventures to other
European countries, that was where I had lived until I was about thirty
years old. In many ways, my transition was easy. My English was con-
versational when I first came to the States, because I had used it profes-
sionally. My American colleagues at the University of Michigan could
not have been nicer. The day I arrived, they welcomed me with a faculty dinner. One of them invited me to their Christmas family dinner;

others gave me small end-of-the year presents. Yet, I remember my first year in the United States as rocky. I often felt a little off.

In my own country, I was used to being a socially adept and emotionally intelligent person. But when I arrived at the University of Michigan in November 1993, I felt emotionally out of sync. My new colleagues were gracious, happy, and outgoing. They exchanged niceties with each other and with me. I liked their company, and I liked how they treated me. Yet, things were not easy, because I was unable to reciprocate in appropriate ways: I felt my own emotional shortcomings. In conversations, it did not come naturally to me to be outgoing and appreciative, to offer compliments, or to acknowledge effort and intention. I was not happy or grateful enough; not as happy as I clearly felt I ought to be, given the situation and given how everybody else was acting.

It bothered me that I was emotionally underperforming, and I was not merely *imagining* that I was. I simply was not smooth. One day, a colleague asked me if I would like to have lunch with her the next day. I replied in truth, "Tomorrow I can't." My new friend Michele Acker overheard the conversation, and coached me privately that I could have been more forthcoming and pleasant: "I would love to go out for lunch with you, can we do it some other time though? I already have plans for tomorrow. . . ." Instead, she said I sounded rude. Rude? It certainly wasn't what I meant to be; in my mind, it was simply informative.

I also had difficulty making sense of others' emotions. When Michele and I entered a drugstore, and she greeted the store clerk with an enthusiastic "How are *you*?," I asked her if she knew this woman (she did not). The interest she displayed in the clerk's well-being did not seem to fit the situation. The clerk, without missing a beat, reciprocated with a smooth, "Wonderful, and what about yourself?" I was left wondering what I had missed in this enthusiastic exchange between strangers.

Likewise, it was hard to gauge the state of my relationships: Did people like me? Did we have a friendship? I was not sure what the daily reassurances meant exactly, and I could not tell if people *really* cared for me. Or was that even a question to ask? One time, I had new friends over for dinner. The meal was tasty, and the conversation was engaged, and at times intimate. We had fun. It seemed to me that this could be the beginning of a real friendship; that is, until my guests left and thanked me for dinner. I felt crushed, because it had now dawned on me that we had failed to make a true connection. The way I was raised, where there is gratitude (i.e., *thanking* someone for dinner), there is no room for friendship. "Thank you for dinner" felt to me as an act of distancing, rather than an expression of appreciation. I would have liked my guests to say that they were looking forward to spending more time with me, that they really liked the evening together, or that they felt happy or connected to me.

Were these instances merely differences in conventions? Or were my emotions really different from the ones experienced by the American people I encountered? In later years, when relatives or friends from the Netherlands came visiting, I observed how they similarly failed to conform to the social and emotional norms. My dad, accepting a very generous dinner invitation by a local American friend, confirmed it was "fine" to come over for dinner on a Friday night during his stay—not only failing to use a superlative, but also failing to give proper recognition to the extraordinary effort on the part of his host. At that point his behavior made me cringe. Friends, coming to visit from the Netherlands, were friendly and jovial with waiters and shopkeepers, but without praising or thanking them. Their jokes and joviality emphasized the connections between everyone involved, but failed to mark the efforts of the service person.

More interesting yet: Dutch friends and relatives privately commented to me that the American emotions they encountered seemed "fake" or "exaggerated." My son's schoolteacher, Jill, exclaimed excitedly to my mom, who was visiting, how wonderful it was that my mom came to spend time with her grandchildren. She next asked my mom if she were enjoying herself. My mom confided to me that the teacher's excitement seemed "fake." On another occasion, my American colleagues praised the presentation of a visiting European scholar, saying it was brilliant. The European scholar shrugged and later told me that their praise "meant nothing," and that is was likely "fake," or "exaggerated." How else would a European explain the unfailing generosity, interest, praise, and enthusiasm that, in their eyes, many Americans display in circumstances that from a Dutch perspective do not "naturally" give rise to those emotions?

As individuals from these two Western, Educated, Industrialized, Rich, and Democratic (WEIRD) countries, the United States and the Netherlands, we experienced emotions that were different enough that each party judged the other's emotions negatively, as either "rude" or "fake." People from the same national cultures arguably would not have condemned them. The emotional differences at first seemed random to me, but over time they gained meaning.

I came to understand these emotional differences as serving divergent relationship goals. Pleasant emotions that would be appropriate in the Dutch context prioritize the connection between equals. At the end of a dinner party (or throughout, actually), you would emphasize the connectedness between people, referring to the get-together as *gezellig*, a Dutch word that has become a collector's item of culture-specific emotion words. Derived from the word for "friend" (*gezel*), *gezellig* describes both the physical circumstances—being snug in a warm and homely place surrounded by good friends (it is impossible to be *gezellig* alone)—and an emotional state of feeling "held" and "comfortable." Stressing the connection is prioritized over acknowledging the host's efforts. In U.S. contexts, by contrast, appropriate positive emotions often prioritize the articulation of the unique efforts, talents, and contributions of another person. Friends and acquaintances contribute to each other's sense of value or self-esteem. When my son's teacher told my mom she was being appreciated as a grandmother, she emphasized that my mom was special to her grandchildren—a domain over which she could claim to have some authority, being the teacher of my son. This is not fake at all: it is just a feeling that comes from a focus on those features or accomplishments that would give the other person reason to feel good about themselves. You are a wonderful grandmother, or in the case of my colleague, your talk had some really novel ideas ("is brilliant").

In America, you praise and acknowledge each other whenever you can. This too could not be more different from the Dutch context, where no one should feel or act any better than another person. No worse, but certainly no better either, than another person. My mom used to tell me "that acting normal would be crazy enough," usually in response to me doing something that—in her eyes—caught too much attention. Nobody should stand out. When I asked my mom, growing up, if she considered me pretty (hoping she would say yes, I guess), she answered: "I think you are about average." She was telling me the truth, both grounding me and providing "real connection" between her and me.

Differences also show in unpleasant emotions. In the Netherlands, one way of making connection is to speak your mind. It is no coincidence, then, that Dutch people are known to be direct. To be able to identify and express your true feelings (and opinions) is considered both a virtue and a sign of maturity. Rather than making you feel special, a true friend tells you what they feel (about you), whether positive or negative. They say, "You are wrong about that" or "This does not look good on you." You confront each other with the truth, even if the truth might not always be easy to hear. Being told the truth is always better than not, because it underlines that you *have* a relationship, as opposed to not. White lies are less acceptable in the Dutch context: They are not taken to mean that you protect your friend or relative, as they clearly are to some of my American friends. They rather have the meaning of keeping you out, and of breaking connection. True connection also means to share your innermost feelings, even if these do not paint you or the relationship in the most favorable light. Telling close others that you are jealous or angry, or even that you feel hurt by their behaviors, shows you as authentic, human, and willing to make connection. The Dutch virtue of "honest authenticity" is so ingrained in me that I have found myself on many occasions (politely) expressing my views or making revelations about my emotions to American colleagues, school teachers, and friends, only to realize how "Dutch" I had been. Who was asking for those opinions? Who wanted those revelations? (No one!) I often realized that there was no need to share my feelings and thoughts in an American context, only after having divulged my inner self. After decades of living in the United States I still catch myself doing it occasionally. My American friends punctuate my self-disclosure, as when my friend Ann Kring pointedly commented "Thank you for sharing" after I had explained in great detail some convoluted story about my emotions (how I had felt rejected when I thought I was not included in some breakfast arrangement, only to discover that people had tried to include me, and that I was mistaken). She did me a service, the Dutch way, by telling me that my self-disclosure was inappropriate, and in the process, socializing me.

Everybody's Emotions Are Cultured

Coming to America made me aware, for the first time, that my own emotions were not like those of people from this other culture. This would not have been remarkable, because it was the first time I had lived outside of the European continent—save for a small, but important detail: I had just spent the preceding six years studying cultural variations in emotions. Given that my research expertise was the role of culture in emotion, my failure to recognize my own emotions as cultured goes to show the difficulty of recognizing our own emotions as anything but natural. Even to me, as a cultural psychologist who studied emotions for a living, it was impossible to see my own emotions as products of culture, until I had a real stake in being part of another culture—until I became an immigrant to the United States.

Many an ethnographer has similarly run "into painful reminders, of [her] failure to share emotional assumptions or commitments" of the people with whom they stayed. The late anthropologist Jean Briggs described in her now-famous ethnography *Never in Anger* how, only after she got ostracized, she fully grasped how different (and inappropriate) her own emotions must have been from the perspective of the Utku Inuit, who lived in the Canadian Northwest Territories. It was then that she realized that her own emotions were cultured, and unfit to the Utku social relationships.

The Utku Inuit valued equanimity and generosity, and considered

anger to be dangerous. "Satan . . . takes people who get angry easily and puts them in a fiery place . . . We do not get angry here,"
her Inuit foster father informed Briggs. Getting angry was considered offensive, immoral even. It was hard for Briggs to suppress her
everyday irritations. She writes: "I was acutely aware of the high level
of control valued, and to a large extent achieved, by the Utku, and
with secret discomfort I contrasted that control with my own tem-
pery reactions to minor misfortunes. Though my reactions were well
within the boundaries set by my own culture, in a Utku setting they
did not seem harmless." Briggs certainly tried to fit in, but to little avail: "The [Utku emotional] control was much greater than that
to which I was accustomed to discipline myself. . . . Discouragingly
often after hours, or even days, of calm, when I was congratulat-
ing myself on having finally achieved a semblance of proper equanimity, the suddenness or intensity of the feelings betrayed me." The
final blow to Briggs's position came when a group of *kaplunas* (white
men visiting the Inuit territory) broke one of the two boats that Utku
owned and asked to borrow the remaining one. Briggs describes this
episode in her book: "I exploded. Unsmilingly and in a cold voice I
told the kapluna leader a variety of things I thought he should know:
that if they borrowed the second canoe we would be without a fishing boat; that if this boat was also damaged we would be in a very
difficult position. . . ." Her litany was longer, but she ended claiming
that the owner of the boat did not wish to lend it. The Inuit owner
of the boat looked dismayed all along, but when Briggs asked him
to confirm, he responded in a voice that was "unusually loud": "Let
him have his will!" The incident had dire consequences, as Briggs
was ostracized for three months during the second year of her field
trip. Although nobody had entered her tent for a few days, Briggs
did not realize that she was ostracized until she read a letter by one
of her hosts to an Utku liaison at the mainland that read: Jean "is a
liar. She lied to the kaplunas. She gets angry very easily. She ought
not to be studying Eskimo's. She is very annoying, because she scolds
and one is tempted to scold her. Because she is so annoying, we wish
more and more that she would leave." At first Briggs had not noticed

the changes in her hosts' behavior, but her book carefully paints a portrait of her stay with the Utku that resonates with the idea that "To understand another emotional world is an often painful process of self-discovery as well."

Though never ostracized myself, my own experiences of emotional misfit have helped me to see that my emotions are not the default, no more logical or authentic than the emotions I observe in other cultures. Abandoning the assumption that my own emotions are the universal default has been a first step to better appreciate how others' emotions are different. It helps me keep an open mind.

My Scientific Journey

My quest to understand cultural differences in emotions began in the late 1980s. I was a graduate student at the University of Amsterdam, the Netherlands, and my advisor was the internationally renowned emotion psychologist Nico H. Frijda. We wondered at the time: Would emotions in different cultures be different in any way at all?

At that time, psychological research had been geared towards finding a small set of emotions that were "hard-wired." The thinking was that these emotions were the result of evolution, as they had improved the chances for survival for our ancestors, and might still be beneficial. Anger might have evolved because it serves individuals to defend themselves against competitors; fear because it helped our ancestors, or may still help us to escape from danger; and happiness because it helped us to seek out, and stay or move close to what seems good for us—the source of happiness. And so, in psychology, the search was on for these universal emotions.

No part of this search for universality has sparked the imagination as much as did studies on the face. Paul Ekman and Wallace Friesen popularized this research in their 1975 book *Unmasking the Face*. They proposed that six emotions—*anger, fear, disgust, surprise, happiness, sadness*—could be read from the face (see figure 1.1). "When people look at someone's face and think that person is afraid, are they wrong

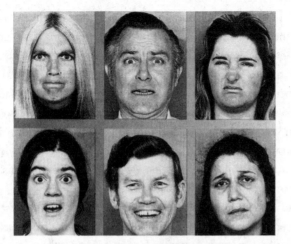

FIGURE 1.1 Ekman's facial expressions
(Image courtesy of Paul Ekman Group, LLC)

or right?" Ekman and Friesen wondered. And their answer was that, on average, people are right about the emotion: they can read emotions from the face. To be sure, the face was thought to be merely a signal of an emotion, not the emotion itself.

To prove that emotions were *biologically given*, and not culturally learned, Ekman and Friesen extended the scope of their research to include other cultures, some of which were remote from their own. They reasoned that *if* people who had never been exposed to Western faces before still recognized the same emotions, this could not have been the result of something they had learned. "When someone is angry," they asked, "will we see the same expression in his face regardless of his race, culture, or language?" And their answer sounded loud and clear: " . . . scientific investigations have conclusively settled this question, showing that the facial appearance of at least some emotions . . . is indeed universal, although there are some cultural differences in when these expressions are shown." They go on to conclude: "The universal feature is the distinctive appearance of the face of each of the primary emotions. But people in various cultures differ in what they have been taught about managing or controlling their facial expressions of emotion." Ekman and Friesen granted that the social and cultural norms for emotion *expression* could be different, or some-times, the *precise situations* that gave rise to emotions. They acknowl-edged that the emotional lives around the world *looked* different, but they attributed these differences to processes peripheral to the emo-tions themselves. Emotions themselves were universal, and faces were "windows to the soul"—the universal emotions being in the soul, or its modern version, the brain. The original research started with six facial configurations, but later research based on the same methods of rec-ognition has claimed several other "so-called" basic emotions: *shame, embarrassment,* and *pride* among them.

There is now a lot of evidence that these findings of universal "emo-tion recognition" are an artefact of the methods that were used, and I will describe some newer work on face perception in later chapters. For now, I want to note what is most puzzling about the emotion recog-nition paradigm: it actually never examined "emotions" or "emotional experience." Research participants matched a still face with an emo-tion word that they selected from a list. These words were translations of each other in different languages, but the meaning of these words across different languages and cultures was not subject to investigation in these studies. So, even if people in different cultures match the same still faces to translations of emotion words, what it means to "have that emotion"—and whether it meant the same across cultures—was altogether unclear.

Around the time, I started my emotion research, psychologists were approaching the universality question from a different angle, by exam-ining the words for emotion. Why study these words? The idea was if we were to find words for *anger, fear, sadness,* and *happiness* everywhere, this could be a sign that language "cuts nature at its joints."

When you ask respondents to give an example of an "emotion," psychologists asked, which *emotions* come to mind? In U.S. research, *happiness, anger, sadness, fear,* and *love* emerged most (as well as first). These were the best exemplars of the category of emotions. Note the overlap with Ekman and Friesen's basic emotions; except for *love,* all these concepts had been found to have a unique facial signal.

Another question psychologists asked themselves was which emotions were central to the emotion domain. If there are better and worse "exemplars" of emotions, which ones are the better—or the central—ones? In one study, respondents were asked to sort emotion words in piles—as many piles as they wanted. The researchers examined the content of these piles, and found that the common denominators of the piles overlapped with the "best exemplars" of the category of emotion from earlier research: U.S. samples sorted 135 emotion words into piles corresponded to *happiness, anger, sadness, fear,* and *love*. For example, the *anger* pile consisted of such words as "aggravation," "irritation," "annoyance," "grumpiness," "frustration," "anger," "rage," "scorn," and "spite": a total of twenty-nine words. The *love* pile had words such as "adoration," "affect," "love," and "lust": a total of sixteen words.

In another study, Chinese participants were asked to do the same task. They sorted 110 words, judged to be good examples of emotions in a previous study with Chinese participants, into piles. Four of the Chinese piles overlapped with the U.S. American piles; they could be interpreted as *happiness, anger, sadness,* and *fear*. These piles were not identical to their U.S. counterparts, but they were similar enough in meaning. For instance, the Chinese *anger* pile counted words for "dislike" and "anger," but also consisted of some unique words, such "rage from shame" and "sadness/resentment." Occasionally, emotion words cross-culturally found themselves in different piles: "rejection" was part of *anger* in China, but part of *sadness* in the U.S. More importantly, there were some unique Chinese piles as well. The Chinese lacked a separate pile for *positive love* (positive love was part of happiness), but had two emotion categories on the negative-valence side that the U.S. data did not yield: one for *shame* and one for *sad love*. Still, the cross-cultural overlap between the piles was impressive. And, moreover, the piles that both cultural groups had in common corresponded to facial expressions that were believed to be universally recognized. It strengthened the field's belief that, deep down, we all have the same emotions.

It was against the background of Ekman's impressive work on faces and the work on emotion words that I started my quest for cultural differences. My first question was if *happiness, anger, sadness, fear,* and perhaps *love* and *shame,* were the most important emotion concepts across cultural contexts. I started my research close to home. Even at that time, Amsterdam was a multicultural city. We set out to study the emotions of three of largest cultural groups: Dutch-majority men and women, and men and women from two of the biggest minorized groups in the Netherlands: Surinamese and Turkish immigrants and their families. Surinam is a former colony of the Netherlands, and my Surinamese respondents were of African origin (from families of formerly enslaved people). My Turkish respondents were from families of guest workers who had come to the Netherlands in the '60s and '70s.

I used a method that had been introduced by others to examine the most important emotion concepts. My Dutch-majority, Surinamese-Dutch, and Turkish-Dutch respondents listed as many "emotions" as they possibly could within fifteen minutes. And I simply tallied how often certain emotion categories were mentioned in each cultural group. Were *anger, fear, happiness,* and *sadness* among them? After all, if these were the hardwired emotions, you would expect that they would be universally among the emotion categories that come to mind first. Were *disgust* and *surprise*? Was *love*? As it turned out, the Surinamese and Turkish respondents were not "as good" at the task as the Dutch-majority respondents, or so I thought. They listed a great many words that, even if they were *related* to "emotions," did not refer to emotions proper (by which I meant at the time that these words failed to describe a phenomenon which happens "on the inside" of the person). Surinamese and Turkish respondents listed "laughing" (*lafu/gülmek*) more often than "happiness/joy" (*breti, presiri/mutluluk*), and "crying" (*kre/ağlamak*) more often than "sadness" (*sari/üzüntü*). Many of my Turkish respondents came up with "yelling" (*bağırmak*) and "helping" (*yardım*) as emotion words. I considered these words emotional behaviors, but not really emotions, and being the diligent researcher I was, I disregarded the words that did not refer to "real" emotions in the remainder of my research. Interestingly, even my Dutch-majority respondents occasionally had trouble understanding what emotions "really were." Many of them mentioned *gezellig* (the unique Dutch word that describes a social setting and a feeling at the same time) and *aggressief* ("aggressive").

And did I justify not including the emotional behaviors (e.g., crying, laughing) that my respondents in all cultural groups considered important emotions? No, not really. In retrospect, I realize that I was blindfolded by my own culturally informed ideas of what emotions were, and by a scientific consensus that originated in that same culture. I decided that my focus would be on emotions as phenomena which happen "inside" the person, and in doing so, I focused on emotion categories that coincided, to a large extent, with scholarly definitions of emotions as they exist in Western (mostly U.S.) science. In retrospect, I could have learned much more, had I been more aware of my own cultural assumptions.

There was more that I missed. Many of the Turkish participants in my word-listing study *did* list emotions proper—the phenomena that happen inside the person—but the emotions that were high up in their list barely overlapped with the basic emotions as psychology knew them. The emotions listed by most of the Turkish respondents were "love" (*sevgi/sevmek*) and "hate" (*nefret*); also prevalent were, in descending order of frequency, "pitying" (*acımak*), "desire/longing" (*hasret*), "sexual love" (*aşk*), and "sadness" (*üzüntü*). The most frequent emotion words looked nothing like the list of emotions that were recognized in the face: *anger, fear, disgust, surprise, happiness, sadness*. They showed only slightly more overlap (i.e., *love*) with the emotion concepts found to be basic by research on emotion concepts.

Despite the differences in what Turkish, and to some extent Dutch-majority and Surinamese-Dutch participants, considered to be emotions, in the next steps of my research I focused on five emotion concepts that had translations in each culture, that had maximal overlap with the basic emotions that Ekman and Friesen proposed, and that emerged as the best instance of emotions: *anger, sadness, happiness*, and *love*. I added *shame*, which was a basic-level category of emotions (i.e., a pile) in China. At the time, I attributed the absence of *shame* from the lists in other languages to its taboo status. *Anger, sadness, happiness, love*, and *shame* became the foci of my subsequent research.

I had some good reasons to focus on these emotions. First, the proposition that these were some universally important categories seemed reasonable enough: they were close to the ones established by other studies that asked laypeople in the United States, and even China, what the best instances of "emotion" were. Second, in including these concepts, my research findings could be tied to the existing emotion literature, which allowed for direct comparison and contrast with existing findings—another big advantage.

Yet in hindsight, I could have learned more about Turkish emotions if I had also pursued studying the emotion concepts that my Turkish participants most frequently mentioned: *hate*, *crying*, *pitying*, *desire*, and *sexual love*. I've learned in the course of my research career that it pays to take cultural differences in emotions seriously: The data are right. Never distrust your findings just because they are different from what you imagine to be true in your own culture. My current self would have told my past self to dig deeper into the finding of differences.

Just around the time that I had started my research into cultural differences in emotions, there was a resurgence of interest in the topic among anthropologists as well. Different from old-school anthropologists who described emotional events using their own culture's understanding of emotions, the new generation took an interest in how the people they studied themselves talked about emotions. No longer did these anthropologists start from the assumption of universal, pre-cultural, and natural emotions, and no longer did they rely "on empathy as a method and on the unquestioned use of American-English emotion concepts in descriptions of other cultures' emotional patterns." This new generation of ethnographers did not write on *anger*, as Jean Briggs had done, but instead paid close attention to indigenous emotion talk. They wanted to know: How did people from other cultures themselves talk about their own and others' emotions?

As it turned out, talking about our emotions as internal experiences is quite exceptional in the world. People in many cultures talk about emotions as more "public, social, and relational" than people do in contemporary Western cultural contexts. In cultures remote from our own in time or place, emotions are often seen as acts in the social and moral world. Take the emotions of a group of Egyptian Bedouins, as described in the late 1980s by the anthropologist Lila Abu-Lughod, a Palestinian-American anthropologist. Emotions among those Bedouins are the moral and social instruments of their culture of honor. Honor Bedouin-style is closely tied to "being strong"; therefore, any appearance of weakness is a vulnerability. And there are many situations in Bedouin life that render one vulnerable, such as the mere encounter of people higher in the hierarchy. Since men are considered higher up in the hierarchy than women, any time a woman meets a man, her (relative) weakness is highlighted and she becomes vulnerable to humiliation. *Hasham*, an all-important emotion, is tied to the Bedouin honor code: it occurs upon "the realization of vulnerability to humiliation," and consists of the modesty behaviors prompted in such situation. The emotion *hasham* is defined by its function in the social and moral order, not by its subjective feeling. Naturally, *hasham* may come with inner feelings (e.g., uncomfortable, shy, and ashamed), but inner feeling is not what defines it most.

I read many similar ethnographies in the late '80s, and I certainly picked up that people talked about emotions differently across cultures. I summarized the work of many ethnographies of emotion, such as the one by Abu-Lughod about *hasham*, in a review article on culture and emotion that I co-authored with my advisor Nico Frijda. Catherine Lutz, one of the main anthropologists studying emotion at the time, complimented me once on these summaries, saying they presented a fair description. And yet, it was not until later that I came to subscribe to the main implication of cultural differences in talk: that talking about emotions matters for how you do them. I still own some hard copies from the '80s and '90s with my own incredulous notes scribbled in the margin, notes such as "This is emotion talk, not emotions themselves" or "The fact that they do not talk about this emotion does not mean that these emotions do not exist." They bear witness to my early disbelief that the way people from these cultures far from my own talked about their emotions constituted a truth—their truth. I believed that, deep down, all people would turn out to have emotions just like mine. I no longer do.

Some ten years after I had first read anthropological accounts on emotions, a collaboration with fellow psychologist Mayumi Karasawa brought them to life. By that time, I lived in the United States, and psychology had started to discover the power of culture. Driven by opportunity mostly, many psychological studies had started to test if "fundamental" psychological processes could be replicated in East Asian cultures; most studies were done in Japan, but some comparative research looked towards China and Korea. The opportunity was created by East Asian researchers trained in the United States, who together with their American colleagues and advisors, started to challenge the textbook psychology in which they did not recognize themselves.

Karasawa was not one of them: she was trained in Japan. We met at a conference, and started to collaborate. She was an assistant professor in Japan at the time, and I was an assistant professor at Wake Forest University in North Carolina. Her questions were often uncomfortable because they challenged my training as an emotion scientist. How could I reconcile her questions with what we "clearly knew" as emotion psychologists?

We started our collaboration by organizing interviews on emotions. We asked participants to describe emotional events from the past, how they felt at the time, how intense their emotions were, what the events meant to them, how they and others present in the situation had acted, how the events and their feelings had evolved, and how the events changed their beliefs, relationships, and outlook on life. Similar interviews had turned out to be very informative during my emotion research with different cultural groups in Amsterdam (more on this in chapter 2), and for interviews in Japan and North Carolina, we decided to use a slightly adapted version of the interview schedule I had developed earlier. We first tried out the questions on three respondents in each of the cultural contexts.

The results of these pilot interviews in Japan returned several surprising findings—so surprising that I briefly suspected the questions had not been correctly translated (they had been!). The Japanese respondents in the pilot study had trouble answering the simple question about the "intensity" of their emotion. Karasawa insisted that there was a reason the Japanese participants weren't able to report the intensity of their emotions: the question did not make sense in Japan. For the time being, we ended up settling for another translation: "How *important* was the emotional event?" The Japanese respondents were okay with that translation, and I could forestall dealing with the inconvenience of Japanese not understanding the question of intensity. The intensity question was not the only issue for the Japanese respondents: they were equally puzzled by questions about the *consequences* of emotions, such as "Did your emotions change your beliefs about the other person?" Again, we settled for an alternative translation, asking: "Did the situation cause you to feel or think differently about the other person?" We received answers to those questions, also from our Japanese interviewees, and for the moment the "problem" had been silenced.

If I had been asked to articulate my views at that point, I would have told you that the *phenomena themselves*—the intensity of emotional feeling or the causal consequences of the emotions—were universal, but that Japanese language had difficulty expressing them. I would have told you that, of course, emotions influenced and changed beliefs, but that Japanese somehow did not allow for a literal translation. I believed the Japanese translations on which we settled were roundabout ways of expressing the same thing I had set out to measure in my original questions. In other words, I would have told you that these aspects of emotions themselves were natural or pre-cultural, but that my own language, which was English at that time, had a better way of expressing them than did Japanese. I would now disagree with my past self. The cultural differences go beyond semantics.

Collaborating with Mayumi Karasawa gave me not only a perspective on Japanese culture, but also a perspective on emotions in the Western cultures in which I had lived and was brought up. It drove home to me that emotions need not even be constructed as inner feelings within people. It was at that point that I came to fully understand how much the psychology of emotions is a science of and for WEIRD cultures. It defines emotions as inner states: essences that cause behavior and cognition. The questions I tried to ask my Japanese respondents came from that Western idea of emotions. The language of "intensity" applies to inner states, as does the idea that inner feelings cause (other) thoughts and feelings to change. My collaboration with Karasawa—and her fine sensibilities—helped me make sense of the anthropological writings of the late '80s that emotions may live "between" people rather than "within." When emotions are between people, when they are primarily seen as systems of social interaction, questions about their intensity and their causing individual thoughts and feelings may be moot. I had wanted to ask my Japanese respondents to describe their emotions in terms that made sense in my culture's conceptualization of emotions only.

A Working Definition of Emotions

I wrote this book to show how we can benefit from a careful consideration of cultural differences in emotions. Emotions are part and parcel of our social and cultural lives, and they are shaped by our cultures and communities. The differences in emotions go beyond merely superficial differences in manifestation—emotions do not only *look different*; the differences pertain to the very constituent processes and the course of emotions itself.

But wait. Is it possible that people across cultures have different emotions? Doesn't the human body prepare us for emotions? It does and it doesn't. Our brains and bodies do not come pre-wired for certain emotions, but they do prepare us each to have emotions that maximally serve us in our respective social and material lives—emotions that are adjusted to our communities and cultures. In the most up-to-date science, nature is no longer contrasted with nurture: it is equipped for nurture. Our brains are dynamically wired through our experiences in specific social and cultural contexts, and this brain plasticity allows us to live in particular communities. It is our nature to be social—to make meanings and act with others in our social world. The wiring of emotions happens through experience and learning. Different experiences make for different emotions, and so a firm definition that fits the wide range of variation is out of reach, at least for now. And yet, the outlines of the domain of interest are clear.

Emotions involve interruptions of life as usual: things happen that threaten or interfere with the person's expectations, plans, and goals. *Hasham* in the Egyptian Bedouin was the recognition of a threat to their honor—for instance, for women encountering men. *Hasham* also meant to do anything to restore honor—for instance, by trying to hide, or by looking down. Alternatively, things may go *exceptionally* well and be of high relevance to a person's expectations, plans, and goals. For instance, when I find myself perfectly in sync with others. *Gezellig* would describe an evening with friends when everybody seems attuned; it consists of further engaging with my friends, and settling where I am. What we call pleasant emotions usually involve the novel, the out-of-the-ordinary, the nearing of an ideal, the desired. Emotions are about important and personally meaningful events that are out of the ordinary, and they consist of meaning making as well as a reorientation, a preparation for action, or a realignment to those extraordinary events.

Where does this definition leave the body? *Everything* psychological comes with bodily changes. Furthermore, by definition, emotional events require adaptation, reorientation, preparation for action, and realignment in the face of out-of-the-ordinary and relevant events, and they will recruit many body processes, often acutely. When I am preparing to resist or fight, as in some instances of anger, my muscles tense and my jaws clench. These bodily changes may themselves become part of our conscious experience within an emotional situation. Whether these bodily changes become part of the emotional experience may depend on your culture. When someone cuts me in line, my tensing muscles may be part of how I experience my anger, but it is equally possible that my conscious experience foregrounds the social implications of the event. I may experience that they are bullying me, and I am not going to let them take advantage of me; my focus may not be on bodily changes at all (more on this in chapter 2). The example makes clear that this definition of emotions as meaning making, reorientation, preparation for action, or a realignment does not leave the body out, but implicates it. Yet, bodily changes may or may not be center stage to emotions as they play out in our everyday interactions.

Importantly, emotions are always meaningful in our relationships with other people. When I feel (or do!) *hasham* as a Bedouin woman, I expect the response will be favorable. I anticipate regaining my honor and dignity, because *hasham* shows I adopt the normative way of interpreting and responding to my potential breach of honor among Bedouins. When I feel (or do) *gezellig* in my Dutch environment, I assume the feeling to be shared and reciprocated. Actually, if it is not, the situation may abruptly stop being *gezellig*. When I *love* someone, at least in a U.S. American context, I want to share time and experiences with them, say "I love you" and hug, hold, and cuddle this person. The experience becomes a very different one if it is not reciprocated. In all cases, the emotions mark socially (in addition to personally) meaningful and important events, and involve the mutual alignment of people to each other.

Any community that provides a set of experiences, understandings of the world, relationship practices, moral sensitivities, and values and goals may shape the emotions we have as individuals. Different cohorts, different socioeconomic groups, different religions, different gender cultures, and even different family cultures may provide emotions with their meaning. I have highlighted the way my Dutch upbringing has shaped my emotions, and contrasted it to my experiences in several North American contexts. I could have chosen any other perspective which undoubtedly helped to shape my emotions as well—as a woman, from a middle-class background, a boomer, the daughter of (secular) Holocaust survivors, a mother, a wife, a friend, or a professor. Meaning and the context of action would have been shaped by any and all of them.

Are Emotions the Same Deep Down?

So, what about this idea, that once you take the time to get to know somebody from another culture, once you surpass the superficial differences, you will recognize the feelings of people from other cultures, and comprehend their emotions? Is it true that we are all the same when it comes to our feelings? No. And we do *not* necessarily find out how similar we are once we try to communicate, either. When people come to the conclusion that others have feelings just like them, that conclusion may stem from their own projections. Scientists have been as guilty of projection as laypeople. Many psychological and anthropological explanations for cultural differences in emotions come down to saying that people in other cultures mislabel or misattribute their feelings, or alternatively hide them—the assumption being that their "real" feelings are more like ours. As will become clear in later chapters, the very concern for the real, deep, inner feelings of an individual may itself be exclusive to WEIRD cultures.

When we communicate, we should do so in the expectation of finding differences, not only similarities. *We should also expect to have to explain our own emotions*, as they are neither natural nor universal. When I first presented this idea to a group of scholars a few years back, some responded with distress. How can we ever hope to connect to each other, if our emotions do not even line up? Their response made me aware of the idealism that often hides behind the assumption that emotions are universal. It is not only emotional imperialism that drives the projection of our own emotions onto those of individuals from other cultures. Equally important in a globalized world is the desire to build on emotions for a shared understanding of humanity.

There is no need for despair: It is possible to find humanity, even in the absence of universal feelings. It is possible to get familiar with the emotions of people from other cultures. Cultural differences in emotions have a logic: they become understandable once we know what people in these different contexts care about—that is, once we understand their norms, values, and goals. Most importantly, once you understand the emotions of people from other cultural groups, you will realize that your own emotions are not the universal default. Emotions—our own included—are as dependent on our culture as our clothes, our language, and the foods we feed our children.

The mosaic of emotional life is too complex to ever fully map in a go-to reference manual and this is certainly not the goal of this book. What I want to convey, instead, is that there is a logic to cultural differences in emotions. We can teach ourselves to expect differences in emotions, and to keep an open mind. By embracing emotional difference, we lay the groundwork for truly bridging cultures and finding common ground.

Chapter 2

· · · · · · ·

EMOTIONS:
MINE OR OURS?

THE PIXAR MOVIE *INSIDE OUT* (RELEASED IN 2015) CASTS FIVE emotions—Joy, Sadness, Fear, Disgust, and Anger—that live inside the mind of a little girl, Riley Anderson, and compete with each other to guide her actions. The movie is delightful, and delivers several wise lessons. Here I want to focus on its portrayal of emotions themselves: In each person's mind, the same emotions are hiding, awaiting an opportunity to act in their own typical ways. Each emotion is represented by its own little figurine, their essence, and with a set of fixed properties. Anger, for instance, is a red figurine. Regardless of the situation in which it occurs, and also regardless of the person in whom it manifests itself, anger is the "same thing." When Riley and her parents are in a heated conversation, a red anger figurine is activated in each of them. Anger is a Platonic essence that gets instantiated in the same way across different individuals and situations.

Inside Out closely captures emotions the way they are experienced and understood in many Western cultural contexts, as MINE emotions: Mental, INside the person, and Essentialist (the latter meaning that they always have the same properties). I pointed this out to my children, then teenagers, when my family went to see the movie. I suggested that the emotions might have looked very different had the movie been made by a non-Western film director or had Riley been anyone other than a white, middle-class American kid. I was accused

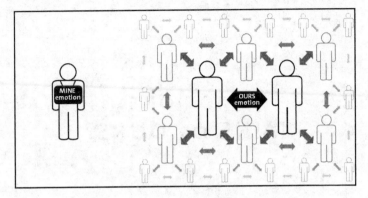

FIGURE 2.1 MINE vs. OURS model of emotion

of being a spoilsport: "Never go see a movie with a psychologist," my kids told me.

Short of presenting you a movie as appealing as *Inside Out*, this chapter will take you on an intellectual journey to discover this other type of understanding and doing emotions: emotions as OUtside the person, Relational, and Situated (the latter meaning that emotions take different shapes depending on the situation in which they take place). The OURS model of emotions prevails almost everywhere outside of WEIRD cultures. It is the way in which emotions are typically conceived in non-WEIRD cultures today, but also the way emotions were historically approached. Understanding emotions according to an OURS model is looking outward, rather than inward. It is more than "just" a way of talking about emotions, it is a way of doing.

INside or OUtside the Person?

My first encounter with OURS emotions in non-WEIRD communities occurred during my follow-up research in the Netherlands, the work described in chapter 1, with Surinamese- and Turkish-minority and Dutch-majority individuals. We interviewed new respondents from the three cultural groups about different emotional instances:

They had received admiration or compliments; they had been successful because of some achievement; they had been offended or not treated respectfully; they had been treated, or had treated someone else, unfairly or improperly. These types of situations had in previous studies been established as emotionally meaningful across the three cultural groups; we wanted to compare the associated emotional episodes in detail.

What struck me most was that emotions happened *between* people. Take Levent, a Turkish young man, who recalls receiving compliments and admiration because he had ended in the highest percentile of a nationally competitive entrance exam, giving him access to the best Turkish university. The pride that follows is entirely shared by his parents.

> [That I won the competition] was important to my mom. It was my mother's pride that she could use my success against lots of people. They asked her if they could see my university ID and without me knowing it, my mom had taken it to show them. My parents had invited all their relatives and neighbors over to their house to celebrate this success.

The emotional experience is between people because it ties Levent to his parents, gives them respectability or honor, while also challenging the honor of the distant relatives. Levent's emotions "live" in the social world:

> My [extended] family did not want me to compete . . . , as this would lower the chances of their own children to get into good programs. There was resentment [about me participating], and so my honor was challenged . . . I was forced to be competitive with the children of my relatives . . . My relatives asked me questions to humiliate me: "Are you going to finish this time?" They kissed me, and wished me well, but I knew that they privately thought: "Damn it, you won again" . . . After I won [the competition], many families

were prepared to offer me their daughters to marry. Of course, my self-esteem increased.

Clearly, the primary force of Levent's emotional experience lies in the social world, in the changing of relationships between people, not in the subjective, inner feeling. This was the picture emerging from many of the Turkish and Surinamese interviews: Emotions were described as shifts in relative status, honor, or power, or as status, honor, or power negotiations. They were not, or not in the first place, private individual feelings, but ways of relating between people.

Contrast this with Martin's account of a time when he received admiration or compliments. Martin is a Dutch-majority young man, who had given his final presentation for his master's in civil engineering, and this is where his emotion started:

> You feel like you have really done it. Yes [you wonder] how you have managed to do it . . . I felt like enormously relieved . . . Not really excited, but more like "It is finally over!" . . . I had set myself this deadline and it made me feel good that I made it this time . . . Afterwards I went out with some friends and relatives, seven people. We did not talk about my presentation. Yes, sure, they are friends of mine, so they know that this is important to me . . . They had come to listen to my presentation, of course, and so they did tell me that I did a good job. They also said "You are done now, it is over," that kind of things . . . Other than that, we just talked about other stuff . . . For a few months, when I would run into people, I would tell them. It gave me a good feeling. Each time it dawns on you a little more that you are really done with it.

The seat of Martin's emotion is primarily INside: the feeling of relief, and the feeling of joy (by whatever name) define his experience. Of course, he shares and celebrates his accomplishments with others. But the focus of the emotion is on his inner feelings.

A critic could object that Levent and Martin do not so much have different emotions, but rather different ways of talking about them. Is it not possible that Levent feels the same as Martin (e.g., enormously relieved, good), but is merely expressing these feelings in a different way? Does Levent talk about his family because this is the way in which Turkish people are *supposed* to talk about their emotions? How different from the involvement of Levent's social environment is the role of Martin's friends and the people he ran into in the weeks and months after his accomplishment? Back in the late '80s, you will recall from chapter 1, I myself might have been that critic, as I was writing in the margins of my colleagues' manuscripts: "This is emotion talk, not emotion itself."

And it's true, many emotional events have both MINE and OURS features. As the accounts of Levent and Martin show, emotional events often involve both a Mental and a Relational component, and as such take place both INside and OUtside the person. Yet, there is a real cultural difference in the locus of emotions as either inside, in feelings, internal sensations, and bodily symptoms, or outside, in actions, the relationships with other people, and the situation.

When your culture's model of emotions is MINE, this means that what counts as an emotion, what is important about the emotion, what will be noticed or remembered, and what is acted upon are internal feelings and bodily sensations. But when your culture's model of emotions is OURS, then relational acts and situational norms and requirements may count as emotions, they are noticed, remembered, and acted upon. A MINE cultural model translates into a very different way of doing emotions than an OURS cultural model. Anybody who is used to a MINE model will recognize that Levent's episode of pride is different than what they are used to. Why would we assume that Levent is just talking about his emotions a certain way because of social convention? Could we just as readily imagine Martin really having emotions like Levent, but talking about them the way he does because that is the cultural convention among the Dutch-majority people? Probably not.

Here is another example of OURS emotions from one of my Surinamese-Dutch respondents, an artist named Romeo. Romeo is reporting inconsiderate behavior by someone he was close to, a fellow artist. Central to Romeo's story is that this fellow artist tries to gain status and resources by denying them to him, Romeo. Romeo describes his own feeling as "bad, really unpleasant," but the core of the emotional episode is happening between people, as a contest of status and of access to resources:

> When a guy comes from an American university. He comes to the Netherlands . . . that guy has heard of me . . . he reaches my friend first, before he has the time to reach me. He has seen a book, a catalogue of my work, and he is really touched by it. [He says:] "I want this man, I want to see him." And this friend of mine, he knows my phone number, but he never gives it to him. Only after this guy returns to the United States, having bought some art by my friend to take home with him to the university, does my friend say to me: "I gave this guy your phone number, but you never answered the phone. Never, never." That guy was never able to reach me, because my friend had withheld my phone number.

Romeo's friend who, in Romeo's eyes, had been jealous of the attention and appreciation that came Romeo's way, had enhanced his own position by simultaneously lowering Romeo's. He had willfully tried to gain attention, appreciation, and opportunities *at Romeo's cost*.

Romeo's story is not unique. In fact, Surinamese respondents in my studies often reported how jealous friends and relatives sabotaged their status or opportunities. The emotional accounts by my Surinamese respondents are reminiscent of Glenn Adams's studies of enemyship in Ghana, and in fact the Surinamese respondents I interviewed were of West African descent. Adams, describing Ghana, notices the ubiquity of signs—on buses, on cars, on billboards—with text "about enemies in intimate spaces": "Your most intimate friends can turn out to be the most treacherous . . . actually at the helm of your downfall. . . . There is no man without an enemy," a well-known poem reads. At the root of an enemyship can be envy of your good fortune, hatred, discord, or simple malice, which in turn may be understood against the backdrop of local reality where people live in cramped quarters and are inescapably interdependent. In those circumstances, one may gain from bringing another person down, and thus gaining either resources or reputation relative to this other person. It is a zero-sum game.

Romeo eventually confirms his suspicions: his colleague had withheld Romeo's contact information from the art collector. Did Romeo confront his colleague, did he express his anger or frustration, or act it out in any way? No. Romeo recounts that he had long stopped trusting "his friend," yet he never confronted the fellow artist, because the balance of the scale had tipped back. Romeo gained the upper hand in the relationship with his fellow artist, as it was he (rather than his friend) who ended up in close contact with the art collector. Given Romeo's superior position in the relationship, no further action was needed. The state of the relationship dictated his actions or, in this case, inaction.

Here may be a good point to address what anthropologists have called "Stereotyping 101." When I talk about Surinamese respondents of West African descent or about Ghanians, I do not mean that all West Africans are similar, nor do I mean that culture is a homogenous, unchanging, and unchangeable entity. My friend, the anthropologist Kate Zaloom, pointed out to me that the way psychologists like me talk about cultures is essentialist. What I am trying to show is not "how Surinamese or Turkish or Ghanese *really are*," as though cultures are homogenous and unchanging, but rather that there is a wide range of different emotional experiences across the cultural universe. It is the contrast with "other cultures," however simplified, that made me aware of an OURS model of emotions. The contrast allows me to hold a mirror to MINE emotions, and suggest that the MINE model of emotions in WEIRD cultures is only one cultural variant. (I will return to the issue of cultural essentialism in later chapters.)

An OURS model of emotions is consequential for when you perceive an emotion in yourself and others. A now classic study showed how Minangkabau individuals in West Sumatra, Indonesia, constructed emotional experience as OUtside the person, in particular, as "between people." In 1986, Karl Heider, a well-known anthropologist, took along two of his psychology colleagues, Paul Ekman and Bob Levenson, to his remote field site. Levenson and Ekman intended to test their theory that a few basic emotions were hardwired and evolved through natural selection (as referred to in chapter 1): among these were *happiness, sadness, disgust, fear*, and *anger*. Basic emotions, so the hypothesis goes, are each characterized by specific brain patterns, a unique subjective feeling, a characteristic autonomic activity (e.g., heart rate, skin conductance, respiration), and also a unique (facial) signal. The different emotional modalities were thought to be strongly connected—so strongly, in fact, that if you activated one, say facial expressions, the others should automatically emerge also. Levenson and his colleagues sought the strongest test of their theory by trying to replicate a former study on a cultural site that was very different from the Western context: the Minangkabau are both matrilineal and Muslim, and lived their lives as agrarians.

Without ever mentioning the emotion words, respondents were coached to produce facial configurations that, to a Western eye, would make them look *angry* or *disgusted* (or any of the other "basic" emotions). For disgust, the instruction was: "(a) wrinkle your nose and let it open, (b) pull your lower lip down, and (c) move your tongue forward, but do not stick it out." Levenson and his colleagues wanted to know: Did a person who looked disgusted also have the associated autonomic arousal of "disgust," and did they feel disgusted? In the United States, the answer to both of these questions had been "yes": when trained actors and undergraduate college students looked disgusted, they also felt disgusted, and their autonomic arousal tended to be distinguishable from the pattern associated with different expressions.

And was their hypothesis confirmed? The answer is *no*. Even if we disregard the lower quality of both facial configurations and the physiological data produced in the Minangkabau group, the Minangkabau men did not report any emotions when asked "if any emotions, memories, or physical sensations had occurred during the facial configurations." As the Levenson team acknowledged, an important reason may have been that "the task [was] missing the critical element for emotional experience as defined by [the Minangkabau] culture, namely the meaningful involvement of another person." Heider himself had observed in his fieldwork that: "[i]n comparison with Americans, for whom the internal experience of emotion is very important, Minangkabau more commonly emphasize the external aspects of emotion, focusing on the implications of emotion for interpersonal interactions and relationships." Minankabau emphasized OURS emotions—emotions as relational acts between people. The test in isolation that had worked so well to elicit emotions in American respondents failed to cue emotional experience in the Minangkabau. Physiological and bodily markers may well play a role in Minangkabau emotional experience, but only if socially contextualized or shared.

Japanese emotions may be similarly shared with others. Yukiko Uchida, a professor of psychology at Kyoto University, watched the media coverage of the Athens 2004 Olympic Games in Japan and the United States and was struck by a difference in the ways Japanese and American athletes talked about their emotions. When Americans talked about their emotions, they located their emotions inside themselves, but when Japanese talked about their emotions, they often located them in relationships with others. A female soccer player who came back from the Olympics after the team had lost was asked by an interviewer:

Now you are back in Japan. How did other people react?

And she answered in response:

We came back without any medals. But when we arrived at Narita airport, many people told us "you did a good job"! I was so grateful for their encouragement, but at the same time, I really felt sorry we had lost the game. . . . I wished I could have met their expectations.

Uchida decided to study the phenomenon more systematically. She started by analyzing the very interviews that had inspired her, and counted how often and when Japanese and Americans mentioned emotions. These were broadcast interviews held right after the athletes had competed, and in that sense, very comparable moments for the Japanese and the American athletes. When interviewers asked the athletes directly how they felt, Japanese and American athletes did not differ in the number of the emotions they reported. But when the interviewer asked a question about other people (relatives, coaches, or friends), something Japanese interviewers did more than American interviewers, the Japanese but not the American athletes' responses contained emotions. For example, to the question "What kind of support has your family given you?" a Japanese athlete responded, "My family always supported me, such as calling me a lot. I am really *happy* to meet the expectations of my family." In contrast, an American athlete responded: "My family always supported me. My mother has always encouraged me." Though athletes in both cultures were able to talk about their emotions, Japanese reported many more emotions in the context of relationships. Could it just be a difference of convention? Do Japanese simply learn to talk about emotions when asked about their relationships with others?

In a separate study, Uchida and her colleagues showed Japanese and American college students pictures of winning athletes—either a Japanese or an American athlete. The athlete was pictured by themselves or with three teammates.

And when did the students perceive that the athlete felt more emotion? Japanese students saw "more emotion" when the Japanese athlete was pictured with their teammates; for American students, it was the other way around. For Japanese, emotions were OURS; for Americans, they were MINE.

Winning athletes arguably do not have a large range of emotions (they presumably won't be sad!), but in another study, we found that Japanese students see OURS and Western students MINE emotions for a wider range of emotions. In the early 2000s, Phoebe Ellsworth, one of my mentors at the University at Michigan, asked me to list the cultural topics that I considered worthy of studying by emotion psychologists. I had become interested in the notion that Japanese

FIGURE 2.2 Japanese and American athletes
(Copyright © 2008, American Psychological Association)

conceive of their emotions as between people, rather than within. Ellsworth had a very creative graduate student, Taka Masuda, now himself a professor at the University of Alberta. Masuda was of Japanese origin, and my idea resonated with him. We started to collaborate.

Masuda designed and drew a cartoonish task, based on the classic paradigm of emotional perception tasks to which I referred in chapter 1. The stimulus material for this perception task showed one of two boys: a Caucasian boy whom we called Jon and an Asian boy to whom we referred as Taro. In each picture, Jon/Taro was depicted as having one of three emotions: happiness, anger, or sadness. Jon/Taro was surrounded by other people who also showed an emotion. In some of the pictures, the surrounding people's emotions were the same as Jon's, but in many cases, they were different. We asked our participants, U.S. American and Japanese college students, what the middle person (Jon or Taro) was feeling.

FIGURE 2.3 Happy Jon/Taro with angry others

Different from the earlier study with athletes, our study examined *which* emotions the participants perceived, not just how many. Asked what Jon or Taro felt, our American college students gauged Jon's or Taro's expression exclusively. If Jon (Taro) looked happy, they rated him to be happy. If Jon (Taro) looked angry, they rated him as angry; etc. American students perceived MINE emotions: their ratings were tied to the expression of the middle person. The Japanese college students saw OURS emotions. They looked at the middle person's expression as well, but in contrast to our American participants, they *also* looked at the expressions of the other figures in the cartoon: The Japanese respondents rated Taro (or Jon) as happiest if the other people's expressions were happy as well. They judged Taro (Jon) to be less happy when the other people in the picture looked angry, but moreover, they judged Taro (Jon) to be angrier in that case. To Japanese, the emotion was inferred from all the people in the picture; the emotion was not just inside the person—in Taro or Jon—but also in the other people in the picture. In fact, an eye-tracking machine (a special device that tracked the gazes of our participants while they were judging what Jon or Taro felt), showed that Japanese spent some time looking back and forth from Jon to the people surrounding him, but Americans never took their eyes off the target person.

Taka Masuda went on to replicate this study, using pictures of real faces instead of cartoons. As before, North Americans (Canadian students this time) saw MINE emotions—they based their judgment on the facial expression of the person in the middle—but Japanese saw OURS emotions, referencing both the middle person's facial expression and the expressions of the four surrounding faces. Even though the instruction for North American and Japanese respondents alike was to judge the emotion of the target person—Jon or Taro—North Americans constructed his emotions as something happening within him, and separate from others, and Japanese as something happening between different people.

Mental or Relational: Feelings or Acts?

The idea that emotions are first and foremost mental states is not as ubiquitous as I once thought. In fact, talking about emotions primarily in terms of *feeling* appears to be rather exceptional, both historically and geographically. People in many cultures focus on emotions as (relational) acts when describing emotions. Historically, this seems to be the common way. Homer described Penelope as tossing and turning, and unable to sleep, rather than by the corresponding mental state (indecisive? tense?). And according to experts on ancient Greece, the Homeric Greeks generally preferred to represent emotions in terms of concrete, observable, behaviors, rather than as *inner* mental states.

We do not have to go as far back as the ancient Greeks to find that emotions were located in action as much as in feelings, and that there was no clear distinction between the two. Even early modern people in the United States (prior to the nineteenth century) did not think of anger or love as deep feelings, but would rather identify them with actions such as a "cold stare" or a "warm embrace." Emotions were closer to relational acts than to mental states.

Cultures remote from ours in place (rather than time) also appear to describe emotions as social acts rather than feelings. Anthropologist Edward Schieffelin describes the Kaluli, living in Papua New Guinea, as "expressively passionate" but reluctant to attribute feelings, motivations, or intentions to other people. Kaluli men would have full temper tantrums when they felt they had been wronged, or simply frustrated, by others. They would yell at, recriminate, and threaten each other. Expressive displays of emotion could count on the sympathy and support of bystanders. Yet, despite the openness of affective displays, informants would not answer questions about how another person feels. They would say, "I don't know." They would refrain from going beyond observations to infer feelings.

Likewise, the Samoans whose emotional lives were described by anthropologist Eleanor Ochs use "love" (*alofa*) when they describe acts of generosity: giving food and money and labor to others. Again, no reference made to the subjective feeling. Anthropologist Sulamith Heins Potter suggests that the members of a rural Chinese community affirmed their caring relationships by working. Work, and the suffering that is intrinsic to hard work, both symbolize love and affirm the relationship with another person. What counts is not so much the inner experience of sacrifice and working hard, but the "outward results, especially measurable ones." When Potter asked her informants about their emotional experience, they often responded, "How I feel doesn't matter." As she explains: "By this they mean that their feelings are not important for understanding those aspects of experience that they, themselves, regard as worthy of being understood." The Chinese of Potter's field site certainly recognized the existence of mental states, such as love, but what really counted was the readiness to sacrifice by work.

The skeptical reader may wonder if this is all just emotion *talk*: Aren't the real emotions—the mental states—hiding even if they are not the center piece of cultural discourse? Even in cultures where mental states are not discussed or referenced, wouldn't individuals still recognize the mental states from the face, the voice, or the body? Would they really see relational acts? Maria Gendron, now an assistant professor at Yale University, studied how Himba individuals perceived emotions in others. The Himba, a seminomadic pastoralist group in the mountainous northwestern region of Namibia, have hardly been exposed to the West and are preliterate. The study by Gendron and her colleagues, similar to other face studies, consisted of showing the Himba pictures of faces selected to reflect happiness, sadness, anger, fear, disgust, and neutral affect. Different from the regular face test, she asked her respondents to freely sort the thirty-six pictures (six for each "basic emotion" concept) in piles so that "each person in the pile experienced the same emotion." She then asked them to label each pile they had formed by simply asking: "What is in the pile?" The Himba did mention some emotion words to describe the piles, but more often they referred to them as acts: "They are all laughing," they would say, or "they are all looking at something," where they could have said "they are all happy" or "they are all afraid."

Gendron and her colleagues had U.S. American respondents—visitors to a Boston museum—perform the same task. The American respondents described their piles in terms of mental states. On average, the American respondents used more than twice as many feeling words (like "happiness") as the Himba, and the Himba used more than twice the number of action words (like "laughing") as the Americans. Gendron and her colleagues reasoned that if in fact the connections between faces and feelings had been strong and naturally evolved, then showing the Himba an angry or a disgusted expression should have led them to perceive anger or disgust in the other person. It did not: the Himba focused on acts rather than mental states. Why did they?

Interestingly, Gendron and her colleagues turned the question around, and asked: Why do U.S. Americans see mental states in those faces, when clearly what is depicted are facial behaviors? And her answer is (as mine would be) that contemporary Americans have learned to infer "mental states" from pictures of facial behavior. They have been asked, time and again, to focus on their own and other people's feelings. This has taught them to infer mental states from behaviors. To be sure, individuals in cultures emphasizing MINE emotions *can* read acts from faces, and individuals from cultures emphasizing OURS emotions *can* infer mental states from acts, but their respective inclination to do so is different. Yet, differences in focus on either MINE or OURS aspects of emotions are consequential: in this case, for reading what is going on in another person's face.

Rather than trying to explain why individuals in many other cultures talk about feelings more sparsely, I will turn the question around and ask why individuals in contemporary Western cultures put so much emphasis on the feeling aspect of emotions. The short answer is: We have learned to do so.

Starting in early childhood, children in Western contexts are taught to focus attention inwardly. Psychologist Qi Wang describes an exchange between a three-year-old boy, whom I will name George, and his mom. Mother and son discussed how George got mad on a shopping trip for Christmas presents. "Did you want to be there?" George's mom prompts him. "No," George remembers. "And what did you start to do?" his mom leads him along. "Hit," he answers. Prompted for more, he adds "scratch." Upon which George's mom brings the conversation to the source of his feelings: "Do you remember why you were so mad?" It does not come easy to George. He keeps adding behaviors: "Yell," he tries, and then "cry." George's mom brings the conversation back to his mental state: "Why were you so mad?" she asks again. George gets it now: "Because I just want to do whatever I want to do," he says. That answer seems to satisfy his mom: "You want to do whatever you want to do. I see." George's mom encourages him to focus on his feelings, and then helps him understand and relate to those feelings. This is the pattern that Wang finds time and again for U.S. American mothers that she studies: These mothers help their children figure out how their emotions relate to what they want or think. They help them to focus on, and articulate, their insides.

Not so for Chinese mothers in Qi Wang's studies: rather than helping their children understand the reason they feel in a certain way, these mothers focus on the social consequences of their behavior much more so than the American mothers. Take little Jiang's mom, who reminds her child of a time he got mad also. It was the night before, when Jiang started crying because his mom and grandma had not let him watch TV. Rather than dwelling on his feelings, Jiang's mom asks: "Do you know why we didn't let you watch TV?" Jiang promptly gives her the reason: "You are worried that my eyes would get hurt. I wanted to watch 'Chao-Tian-Men.' I was mad. I insisted on watching it." Jiang's mom responds not by relating to Jiang's feelings or preferences, but by reminding him of the social consequence of his protest: "So you got spanked, right?" she asks. Jiang nods in acknowledgment.

Many of the Chinese mothers in Qi Wang's research use the emotional exchange to point out to their children what the right and wrong behavior is in a way the American mothers in that same research did not. Jiang's mom points out that Jiang was wrong to protest her decision that he could not watch TV, and she reminds him of the negative social consequences. There are also mothers who use the exchange to point out the positive social consequences. Xuexue's mom, for instance, uses the conversation to underline the virtue of her three-year-old's emotional response—sadness in this case. "Xuexue is a good child. You understand that you made a mistake," she says, after Xuexue acknowledged she was "very sad" upon fighting with her sisters because they would not let her pull the grass (something that was forbidden). Where American mothers helped their child to notice and understand their own feelings, Chinese mothers encourage their children to understand their emotions as acts with social consequences. American caregiving practices facilitate looking inward to the MINE emotions, and Chinese lead the attention outwards towards OURS emotions.

The almost exclusive focus on emotional acts and their social consequences is certainly not limited to Chinese mothers. The anthropologist Andrew Beatty describes how on Java, Indonesia, adults use emotion words to describe how children should be acting, given the precise circumstances, rather than using these same words to refer to any feeling or mental state. For instance, they will use *isin*, "shame," to indicate to a small child that they are expected to show inhibited and polite behavior in the presence of strangers or elders. *Isin* is not used to describe feelings, not even emotional behaviors (or "expressions"), but rather a norm for behavior given a certain set of circumstances. Adults encourage children to align their emotional behaviors with the social norms; again, the attention is outwards to OURS emotions, not inward to private feelings.

It is safe to assume that, even after early childhood socialization, other people continue to play a role in focusing the individual's attention either inwards to their feelings or outwards to the consequences of their actions, depending on the culture. In research that I conducted with Belgian psychologist Bernard Rimé many years ago, we found that people across very different cultures share most of their emotional episodes with others. But what sharing meant was very different for Dutch and Turkish individuals in ways nicely illustrated by the earlier examples of

Martin and Levent. Martin talked to his friends and family about his emotions, and they in turn helped confirm, justify, and further articulate his feelings. Levent shared with his parents, who helped orchestrate the broader announcement and the celebration of his success, thus making sure that the wider social environment noticed Levent's success and paid proper dues. Social sharing helps to focus the emotion either inwards to MINE aspects of emotions, or outwards to OURS.

Research on health and wellbeing suggests that the focus inwards, on feelings, or outwards, on acts, may in the long term be a matter of life and death. In cultural contexts that emphasize a MINE model of emotions, people who *feel* happy tend to be healthier. But would this be true for individuals in cultures with OURS models of emotions? A group of researchers from the U.S. and Japan addressed precisely this question in a large-scale study including representative samples of Americans and Japanese in their midlife (average age between fifty-five and sixty). The findings of this study are succinctly summarized in its title: "Feeling Excited or Taking a Bath." The best predictor of physical health in the U.S. American sample were positive *feelings*; the best predictor in the Japanese sample were positive *behaviors or activities*. The details of the results need a bit more elaboration, because they show another difference in emotions that has been well established in cultural psychology: different kinds of positive emotions are valued in U.S. American and in East Asian contexts. Excitement is more valued in American than in East Asian cultural contexts; the reverse is true for calm emotions. With this in mind, the findings have some logic. In the U.S., the healthiest individuals were the ones who *experienced more positive feelings*, especially of the excited kind (e.g., enthusiastic); they slept better, had fewer physical limitations, and showed better values on some key health measures such as inflammation and body mass index. In Japan, the healthiest individuals were the ones who *engaged in positive activities*, especially of the calm kind (e.g., taking a bath). Calm *feelings* were much less important than activities for health in Japan. A lifelong focus inwards may make feelings the measure of all good in the U.S., whereas a lifelong focus outwards may make acts the measure in Japan. Feelings in the U.S. and activities in Japan become health indicators. An emphasis on either MINE or OURS emotions may come to embody different health trajectories, and contribute to longevity.

Essence or Situated: Inside Out or Outside In?

Bottling up your feelings is unhealthy. This notion is so powerful that one of my friends had to convince the social worker of a Dutch adoption agency that he and his wife were suitable parents for adoption, *despite the fact* they never argued. The social worker could not imagine that, in a healthy marriage, the partners would never be angry at each other—and if they were, at what cost had they been suppressing it? (The couple did end up convincing the agency that they had some minor conflicts and were allowed to adopt their son.) And of course you should cry when you are sad. When one of my friends could not stop crying after she found out her husband had had an affair, she was encouraged to "just let it out, it will be good for you." The English language is full of reminders: without "letting off steam," we know that "the pressure could build up," or "our feelings are pent up inside us."

The notion of "grief work," introduced in the early twentieth century by Sigmund Freud, is based on a similar idea that inner feelings need to come out and run their natural course. "Grief work" was seen as an indispensable part of recovery after trauma and loss, and consisted of giving way to negative feelings such as anger and sadness. Bottled up, these feelings would start interfering with a person's wellbeing and ability to lead a normal life: they might turn up when least desired, and paralyze or interfere with daily life. Freud's work has been the catalyst for the idea that suppression disrupts the natural flow of emotions, and is somehow harmful to the individual.

Freud's idea that emotions need to run their natural course has received some support from modern psychological research. A 2004 study with around 1,000 U.S. Americans found, for instance, that suppressors (i.e., individuals who did not give their emotions full rein) felt bad about themselves for being inauthentic and had a harder time experiencing closeness to others compared to non-suppressors; relatedly, suppressors had an impoverished social network. The researchers, psychologists Oliver John and James Gross, conclude from their study that suppressors' outer expression may be discrepant with their feelings, causing them to feel ingenuine or inauthentic. This inauthenticity may lead them to feel bad about themselves as well as alienate them from others in their social environment, to the detriment of close relationships.

Sociologist Arlie Hochschild's landmark book, *The Managed Heart*, first brought attention to a very similar problem for workers in the service industry. Hochschild explored two opposite ends of the continuum of "emotion labor." On one end, flight attendants were to be warm and caring with their customers. "Our smiles are not just painted on," proclaimed one airlines company, trying to sell not just the flight attendants' *smiles*, but their true feelings. As another company put it: "Our flight attendants' smiles will be more human than the phony smiles you're resigned to seeing on people who are paid to smile." On the other end, bill collectors enforced payments with their anger. In collection agencies, "[o]pen aggression was the official policy for wringing money out of debtors."

In both industries, companies worked hard to cultivate the emotions needed on the job. Strikingly, both industries targeted *feelings*, not just *displays* of emotion. Flight attendants were taught "to see the passenger as a potential friend, . . . and to be as understanding as one would be with a good friend." Bill collectors were taught to think of their customers as "loafers" and "cheats." The companies' understanding was that the best results were reached if emotions came from the inside out. Despite companies' best efforts, however, many a flight attendant could "not bring themselves to think of an airplane cabin as their living room full of personal guests [because] it seemed too much like a cabin full of 300 demanding strangers." And some bill collectors felt empathy rather than disdain for their debtors. While meeting the demands of the job at a superficial level, they would have "a sense of being phony or insincere," and ultimately fall victim to burnout.

Sounds right? That would be because a MINE model of emotions prevails in Western contexts. Having the emotions that are required by others or by the setting is thought to be demanding and unnatural in MINE contexts. It is quite the norm in contexts that favor an OURS model. Take the example of a Buddhist community in Northern Thailand. During her field trip in 2005, anthropologist Julia Cassaniti recorded the emotions of a family of an alcoholic thirty-three-year-old man named Sen. After a long period of disease, Sen was finally taken to the hospital, where the doctors found that he suffered from advanced liver disease, and was untreatable. Sen's family gathered around his bed, being "upset by the turn of events: Most had expected that he would eventually get help and be healthy again." Despite the general sense of devastation, Sen's relatives "crafted their emotions so that they could accept what had happened. . . . Sen's father and sister went to the temple to make offerings every morning. His sister, brother, relatives, and friends, at least at first, for the most part, displayed what seemed to be blank faces: faces that did not show emotion at all." Cassanti assures us that the blank faces of Sen's friends and family neither meant that they were indifferent, nor that they just faked it for others' benefit. Instead, she writes, they were working towards a state that they felt to be appropriate—to accept what had happened (*tham jai*), and to be calm (*jai yen*).

Acceptance is quite the opposite idea to "grief work." Where grief work makes sure that inner feelings are expressed, acceptance is the effect of becoming detached from these inner feelings. Julia Cassaniti tells us that family and friends who show distress when Sen was hospitalized (herself included) were kindly reminded by others to "not think about it" and "not talk about it." The Buddhist Thai community thought that talking and thinking about negative feelings would exacerbate them, and this was to be avoided at all cost. It was important to accept, be calm, and detach, rather than getting the grief out.

The Buddhist Thai practice of grief is reminiscent of the Utku Inuit stance towards anger: anger was unacceptable among the Inuit, and equanimity was valued instead. Briggs could not force her feelings, or so she felt—her inner feelings needed out. In contrast, her Inuit hosts managed to achieve the valued state of equanimity, even in the face of frustrated goals.

In a similar way, when Mayumi Karasawa and I conducted interviews with Japanese respondents, Hiroto, a Japanese man in his early fifties living in Tokyo, described his experiences as a member of the organizing committee for his high school reunion. He was in charge of inviting the alumni. At the committee meeting, Hiroto was told by another committee member, a woman, that he had not been doing a good enough job calling alumni and inviting them to the meeting. He felt "offended and annoyed." Yet when he elaborates on the incident during the interview, it becomes very clear that he does not act on these feelings. Instead, he tries to understand the perspective of his fellow committee member:

> She is the kind of person who is eager to do anything that is necessary for the organization. When I tried to call alumni, I often found that they had already been contacted by this other person. . . . She was worried about me, and she might have thought I was unreliable. She is a very strong person. Perhaps I am not that strong; I tend to worry that my phone calls will come at an inconvenient time, so I find it really hard to decide when to call these alumni. . . . She must have thought that she'd rather make those phone calls herself than asking me to do it.

Hiroto finds out that not only is he being criticized, but his critic had actually been doing his job. Hiroto is annoyed, he tells us, but he maintains harmony within the organizing committee; relational harmony is highly valued in Japanese cultural contexts. Perhaps Hiroto even suppresses his initial feelings of anger or annoyance; he does not say. But at any rate, he does what the situation requires from him: as a committee member he meets the social obligation of getting along and maintaining harmony.

Hiroto does what the majority of our fifty Japanese interviewees told us they did in emotional episodes of anger: they tried to understand the perspective of the other person (i.e., their fellow committee member), and simply adjusted. According to their own reports, they did nothing else, even if they felt strongly. "Doing nothing" was far more frequent among Japanese respondents in "anger" situations than any type of aggression or assertiveness, or even than moving away. Although accep-

tance was not the term Hiroto used for this, what his response has in
common with the Thai Buddhist family of Sen and with the Utku Inuit
hosts of anthropologist Jean Briggs is that they did what needed to be
done, and their feelings mostly followed. The emotion was outside in.

Another example from our interviews illustrates the outside-in emotions well. Chiemi, a twenty-year-old Japanese student who lives with
her grandparents, tells us she always tries to be home on time for dinner.
Recently though, she has joined an extracurricular activity for which she
stays out late a couple of days a week. When she mentions to her grandparents that she will be late that night, they complain that she is "*never*
on time*." Chiemi is annoyed about this exaggeration, but she tries to
understand her grandparents: They must be worrying; they surely mean
well; they care about her. When the interviewer asks her what she does
or tells her grandparents, Chiemi answers she never mentions to them
that she is annoyed:

> How can I say . . . I want to say "I want to have more fun, I
> want to have fun until late at night." But at the same time, you
> know, I know how much they worry about me. So I try not to
> say anything like that. I just try to laugh it off/smile it away.

Chiemi accommodates to her grandparents' wishes, and starts making even more of an effort to come home early. She plays her role.

Sen's relatives, the Utku Inuit, Hiroto, and Chiemi are all focused
outwards, not inwards. When an OURS model of emotions prevails,
emotional acting is Situated: individuals accommodate to the social
norms, expectations, and roles in their social context. What matters
is whether your emotions match up to others' needs and expectations,
whether you fit with the norms, and whether you fulfill your role.
In fact, in a large-scale international questionnaire study, psychologist
David Matsumoto and his colleagues found emotional suppression to
be highest in national cultures that are strong on social order, norms
and traditions, and power hierarchy, and lowest in national cultures
that prioritize the individual and their feelings.

Does this mean that Sen's relatives, the Utku Inuit, Hiroto, Chiemi, or all the international students in order- and hierarchy-loving countries feel alienated from their feelings? When Sen's relatives showed no emotion, did they feel unnatural? When the Utku Inuit stayed calm in the face of frustration, did they feel alienated? When Hiroto nodded in the committee, or Chiemi smiled to her grandparents, did they feel phony? Does it make them unhappy to *not* express their emotions? Does their anger or grief resurface at other, improper times?

It does not seem so. In many cultures, people consider their emotions to be "negotiated" with the social environment, rather than leading a separate life inside them. During emotional episodes, individuals from these cultures would start from an expression of no emotion and work towards acceptance, start from doing nothing and try to cultivate empathy, and start from adjustment and accommodation and try to maintain harmony in the relationship. The OURS version of the Pixar movie would likely be entitled *Outside In*. If authenticity—expressing one's inner feelings—is regarded as a virtue in Western cultures, it is constructed as a sign of personal immaturity in many non-Western cultures, such as Japan.

The outside-in perspective may also explain why Chinese service workers seem to cultivate the emotions desired on the job with greater ease than their American counterparts. In a cross-cultural study, Chinese and U.S. service workers alike reported that they "put on an act in order to deal with customers in an appropriate way"; in this case, it concerned service work that required a positive outlook. For Americans, putting on an act felt like faking that they are in a good mood, but Chinese service workers did not see it as faking at all. To the Chinese service workers, aligning their emotions with the requirements of the situation may have been nothing out of the ordinary. Emotional attunement to the needs of others and the situational requirement is having an OURS focus on emotion, and is quite different from faking it.

Several other findings bolster this interpretation. The first is that, like Hiroto and Chiemi, the Chinese service workers seemed to have gone beyond suppressing their feelings, or managing their display, to actually feel what the job required. American service workers in many cases just managed their display, but Chinese service workers who pleased their customers managed to have the emotions to match their display. Second, managing emotions on the job was much less costly for Chinese than American service workers. American workers, most of whom merely managed their emotional display, suffered from burnout: they felt alienated and exhausted, and also not very effective interpersonally. American service workers who tried to change their feelings were certainly better off than those who just faked their display, but still felt interpersonally ineffective. A very different picture emerged for the Chinese service workers: managing the display (or "surface acting") took some effort, but service workers who put on an act to deal with their customers in a way considered appropriate were no less effective interpersonally than those who did not. Furthermore, deep acting was a good thing for Chinese service workers: it made them energetic and interpersonally effective. Outside-in emotions, while costly in contexts where a MINE model of emotions prevails, aren't necessarily bad or unnatural in contexts in which OURS emotions are highlighted: on the contrary, these outside-in emotions seem to be beneficial in cultural contexts that view emotions as socially negotiated.

Inside-out emotions may be healthy when emotions are understood as MINE, but not so much when they are OURS. In an elegant study, psychologists Iris Mauss and Emily Butler made European American and Asian Americans undergraduate students angry in the lab. On average, Asian American students put a higher value on emotional control than their European American counterparts, agreeing more that "It is wrong for people to always display how they feel." In contrast, European American students put a lower value on emotional control, and agreed more than their Asian American peers that "It is better for people to let out pent up emotions." Generally, students who valued (high) emotional control *behaved* less angry during the experiment (as perceived by judges who were blind to the hypotheses of the study). Turning that same finding around, it can be said that the individuals showing most anger were the ones to endorse the Freudian notion that it is better to let out pent-up emotions. Most of these were European American.

Even more interestingly, Mauss and Butler tracked anger experience and cardiac output during the same experiment. Low cardiac output is often a sign that the individual has difficulty coping with the situation (the situation is a "threat"); high cardiac output can mean that the individual feels well equipped to cope with the situation and that the situation feels under control (the situation is a "challenge"). Judging by cardiac output measures, anger affected the cultural groups in the study differently. European Americans who showed little anger had stronger anger feelings and felt more "threat" than European Americans who did show anger. In contrast, Asian Americans who showed little anger felt less angry and better equipped to cope than Asian Americans who did show anger. These findings suggest that emotional control, while effortful, allowed Asian American individuals to achieve the emotional state that they were aiming for. Moreover, the outward-in adjustment felt under control.

Outside-in emotions do not always move away from strong to weaker emotions. Norms, other people's needs and expectations, or relationship concerns may call for expression rather than suppression: either for an emotion that was not there in the first place, or for amplification of an existing emotion. Among the Ifaluk, who live on a small Micronesian island in the southwest Pacific, another person's needs call for *fago*, the readiness to care for others. *Fago* can be translated as a mix of compassion, love, and sadness. A sister who feels *fago* for her brother comes to his aid. When Tamalekar, an Ifaluk man, was shamed by his ten-year-old son who had thrown rocks at a man who lived on the island and suffered from psychosis, this elicited *fago* in Tamalekar's sisters. The sisters "hurried to his house with gifts and cloth to be given, by way of apology, to the family of the 'crazy' man."

My colleague Alba Jasini tells me that in her country of origin, Albania, the relatives of deceased people hire "professional mourners" to wail for (and with) the family, and thus raise the level of grief display to the right cultural standards. Outside-in emotions may involve excitation rather than suppression. Arguably, many rituals have a similar function of collectively supplying individuals with situationally appropriate options for behavior during emotional events.

Among the Indonesian Minangkabau, people are expected to show *malu* (roughly equivalent to shame) when they violate any social norms. If necessary, educators force the display by highlighting the norm. *Malu* was induced in thirteen-year-old Andi who had his hair cut in front of the class. In Andi's own words: "Two days ago, the teacher told me to get my hair cut. Today, she called me in front of the class and took a pair of scissors out of her desk. She gave me a haircut and the others [classmates] watched. I had to sweep up the hair and go home. Now I can only run around with a baseball cap on, but wearing caps is not allowed in class." When the situation requires it, people are expected to show *malu*, or else helped to recognize the situation as one of *malu*. The direction of the emotion is outside-in.

A final reflection on the terms *emotional expression* and *emotional suppression* is that they may themselves be suggestive of a MINE model of emotions. They imply that there *is* a deep inner feeling that wants to come out, or alternatively, has to be actively suppressed. *Expression* and *suppression* privilege a view of emotions as inside the person, and naturally wanting to come out. When emotions are conceived of as *acts between people*, rather than feelings within, then no "expression" is naturally privileged over another. There is no essence to be expressed. There is no reason to assume that any emotional act is more authentic, or to the contrary, less. There is also no reason to think it is unnatural to meet social expectations. If emotions live between people, then why would yelling in anger be any more natural than Hiroto and Chiemi's accommodation to the expectations of their environments? Why would silently mourning by yourself be any more natural than wailing with the professional mourners? Why would managing your emotions to accommodate the expectations of the social environment be any more phony than asserting your frustrations?

Emotions: Mine and Ours?

Emotions are not solely feelings deep inside us. The way they have been portrayed in the Pixar movie *Inside Out* is a MINE model of emotions. Many cultures have an OURS model of emotions, which understands emotions primarily as acts happening between people: acts that are being adjusted to the situation at hand. Emotions in MINE and OURS cultures look different.

Individuals in cultures that emphasize MINE emotions identify their own emotions based on their own bodily changes, but individuals in cultures with OURS models infer emotions from what is going on in the relationship between people. Where MINE models prevail, individuals are more inclined to judge emotions from the facial configuration of a single person; where OURS models prevail, they are more likely to judge them from a combination of the faces of all people present. Where OURS models prevail, individuals are more likely to infer behavior from facial configurations than in places where MINE models prevail. Where MINE models are foregrounded, *feeling* good is healthy; where OURS models are first, positive *activities* are more important for health. Where MINE is the received model, emotions are seen to seek expression and take charge of the situation; where OURS models are accepted, emotional acts seek to meet given situational needs. Consistently, where MINE models dominate, emotion suppression is both less frequent and more harmful to psychological and relational well-being than where OURS models dominate. When a culture's focus is inward, emotions are different from when it is outward.

The OURS model has value for describing and understanding emotions in Western cultures as well. It helps us recognize how our own emotions are social and cultural, even though these aspects are often downplayed and under-recognized in the MINE model of emotions. U.S. American students describing instances of emotions reported *fear* of social rejection, *sadness* about the death of—or breakup with—a loved one, *anger* about a power reversal, *joy* about receiving esteem, respect, or praise, and *love* for another person who loves or needs them. When American individuals speak about emotions, they too speak about deeply social, interpersonal events.

Let's reconsider the reason that airlines companies are keen on their flight attendants smiling. It is because emotions play an important role between people: smiling is instrumental in making a connection with their customers, and possibly in reassuring them. When airline compa-

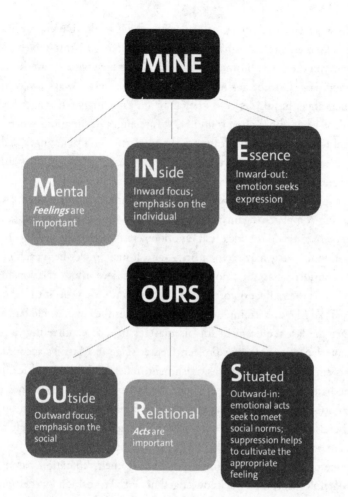

FIGURE 2.4 Schematic overview of MINE and OURS models of emotion

nies want to bind their customers to them and show them that flying is a fun (as opposed to scary) adventure, their flight attendants' smiles are their most effective tools to do so, for the very reason that emotions operate *between* people.

Similarly, the reason that bill collectors get angry is that anger is a pretty effective interpersonal tool for making people back down and do what you (the angry person) want them to do. Dutch psychologist Gerben van Kleef has shown that at the negotiating table, anger gets you the better business deal—certainly much better than showing happiness. Do not get me wrong: people are not always aware that their anger has this effect—they may not knowingly seek anger for its effect—but, more often than not, we are angry in situations where we feel that we are entitled to more than we get, and often, anger makes other people agree with us, or at the very least, submit to our wishes or entitlement. (A personal confession: my husband had the science on his side when he addressed our mortgage banker with irritation; I was acting completely against our financial interests when I smiled at her encouragingly.) The idea that emotions exist between people is not as outlandish as it may seem at first—and it may in fact help each of us to consider what our emotions (want to) achieve in our relationships. What is their effect on other people, or what do we want it to be?

Take Martin's example at the beginning of the chapter. He had just met the last requirement for his master's in civil engineering: a presentation of his master's project. Center stage in Martin's account of his emotion are his own astonishment, relief, and "the good feeling" he had when telling others about his accomplishment. But does the emotion not also live between people? Surely, he makes mention of friends and relatives who were present during his presentation. He told as many as seven people that he had passed his important exam. While none of these people claimed a change in their reputation based on Martin's success, they acknowledged his social transition by their presence and celebration. Is it possible that these other people felt proud of him? Sure. Is it possible that Martin's status changed, and that his success opened up new opportunities? Yes, of course. Is it possible that Martin's inner feelings are strongly related to his changed status in the world? It is not only possible, but likely. Very clearly, then, the social aspects of emotions are downplayed and under-recognized in the MINE model of emotions.

The importance of the OURS model is that it places emotions squarely in our social interactions and relationships. There is no question that *feelings* are important in MINE emotions, but we should not

lose sight of the primary function of emotions: emotions *are* for acting, and particularly for acting in the social world. Yes, we may feel
something, of course we do, but we primarily have emotions in order
to adjust to changes in our relationship with the (social) world. Even in
cultural environments where MINE emotions prevail, our pride seeks
to benefit from the advantage of moving up in the hierarchy and our
shame seeks to do some damage control when we find ourselves sliding
further towards the bottom of that hierarchy; our happiness brings us
closer to others, and our anger is antagonistic; our excitement engages
us in social activities, and our sadness disengages. Holding our own
emotions against the template of OURS models helps us to ask some
very important questions: How do our emotions act to change our
relationship with the world? Or, as one of my students who became a
therapist said, What does this emotion want in the social world?

And what about outside-in emotions? How could we be "authentic"
if we acted on norms or expectations, rather than inner feelings? Perhaps we do this more than we realize. Like many parents, I have felt
that loving my children was the easiest plight of all; it came so naturally.
If other relationships are filled with ambiguity, the bond with my kids
has been one of pure love. But is it possible that my love for my children
flowed so naturally because the feeling rules for a mother towards her
children are crystal clear and uncontestable? Your child simply *needs*
your love and acceptance. The culturally desired emotional mix in the
relationship between parents and children is always clear. This is in
fact what Arlie Hochschild suggests. If this were true, should the most
natural emotions of all—parental love—be considered outside-in? Do
we always cultivate our emotions to fit the social norms? Our emotions
may be more OURS than we acknowledge most of the time.

There are several striking examples from research within Western
Europe and the United States showing that emotions that are rewarded
will become habitual. Temper tantrums occur more among children
whose parents give in to their desires. And children whose parents only
respond to their negative emotions end up showing those emotions
more than children whose parents also attend to them when they communicate less urgency (insecurely versus securely attached children).

Similarly, gender differences in anger expression may be associated with differential rewards for men and women expressing the same emotion. Expressing anger seems to be more rewarding for men than for women. In a psychological experiment, women were made to be more angry and men less by merely reversing the reward patterns. Women received points when they were aggressive, and men received points when they were friendly in an interactive game. When rewarded, women started to be more angry, even within the course of an experiment.

When the cultural focus is inward, emotions become different creatures than when the cultural focus is outward. MINE and OURS emotions go beyond mere ways of talking about emotions. Yet, even if a culture focuses entirely on OURS aspects of emotions, some feeling, some embodiment of the emotion, is surely there most of the time. Conversely, even in a culture that resonates with emotions as little characters in the head—MINE emotions—emotions are also OURS. Emotions, whatever else they do, make meaning of events in the relationship with other people, and they align to these events in ways that meet social norms and expectations. Emotions are social practices, shared to a large extent with other people. So, looking through the lens of an OURS model will give you new insights into your emotions; it will focus attention to all the different aspects of emotions that the MINE model that is dominant in Western cultures overlooks and ignores. An OURS model can also help us understand how each of our emotions is tied to our cultural contexts—understanding is a first step to bridging the differences in emotions that we encounter in a multicultural society and a globalized world.

Chapter 3

. . . .

To Raise
Your Child

WHEN MY SON OLIVER WAS VERY YOUNG, ABOUT TEN MONTHS old, he knew how to hold a book right side up. When friends or grandparents were visiting, his father or I would hand him the book turned upside down, and wait for him to turn it right side up. Without fail, our visitors would praise him and be excited, and he beamed. Was he feeling really proud? Perhaps not in an adult sense (psychologists have found that initial forms of pride still miss many of the adult features). But we, as parents, helped by our visitors, created opportunities for pride. We cultivated an emotion that was culturally valued.

The anthropologist Heidi Fung found that Taiwanese mothers cultivated shame in similar manners. They took and created opportunities for children to feel shame. The mother of three-year-old Didi, a Taiwanese toddler, scolded him when he approached the researcher's camcorder: "Eh, eh, Didi! What has Mama told you? You never [listen] . . . You cannot! I'm going to spank you. You are a child who doesn't obey rules." She threatened to ostracize him, and put him aside: "We don't want you; you stand here." And she told him to control himself: "Look how ugly your crying will be on tape." Didi's sister joined in, calling him "ugly monster" and adding "shame on you." Fung assures us that shaming was not intended to harm or ostracize the child, but rather to "transmit the cultural values of discretion shame [. . .] teaching children how to be part of society, to include them rather than to set them apart."

Just as Oliver's dad and I created opportunities for Oliver to feel the right emotions at the right time, so did Didi's mother and sister. Each in our own ways, Didi's mother and sister and we, Oliver's parents, nudged our children to feel and express the culturally desired emotions. The emotion in each case was a different one, because we valued different socialization goals. Our family lived in the United States, and we wanted our child to think highly of himself, to take his unique place in the world, and distinguish himself. Didi's mother wanted to teach her child propriety, as valued in Taiwanese contexts; the norm for Didi was to be aware of his proper place, by feeling shame. We each induced the emotions that made our children valued members of their respective cultures. In short: emotions help us become part of our culture.

Raising a Child Who Feels Good about Themselves

Anthropologist Naomi Quinn observes that "Small children bask in their parent's, often public, praise long before they comprehend what feats of accomplishment will be required of them if they are going to continue gaining approval from others and feeling good about themselves." She was describing American middle-class families who draw attention to anything worthy of pride, such as turning a book right side up. In one research program comparing middle-class white American moms and kids from the Chicago area with Taiwanese (middle-class) moms and their young children, the U.S. mothers spontaneously brought up self-esteem in interviews about their parenting goals: "I want them to be comfortable with themselves" or "I want them to develop self-confidence." These moms were convinced that self-esteem was the source of all healthy development, essential to making their children happy, resilient, successful, and strong enough to try on new things. In a culture where happiness, success, and excitement are central goals, feeling good about yourself is indispensable.

Not surprisingly, then, the middle-class U.S. mothers in Miller's study noted it was important to actively "build, cultivate or protect their children's self-esteem." And in their minds, a good way of doing this was to "love, respect and affirm" their children in the here and now; all psychological benefits would follow. So this was the project that Oliver's father and I embarked on: we loved, respected, and affirmed our ten-month-old son. We were not alone in praising our child's special accomplishment.

Parents' praising is not limited to events in the here and now. Many moms in Miller's study reminisced with their children, or with the researcher, about events in which their children were the star. Referring to her two-and-a-half-year-old daughter Molly, one Chicago mom relates to the researcher:

> You'll get a kick out of this one. Friday night, we were just sitting around. . . . Jim and I were sitting on the ground. . . . she puts her hand on me and says "Me happy." And I am like, "That is good, Mollie. You happy." [researcher: I love it, it sounds so cute.] I said: "I don't think I ever heard anyone say that," and Jim says, "I know I never heard anyone come up with [me happy]."

In this narrative, Miller and her colleagues tell us, Mollie's mom draws attention to her daughter's funny pronoun use (in Mollie's presence). In doing so, she conveys to both Mollie and the researcher, how endearing and surprising Mollie's expression is, further underlining the novelty (and uniqueness) of Mollie's word choice by citing her own and her husband's response in the moment. She also uses the situation to solicit an audience: the researcher, being a well-socialized audience, affirms Mollie's mother's take on the behavior: "I love it, it sounds so cute." The story sets Molly apart as a special child, and creates an opportunity for pride both for the mom and the child. The Chicago homes of these middle-class European American toddlers were full of this kind of narrative.

Praising is not restricted to homes. Both Oliver and his two-year-younger sister Zoë often came home from their North Carolina elementary school with "best student" awards. As a "new" American mom, I would have liked to believe my kids were "the best," but the awards did not reflect as much. One month they were the best at having mastered the first list of French vocabulary (twenty words), another month they had been the most eager participant of a sports day: the person who, despite having had no chance at winning, had been a good sport. None of these certificates marked major achievements, but the school practiced public praising as a way of giving kids—many kids, I believe—a sense of being valued and seen, or even of being unique at something or other. We may call the associated feeling "pride."

Praising is embedded in a child-focused culture, where a child's perspective is taken quite seriously from very early on. Mothers of white U.S. and European babies have face-to-face interactions with infants, and talk to them, as opposed to mothers from many other cultures who keep their babies on their bodies, instead of facing them.

How much middle-class American families invite even their babies to be full conversation partners is well illustrated by a story of my own family. One of my undergraduate students at Wake Forest—let us call him John—was exceedingly smart, but less than exceedingly organized. Once in graduate school, he asked me for a last-minute favor: he needed a recording of a family dinner conversation, a family with small children. I agreed to help him, but right before the start of our dinner, I realized that the data would be worthless to him. I spoke Dutch to the children, their dad spoke English, so John (not being bilingual) would not be able to make any sense of our conversation. John's deadline was imminent, so I had no choice but to tape our dinner conversation anyway. To my surprise the recording turned out to be very useful to John: he was interested in speaking turns. My daughter Zoë, who was less than one year old, and not speaking yet, was still allowed speaking time. We asked her questions (in either language), and we allowed her time to answer, even if she was not yet able. We prepared her for the role of an individual who was valued in her own right.

There are many practices to let middle-class American children know that they are valued individuals, but praising is a practice that is particularly emotionally arousing. With praise for children's small early successes—such as holding a book right side up and early talking ("me happy")—American middle-class parents not only teach their children the importance of those particular achievements, "but also hope to instill in them a generalized self-reliance that, it is thought, will stand them in good stead in their future pursuit of success and happiness." As one of the moms in Miller's research said: "[It is important to give] them enough love and praise so that they feel good about themselves, and then they can go and master the world." The marking of small achievements by parents and other socializing agents paves the road for the child to feel good about themselves generally; it predisposes children to feel happy, proud, or full of self-esteem.

Parenting websites in the U.S. now tell parents not to praise their children for just anything, and to give them a realistic sense of self, perhaps in an effort to tip the scale back a bit. Despite the new nuance, middle-class U.S. parents still want their kids to be convinced that they can obtain the place in the world that they clearly deserve, to feel secure and loved, and possibly also to feel unique and special. As one website puts it: "Give your child positive experiences. They will have the ability to experience positive experiences themselves and offer them to others. [If you g]ive your child negative experiences, [t]hey won't have the kind of development necessary for them to thrive." The shared wisdom is that positive feelings need to be fostered.

Where I raised my children, it was hard to imagine putting an emphasis on shaming them, or putting fear in them. Like the Chicago moms in Miller's research, I thought that "shaming children, disciplining them too harshly, or making invidious comparisons should be avoided because they damage self-esteem." Numerous psychological studies have supported this view that shame is associated with low self-esteem and proneness to depression. Shaming practices have been linked to the development of aggressive and antisocial tendencies, and to a lack of empathy in children. It is hardly conceivable that shaming—by publicly mocking a child or humiliating them—

would be the "go-to" socialization tool for middle-class white American parents.

The reputation of corporal punishment as a strategy for socializing may even be worse than that of shame in WEIRD contexts. "Do not spank, no matter what," is the popular advice. The consensus today is that corporal punishment leads to a child's immediate compliance, as it induces fear, but fails to bring about the lasting changes in behavior that discipline seeks to achieve; it does not teach the child right from wrong. At the same time, corporal punishment, and the associated fear in the child, hampers closeness in the parent-child relationship and puts children's psychological health at risk. Corporal punishment also teaches children to be aggressive themselves, and increases their chances of becoming antisocial and abusive. In WEIRD cultures, the consensus is that neither shame nor fear have the desired effects: they do not render our children into the kinds of people we want in our culture.

And yet, there are communities where these emotions can be desirable, communities in which children are consistently made to feel shame or fear when doing something wrong. In these communities, shame or fear ensure that children become the kinds of adults these communities value. I turn to those next.

Raising a Child Who Knows Shame

In one of the most vivid examples of different socializing emotions, anthropologist Birgitt Röttger-Rössler and developmental psychologist Manfred Holodynski described the central role of *malu* (shame) in the socialization of Minangkabau children. The children come from a small peasant village on West Sumatra, Indonesia (the site where Levenson and Ekman tested their MINE theory). The central goal for socialization among the Minangkabau is to pay respect to parents and anyone else—whether kin or no kin—who is older.

For the Minangkabau, "showing respect" is to be modest and norm-compliant, and children learn this behavior by learning *malu* (closest translation: "shame"). From very early on, Minangkabau parents encourage shy behavior in their toddlers, and call it *malu-malu* ("baby malu"). By calling attention to the behavior, parents also expose their children to the full attention of everyone present, which itself may elicit *malu*. When children are slightly older, public mocking begins. Five-year-old Haifa and her same-aged (male) cousin Is were publicly mocked by their classmates after having been discovered swimming naked in the local pond. The peers laughed and whispered, and then one cried out "They have no shame!" which was met with agreement and laughing. The episode ended no sooner than Haifa and Is were fully dressed. Sanctioning by caregivers and other relatives similarly does not end until the child's norm violations have stopped. A defiant child is completely ignored until their behavior is no longer inappropriate, and the adults involved show vicarious or "shared" shame over their child's norm violations.

When the Minangkabau child is older yet, during early adolescence, they are sometimes actively humiliated. Thirteen-year-old Andi, whose teacher cut his hair in front of the whole class (see chapter 2), was an example of this. The use of progressively serious exclusion techniques ensures that Minangkabau children experience and "know" shame. Inducing shame does not only mark norm violations to be avoided; it also leads to the reserved and modest person that is valued among the Minangkabau: a person who is always aware of the social consequences that their behavior may have.

Taiwanese Didi's mom, whom I cited at the beginning of this chapter, equally used shaming to teach her little boy propriety. She drew Didi's attention to norm violations, and had she lived in the Chicago area, might have been called "critical." Where the U.S. mothers were weary of shaming or criticizing their children out of fear that doing so would harm their children's brittle self-esteem, Didi's mom was trying intentionally to produce a child prone to shame. She was convinced that shame was the "right" thing for Didi to feel. In Taiwan, shame shows that you know your place, and are ready to be deferential. It shows you are committed to preventing the potential negative consequences of norm-violation. In such a cultural context, Didi's mom thought of shamelessness, not shame, as the more worrisome of the two.

Saying that the Taiwanese mothers in Miller and Fung's research did not care about self-esteem does not do justice to their perspective: many of them did not know what the researchers even meant by "self-esteem." There is no good translation for self-esteem in Chinese, and feeling good about yourself is not a prominent goal. A few moms spontaneously brought up protection of the child's integrity, but always in the context of harsh punishment, which was to be avoided. And Taiwanese moms, asked to talk about their children feeling good about themselves, thought children "with self-esteem" would be more likely to be frustrated by failure, and would be more stubborn, and unwilling to listen and to be corrected—all negative traits in their eyes.

But how is it that shaming does not make Minangkabau and Taiwanese children feel bad all the time? Are those children doomed to live their lives in low self-esteem, prone to depression, un-empathetic and aggressive? This does not seem to be the case. One reason is that shame takes place in a different kind of relationship between a child and their parents and relatives: a relationship in which your parents and close relative share your shame, or even have vicarious shame. Shame in Taiwanese and Minangkabau communities highlights the connection with others, such as your parents, and this may partly explain why shame is less painful. Shame highlights your proper place in an unalienable social network, rather than focusing on rejection or isolation. It reminds you how to behave in the network, but it does not push you out.

One reason Didi's mom shames him in front of the researcher is that Didi's behavior reflects on his mom. It is his mom's responsibility to make sure Didi "has shame." When Didi does show shame, this reflects well on the mom. Shame strengthens the bonds between people, rather than reflecting a potential threat to them.

In another study, Fung and her colleague Eva Chian-Hui Chen followed seven middle-class Taiwanese families. The study began when the focal child was two and a half years old, and continued until this child reached age four. A researcher visited the families every six months, and systematically videotaped spontaneous inter-actions between the family and the child. During the more than a hundred hours of video-recorded family interaction, the researchers identified instances of shame more than three times an hour. In the great majority of cases, the parent marks a transgression, thus trying to provoke shame in the focal child. Taiwanese moms in Fung and Chen's research often zoomed in on shame-sharing, as in the exam-ple below where four-year-old Axin and his two-year-old brother refuse to go to sleep, even after their mother told them it was time for their nap:

> Mother says, "School master has said that we should follow fixed work and rest routines, otherwise School master will reproach us." [Both children] wonder if School master will reproach her. Mother answers: "That day, wasn't School master reproaching . . . me?" Both children ask why. Mother replies, "She said I did not raise you two well, and that I did not have you sleep during nap time, right?"

If her children misbehave, it will be the mother who is blamed for not teaching and raising them well. Implicit is the shame-sharing: the child's shameful behavior reflects badly on their parents and family. Many parents articulate the shame-sharing, saying, "You made your mother lose face" or "such a disobedient child." But perhaps more important is that, through invoking an authority figure—the school-master in the case of Axin's mom—the bond between the child and the parent remains intact. It is not the mom rejecting the child, but the child and the mom jointly having to meet external demands. There is a basic alliance between the child and their parents (or relatives). This alliance makes for the wider impact of norm violations, but also means that shame is not nearly as threatening as it is in Western cultures. Shame among the Minangkabau and in Taiwan calls for remedying what is wrong, but it does not challenge the bond between a child and their most important caregivers.

Having shame is seen as a virtue: it reveals that you have a sense of social norms, and it will prevent you from violating these norms. Having shame keeps you attentive to how others see you, but in so doing, keeps you from the misconduct that would have led to social exclusion. Adult Minangkabau cite *malu* as source of normative behavior, saying, "*Malu* makes us behave carefully so that we don't do something bad or wrong." And similarly, the Taiwanese mothers want to teach their children propriety by helping them to feel shame. Across cultures, caregivers want what is best for their child: among the Minangkabau and among Taiwanese families, "knowing shame" best prepares children to be valued members of their society.

Raising a Child Who Knows Fear

A central goal of socialization among the Bara in the southern part of Madagascar is to be docile. Bara society is segmented and hierarchical: the basic segment of the Bara social organization consists of three or four generations of living descendants from a single ancestral spirit. The ideal behavior for Bara children is to be docile, submissive, and compliant with anything their elders want them to do: Bara children are made to follow the directives of their elders without protest. To that end, they should "know *tahotsy*, that is, they should readily fear their elder relatives." Fear, according to anthropologist Birgitt Röttger-Rössler and developmental psychologist Manfred Holodynski, is the socializing emotion.

During their first year, Bara infants are in very close proximity to their mother: there is a lot of body contact, and the baby's physical needs are met and often anticipated. Slight corporal punishment starts when the mother weans the baby during the second year. Mothers enforce bodily distance and administer mild corporal punishment such as pinching their children when the latter do not behave as called for. During this time, older siblings and peers become more important to the toddler. At around four years of age, children are thought to understand both social norms and the sanctions associated with violating them. This is the time when corporal punishments start, and strong experiences of fear (*tahotsy*) are instilled. Beating is the most common form of corporal punishment, but food deprivation (in this context, inducing a fear of starving) occurs as well. Beating is always done by the same person, usually the father. The Bara believe that shaming or public humiliation is harmful for children, and they make sure the beating is done out of sight. In an effort to ensure that the child feels accepted after the beating, the Bara go to great lengths to comfort a child who received a beating. This role is often taken up by the mother; "[t]he child is petted, advised how to avoid the beating in the future, and assured that the beating was due only to her or his misconduct." The Bara punish to induce strong fear for the rule of authority, but unlike the Taiwanese mothers and the Minangkabau, they counteract any feelings of devaluation and they actively avoid threatening their children with social exclusion.

Just as the Bara avoid shaming, so do they avoid praising. When asked what they did when the child behaved well, Bara parents denounced praise. Oliver's dad and I would surely have been seen to spoil our kid, and to raise him to no good end. What did the Bara do instead? Most of the interviewed parents told the researcher that they would not be angry and would not beat their well-behaved children (only a few added they might reward their children with some food, or even a piece of clothing).

How do Bara children fare with the corporal punishment they receive? Do they experience strong fear as a consequence? How can Bara children become good adults when they do not internalize the social norms, and merely comply when a punishing authority is present? Does the widespread use of corporal punishment as a tool for socialization leave Bara children at psychological risk? Again, the answer seems to be that punishment and fear may be effective tools for raising a Bara child, even if they are ineffective to the kind of child contemporary (middle-class) white (U.S.) parents want to raise. To understand this, we need to know more about the society for which the Bara children are raised.

Corporal punishment induces fear in Bara children: merely *thinking* of norm-violating behavior induces a strong fear for the potential consequences. Bara children may be conditioned to avoid those consequences rather than internalizing the societal norms; in that sense, Western research may be right. Yet, internalization may not be necessary in Bara society, given that Bara children are surrounded by the watching eyes of many ever-present adults. Even in adult life, fear may do the job. By the time Bara kids have grown strong enough to fight back, and no longer have to fear corporal punishment from their elders, they have adopted the collective fear of ancestral spirits who seem to replace the elders. Norm violations are believed to "so enrage one's own ancestral spirits that they will inflict diseases and other calamities on the norm violator and his descendants. This rage of ancestral spirits is believed to be potentially fatal if not appeased by sacrificial offerings." The omnipresence of the ancestral spirits makes *tahotsy* (fear) a virtue; individuals with *tahotsy* will remember to respect the social norms.

Tahotsy comes with aggression proneness; in this sense, too, it is consistent with conclusions from Western research. Bara children often report not only feeling *tahotsy*, but also *seky* (translated as "anger") right after the beating. Moreover, there is some indication that children do learn aggression from the beating itself; parental aggression may become a model of behavior. Wielding this aggression on the disciplining elder himself would be punished harshly, as it amounts to further norm violation. Yet, there are alternative outlets for anger: competition between patrilineages is high in Bara society, and children who have just been beaten act their anger out on unrelated peers. It is very plausible, therefore, that strong fear is related to aggression proneness even among the Bara. What may be different for the Bara is that this proneness is not considered antisocial; instead, it can be funneled into socially normative behavior, first by beating up peers from competing patrilineages, and later into socializing new generations of Bara children that need to be socialized to feel *tahotsy*.

Finally, fear may hamper closeness in the child-parent relationships, true even among the Bara. But who says the relationship between parents and children needs to be close? Bara parents meet their children's physical needs as long as the latter are not able to take care of themselves, and after that, they make their offspring fit for the social demands of a hierarchical society, and protect them from the wrath of the ancestral spirits. What more could a Bara child wish for?

We need not go to cultures remote from our own to find this type of emotion socialization. A very similar approach was found in the United States before nineteenth-century Victorian norms came into vogue. Anger and punishment were used "in defense of hierarchy and religious orthodoxy" and to instill in children the respect for elders (including their parents), the fear of doom in eternity, and the fear of God. Child-rearing practices across the Atlantic were hardly different at that time. Louis XIII, a seventeenth-century French king, was brought up in a similar fashion: "[T]he whippings the child constantly received were designed, in some way, to suppress his sense of autonomy, and to prepare him for a role of submissiveness." Regardless of class, the goal of childrearing was to combat pride, and instill feelings of submission. Even a king would have to be servile and please the potentially angry deity.

Only in the nineteenth century did attacks on the disciplinary uses of fear emerge in American middle-class contexts. As historian Peter Stearns eloquently describes in his 1994 book *American Cool*:

> As the God-fearing qualities of religious virtue began to decline in mainstream American Protestantism, a fearful individual was no longer considered appropriately pious. Rather, he or she was emotionally crippled, incapable of taking the kinds of initiatives or displaying the kinds of confidence desirable in middle-class life. Most obviously, if fear became an emotional link between parent and child, long-term affection would be excluded even if short-term discipline was served. Fear, quite simply, became an emotional abuse of parental authority.

It was around this time that affection trumped servitude, and that parent-child relations came to be seen as "loving" in the first place. Maternal love played a central role in this new model of child-rearing, as it contributed to raising a moral child. "God planted this *deep*, this *unquenchable* love for her offspring, in the mother's heart," a reverend wrote in an 1839 issue of *The Mother's Magazine*. The idea was that the appropriate affections of children themselves would spring from this mother love: "Children of a loving mother cannot but desire to conform themselves to such models." Love became an important socializing emotion in Victorian America, and has arguably not ceded its place since.

Raising a Child with Empathy

To a Western eye, it is striking how Japanese parents and educators fail to impose boundaries on children's behavior. In one cross-cultural study, for instance, developmental psychologists Gisela Trommsdorff and Hans-Joachim Kornadt observed Japanese and German mothers responding to their disobedient five-year-olds. Japanese mothers interpreted disobedience empathetically from the child's perspective, remarking that "the child is just a child, is too much absorbed in playing, is too tired." If the child kept disobeying, Japanese mothers repeated their demands in a friendly manner, again showing empathy for the child. Only after some back and forth would the mothers start appealing to the child, and asking their child to consider how they, the mother, felt; even then, they never corrected the child. Interestingly, the Japanese approach to their disobedient kindergartners often ended the interaction in compromise and harmony, and thus led to relatedness. It also was associated with long-term socialization goals for Japanese children: nine years after Trommsdorff and Kornadt initially observed the interactions, they found that the Japanese children were more empathetic than German children.

In Japan, a young child is assumed to initially feel *amae*, which is a complete dependence on the nurturant indulgence of their caregiver, usually their mom. *Amae* is recognized by the Japanese as an emotion. Mothers accept their child's *amae*, and show them *omoiyari*, or empathy, in return. They indulge their child in ways that, to a Western eye, verge on spoiling, giving in to the child's every wish. In doing so, they model the very emotion that they ultimately want their child to display: *omoiyari*. *Omoiyari* "refers to the ability and willingness to feel what others are feeling, to vicariously experience the pleasure and pain that they are undergoing, and to help them satisfy their wishes." The emotion is at the very center of the harmonious relatedness that is culturally valued in Japan.

Japanese mothers instill *omoiyari* in their child by embodying this emotion. While at first children are not expected to show any *omoiyari* themselves, over time the mother will encourage them to take her point of view, and help them to be sensitive to her feelings. Rather than telling the child what to do, Japanese mothers wait until the child is motivated to voluntarily follow the social rules in order to meet her expectations. Modeling and instilling *omoiyari* requires patience on the part of the mother, but is thought of as the only way to prepare a child for their adult role: taking the perspective of others, meeting one's role expectations, and avoiding causing others any trouble. Perspective taking makes a person ponder about how they can improve to better meet others' expectations, and to persevere and overcome externally encountered adversities.

The idea that *omoiyari* has to be cultivated, but cannot be forced onto kids until they are ready, prevails in Japanese preschool practices. Teachers show great restraint, even if the interactions between preschoolers are conflictual, and at times aggressive. Witness an episode between Nao, the newest child at a preschool, and several of her classmates:

Nao pulls a stuffed bear away from another girl, Reiko. [. . . The teacher] Morita tells them to "junken" (to do the game "paper, rock, scissors") to settle their dispute. Reiko's scissors beat Nao's paper. Morita says to Nao, "We'll let Reiko put the bear away today, right." Nao defiantly says, "No!" Morita replies, firmly, "We did 'junken.'" Nao sits on the floor and sulks. Reiko and her twin sister and constant companion, Seiko, approach Nao and tell her that she should not have tried to grab the bear away from them. Nao replies, "Seiko-chan and Reiko-chan are stupid." Seiko replies, "Well it is your fault. You put the bear down. That's why we took it."

After an interruption by some structured class activities, the bear saga continues, with Nao and the other girls grabbing the bear from each other. In the end, the other girls explain to Nao once again that her turn was over when she put the bear down.

Nao, pouting, is led away to the other side of the room by Seiko, who says to her: "You cannot do that. Do you understand? Promise?" Linking little fingers with Nao, the two girls swing their arms back and forth as they sing, "Keep this promise, or swallow a thousand needles."

All the while Morita-sensei, the teacher, watches what is going on, but does not interfere. She stays back and observes. She interprets the episode as Nao expressing *amae,* in a whiny and aggressive way, and the others girls giving her attention and in the end including her, and thus showing *omoiyari.* Interestingly, *amae* and *omoiyari,* but also *loneliness,* are valued emotions in Japan because they "fuel the desire of sociality." Loneliness motivates people to seek the company of others, and when relayed to others through *amae,* provokes the empathetic response of others inviting the person to join the group.

Most Japanese teachers would agree with Morita-sensei and not interfere; in this way children learn to interpret *amae,* and give *omoiyari.* In contrast, U.S. teachers who see the interaction on tape think the teacher should have interfered. They see the teacher's nonintervention as a failure to protect children from harming each other, and they also suspect that the teacher has not been paying attention (or she would have interfered!). But Morita-sensei does pay attention: her goal—different from that of her American colleagues—is to create room for the development of *omoiyari,* not to make sure her preschoolers feel good.

When the (white middle-class) American goal may be to raise a child who is secure enough to become independent, the Japanese goal is to raise a child who becomes sensitive enough to take perspective. If pride and happiness are foregrounded in many American and European contexts, then *amae* and *omoiyari* are socializing emotions in Japan.

Raising a Calm (or an Emotional) Child

Nso mothers living in farming communities in Cameroon told psychologist Heidi Keller and her team that "a good child is one who is always calm." All the mothers had very young children, three to nineteen months of age. These infants were supposed to be calm and inexpressive, so as to enable the mother to pursue her activities and to facilitate other people's caring for them when their mothers were not around. "We do not cry in Mbah" (the village), the mothers told Keller. And in fact, they did everything to quiet their infants down. One strategy was nursing their infants. As one mother told Keller:

If the child is crying at times and you breastfeed him, he will stop crying. Because when a child is not crying it enables you to do your activities . . . I gave him the breast and he stopped crying and started sleeping.

Nso mothers nursed to soothe babies who were crying or to prevent babies from crying. If nursing did not work, Nso mothers showed their babies disapproval, calling them "a bad child" or exclaiming "terrible," and telling them to stop crying. A good and healthy kid is a calm kid, a kid that "stays put." In the process, Nso babies were prepared to adjust to circumstances.

Contrast this to the German mothers in Keller's research. All of them coming from urban, middle-class families, and having infants of the same age as the Nso mothers. They were seen to stimulate and maintain positive emotionality in their children. One German mother, interacting with her three-month-old infant, speaks to him:

You have to smile, little man! Yes, you should smile, Eyeyeye. Come on. Uah. Yes, you are doing great. Do it again. Yes, you are doing great.

Like Nso mother, German mothers acted to achieve their cultural ideal for a child. One mother explains this ideal to Keller and her team:

To smile a lot with the mother boosts the child's trust in his environment; a child needs care and attention and I read that infants laugh most during their first year. . . . Well, we laugh very often with her. I think laughing is healthy.

Keller tells us that German middle-class babies and their mothers spend about 80 to 90 percent of their interaction time with face-to-face contact. In many of these situations mothers made eye contact, smiled, and made positive vocalizations. Of course, as much as German mothers value and stimulate positive emotionality, their children sometimes cry too, and even then, the mothers give room to their babies' emotions. They try to find the reason for the babies crying, and rather than telling them to be calm, they try to find out how the situation needs to be changed or influenced on behalf of the baby. "Don't you want to lie down anymore? Do you need your pacifier?," one mother asked her crying baby. The baby cannot yet influence their environment themselves at this point in development, but the mother can help them moving away from the undesirable and towards the desirable circumstances: for example, by picking them up, or giving them their pacifier. In the process, German babies get prepared to be influencers.

Nso are not the only adjusters and Germans not the only movers, it seems. When white U.S. preschoolers were asked if they would rather be like a picture of a face with a "big smile," or like a picture of a face with a "small smile," almost all of them told Jeanne Tsai, psychologist from Stanford, that they'd prefer to have the big smile. Yet their Taiwanese peers did not have the same preference for big smiles: just as many of them would have preferred the small smile as the big one. Being calm, in other words, was a much more favorable feeling for three- to five-year-old children in Taiwan than in the United States. This greater preference for calm was consistent, regardless of how the question was asked. For instance, when the activity was swimming, the majority of Taiwanese preschool kids preferred sitting and floating on an inner tube over jumping and splashing, but this was not the case for same-aged European American children. Taiwanese children preferred calm over active; European American children did not. Finally, almost all of the European American children found the big smile "happier" than the calm smile, but only about half of the Taiwanese children did; the other half found the calm smile "happier."

In their observations of mother-child interactions in Taiwan, Fung and Chen observed that many toddlers were shamed when they cried. Didi's mom shamed him the next day for crying when he slipped on the wet floor of the bathroom and fell. "Didi is most annoying, simply loves to cry!" Didi's sister echoes the sentiment: "Crying devil," and makes a gesture of shame. Another toddler, Wenwen (three and one-half years old) sits down and sobs when her younger brother destroys her artwork. Her mother tells her she should have cleaned up her stuff before her brother had a chance to touch it. Her father comes into the room, tells Wenwen to calm down. He takes her little brother out of the room, but Wenwen is still whining, upon which her mom says, "I am not gonna care for you if you keep crying." Here too, the norm is to be calm rather than emotional.

But why would anybody want to be just calm? The Nso mothers in Heidi Keller's research summarized it well: a calm child allows you to work, and others can take care of a calm kid. A calm child, in other words, easily adjusts to their environment. This is Jeanne Tsai's theory as well: calmness is a preferred emotion in a culture that expects you to put the group's needs above your own. It allows you to pay attention to what others want, do, or say. It allows you generally to observe the flow and follow it. In contrast, excitement (and movement generally) is more desirable in a culture that expects you to take control of your environment. It allows you to act first and influence others.

Being a good experimental psychologist, Tsai tested whether her predictions would work in the lab. If she *created* a condition in which one participant influenced the other, would that participant seek to be more excited? And if she put a participant in a position in which they followed the other person, would this adjuster want to feel more calm? The short answer: Yes. Tsai asked pairs of students to come to the lab and perform a dyadic card sorting task. Both students received an unsorted stack of cards; the cards displayed unique figures. One student was instructed to be the influencer, and described each card one by one so that their partner could put their cards in the same order. The other student, the adjuster was asked to "get into the mindset" of their partner, and to sort their cards in the same order as the influencer's pile. As Tsai predicted, influencers did in fact want to be more excited, and adjusters more calm.

German mothers wanted their children to be emotionally expressive, because they hoped their children would grow up to confidently express their own preferences, and develop their personal talents; Nso mothers wanted their children to be calm, because their goal was to raise children who respect older people, obey their parents, and maintain social harmony. Similarly, Taiwanese parents admonished their toddlers to be calm rather than crying, and to adjust to (or prevent) undesirable events. In each context, children's emotions were socialized to become socially valued adults in their cultures: autonomous movers or related adjusters.

There is another way of looking at these differences: Nso and Taiwanese children may be socialized to have emotions outside-in, whereas middle-class German and white American children are socialized to have emotions inside-out. Outside-in emotions are cultivated to first meet the needs of the environment, including relationships with others. Inside-out emotions follow the feelings out. By the time mothers talk with their three-year-old children about emotional experiences in the recent past, either emphasizing the social consequences or emphasizing the feeling itself, the groundwork may have been laid. The attention of Jiang, the three-year-old Chinese boy we met in chapter 2, may have been focused outward for a full three years; during the same three years, the attention of George, the three-year-old American boy that we also met in chapter 2, was turned inward. This was the case even before they engaged in conversations with their moms in which the same respective outlooks were reinforced.

Raising a Child with Anger

There is no culture that wants their children angry all the time, yet it is very clear that anger is valued in some and demonized in other cultures. Middle-class white American parents consider anger unavoidable in their children, and cherish the underlying traits. There are the "terrible twos," in which toddlers play with a sense of independence, and go through a "no" stage, in which they become "assertive and contrary." Then there is adolescence, starting as early as ten years old, in which conflict with parents increases, and adolescents have outbursts of anger. In both stages, as well as in between, anger—if not likeable—is a sign of healthy independence. An article on adolescence in *Psychology Today* (by the author of the book *Who Stole My Child?*) reads that "anger is a frequently occurring issue, not just for the young person, but for parents as well. How could it be otherwise?" The reasons according to the author? "Parents can get angry in their frustrating fight for influence, adolescents can get angry in their frustrating fight for freedom." At different developmental stages, anger is an unavoidable part of the power struggle that ensues between middle-class American parents and their increasingly autonomous children.

No one *wants* to be the parent in the supermarket dealing with their out-of-control toddler throwing a tantrum, no one wants to be on the other end of a disobedient kindergartener, and no one wants the be at the receiving end of adolescents' resentment and slamming of doors. Yet, middle-class European and white American parents raise their children to feel as well as show anger, both by modeling the feeling and by cultivating independence.

Psychologist Pamela Cole and her colleagues compared the anger feelings and expressions in U.S. American and Tamang Nepali pre- and early adolescents (nine to eleven years old), and came to a similar conclusion: faced with similar situations, U.S. children from a farming community in the northeastern United States projected more anger than did Tamang children from a Buddhist Nepali community. All participants read vignettes of "difficult situations," and saw a graphical depiction of the situation. One of the situations read:

> You are doing your homework. Your father is sitting next to you. You want to use the eraser and you see it by his hand. You take the eraser and your father slaps your hand and says, "Don't grab things—wait until I am finished!"

The eraser story was one of several in which either the father or a friend figured. After reading the story and seeing the picture, children were interviewed about their emotions. The U.S. children reported they would *feel anger* (as opposed to *feeling happy, ashamed,* or *okay*) in more than half of the "difficult" situations, and that they would communicate their anger. Compared to younger children, older children in the U.S. were more likely to show their anger, suggesting that in full development anger is shown. U.S. children thought that showing anger would help deal with the problem, and influence the situation. A typical U.S. child's reply was to communicate anger to their father "so that he would realize it was only a mistake," and to tell him "you can have the eraser, but you do not need to *hit* me." Cole and her colleagues suggest that in a society that emphasized self-reliance and self-assertion, children have learned that feeling and communicating anger is acceptable and effective.

How very different were the emotions of Tamang children, whose community valued egalitarianism, tolerance, and minimization of psychological distress! In keeping with their values, the Tamang children often blamed themselves for the unfortunate turn of events: "I snatched the eraser," they might say. Whereas the U.S. kids felt and showed anger (and blamed their father or friend) with the objective of changing the situation to their benefit, Tamang children blamed themselves to maintain harmony.

Parents and other caregivers may play a larger role than they imagine in socializing anger. The observational study of German and Japanese mothers and their five-year-old disobedient children (described above) suggested that mothers play a significant role in socializing their children's anger. The German mothers in this study were not nearly as patient with their disobedient children as the Japanese mothers had been. Rather than accepting their children's behavior as immature, as the Japanese mothers had done, the German mothers were quick to infer that their disobedient child had been acting on purpose. Remarks such as "he wants to make me angry" were not uncommon, and many German mothers reacted to their child's disobedience with their own anger. As an unintended side effect, the German interactions often escalated, with the child and the mother both being angry. My reading is that German mothers treated the disobedience of their children as a power conflict between two individuals with different interests (whereas the Japanese mothers felt responsible for their children and the relationship). Notably, the anger that German five-year-old kids showed during these interactions with their mother, predicted their aggression nine years later (and also explained that, nine years later, the same German children were more aggressive than the Japanese children who had participated in the study). The German mothers may not have so much wanted their children to be angry, but by assuming their child's individuality and intention, and by showing anger themselves, they created the circumstances for anger.

Psychologists Peggy Miller and Linda Sperry followed three working-class mothers who lived in South Baltimore, each with a two-and-a-half-year-old daughter. The mothers also encouraged anger, but not completely in the same way as the German mothers. The South Baltimore mothers wanted to teach their girls to "be strong, to suppress hurt feelings, and to defend themselves when wronged."

When narrating their own lives, the Baltimore mothers described experiences in which they themselves had a great deal of anger and aggression. The girls were not protected from hearing about these incidents. The mothers seemed to want their children to know how to respond to the harsh realities of life in which they might find themselves one day (as their mothers had). Tells one of the mothers:

He started that shit, he was embarrassed to walk down the street with me 'cause my stomach was startin' to get big and all that. I said, "Well get the hell out then."

The morale of this story was: If you want to stand your ground, you have to show anger. This was exactly what the Baltimore mothers wanted to convey to their girls: "Don't be a sissy!" When their child was hurt or wronged, these moms encouraged their child's anger, and helped them "not being a sissy." One mother helped her little girl by explaining to an older child: "She ain't got no . . . blanket. That's why she's yelling." On occasion, the moms also trained their children to not be a sissy by teasing them, and provoking their anger. One mother challenged her two-year old girl to fight her: "You want to fight about it? [provocative tone]; Come on then, chicken." And then told the researcher: "I'm trying to get her mad at me." And afterwards to the child: "Mad 'cause you lost?" In this context, the moms were found to encourage their little girls' anger.

Yet there were other contexts in which the Baltimore moms disapproved of their little girls' anger: when their daughters were mad at *them*, for instance, anger was seen as "spoiled" behavior. Two-year old Wendy had a temper tantrum after her mom took her pacifier ("ninny"): "Wendy hurled herself against the chair, glared at her mother with wide, angry eyes, and screamed, 'Want ninny! Want ninny!'" Wendy's mom responded with a stern "Hey!" and a warning ("Go ahead, You're gonna knock that chair over . . ."). In situations like this, moms used many techniques to stop the anger they perceived, from the kind of warning that Wendy's mom gave to Wendy to threats of punishment ("Want me to beat you?") and justifying explanations of their own behavior ("I needed to wash it off"). Moms were also disapproving of their kids' anger at a peer who did nothing wrong. The message here was a different one: "Don't be spoiled." The Baltimore moms considered the ideal child one who was not easily taken advantage of by others, yet knew their place.

Where many Western caregivers may assume that anger is an unavoidable concomitant of the child's maturation as a person with their own needs and goals, or a necessary response to injustice, caregivers in many other cultures consider anger childish; they believe that it is their role to help children outgrow and conquer their anger. Utku caregivers indulge the emotionality of little children who have "no *ihuma*: no mind, thought, reason, or understanding." Anthropologist Jean Briggs describes how Saarak, who was the youngest of her host family and three years old around the time Briggs arrived at her field location, "screamed in anger and frustration." Saarak's family indulged her, trying to meet all her needs, and soothing her when they could not. It was common knowledge that small children are easily angered and frightened, and cry a lot. It was also shared wisdom that there is no point in teaching children *ihuma* before they show signs of possessing it, which was thought to happen around the age of five or six. Saarak's older sister Raigili, who was six when Briggs arrived, was treated very differently: she was expected to have *ihuma*. Raigili acted as one who has *ihuma* most of the time: her behavior was pleasant and inconspicuous, and she tried not to give offense or inconvenience anyone. Maturity meant to contribute to the equanimity of the group, which meant to ban anger.

Of course, older children's control was still imperfect. Raigili did express anger or frustration sometimes, though her "hostility took the form not of attack but of sullenness: a passive, but total resistance to social overtures." These feelings were never considered justified by the surrounding adults, and her parents ignored the behavior. Adults assumed that the child would end up finding reason, and seeing their errors, even if they did not at the moment. Adults' disapproval of children's actions, although clear to see, did not lead to sanctions. If a child chose to pay no attention to the disapproval, sometimes expressed in the form of fake threats, the subject was dropped, no penalties inflicted. Utku parents modeled the calm and rational response that they valued. They expected that over time their children would become calm as well. Like the Japanese mothers before, Utku caregivers socialized their children to *"never (be) in anger,"* first by modeling an understanding equanimity, and later by disapproving of any anger expressed by their children.

It may be harder to believe that parents in U.S. and European cultural contexts socialize their children to be angry than it is that they socialize them for pride, happiness, and self-esteem, hence the idea that anger is unavoidable; however, research seems to suggest many American and European parents do. Anger embodies the self-reliance and assertiveness that is valued in these cultures, and many parents model, allow, and explicitly teach their children anger, even if they do not like to be at the receiving end.

Emotions Are OURS, Not Just MINE

We raise our children to be good adults in our communities: adults who live their lives according to cultural norms, values, and expectations. Having the right emotions is an important part of being a good adult. In each culture, caregivers teach their children the emotions that support the cultural social norms and values. Having these emotions makes you part of your culture. The moral force that surrounds these emotions is remarkable. In some communities, there is great consensus that a child ought to be made to feel good about themselves; in other communities, there is great consensus about the value of shame, fear, or calm.

Parents and other socializing agents instill these emotions by creating opportunities to experience them, as Oliver's dad and I created opportunity for Oliver to feel pride, and Didi's mom and sister afforded shame. Often, these opportunities are created with emotionally arousing practices, such as praising, beating, frightening, and shaming. Even the methods to reach these emotional outcomes are strongly moralized: in middle-class European American families it is good to praise, and bad to unnecessarily criticize, your child; among the Taiwanese mothers, it is good to shame your child, and wrong to praise them.

Children learn that some emotions are right, when having or showing these emotions meets with approval from the parents and the larger community, or when not having or showing them meets with disapproval. Think about the South Baltimore mothers who encouraged their little daughters to be angry when taken advantage of, and teased their girls to provoke anger. Children also learn *not* to feel or show certain emotions, when having or showing these emotions is met with disapproval or when they are being ignored altogether when showing these emotions. Utku Inuit children, Taiwanese toddlers, and Nso babies learned that being upset was wrong because they met disapproval or were being ignored when they were. Children also learn which emotions are right by observing parental emotions. Parental love, anger, and shame provide children with models for their own emotions.

Becoming part of a culture means having certain kinds of emotions rather than others. Which kinds of emotions are foregrounded depends on the type of adult that is valued. In communities that foreground individual achievement, children need to feel good about themselves (pride). In communities that value obedience, or view the world as a dangerous place, children need to know fear. Communities focusing on propriety encourage shame. Inducing a given emotion is never good or bad in broad terms, but good or bad in a certain cultural context or community, depending on the goals of child-rearing. Beating, and inducing fear, are not bad in general, but bad in a culture that values self-confident and self-propelled children. (White American middle-class families constitute one such context.)

We experience such emotions as *pride, shame, fear, love, amae, omoiyari, calm,* and *excitement* because they are instilled in us by our parents and other cultural agents. Rather than emerging from someplace deep within us, these emotions have been conditioned by recurrent experiences within our cultures. Emotions in early life are better described as relational acts between people than as mental states within an individual. In this particular way, all emotions are OUtside as much as INside the person. This is no less the case for Oliver's *pride* or German babies' *happiness* than it is for the *shame* instilled in Didi, the *malu* instilled in Minangkabau children, the *tahotsy* instilled in Bara children, the *love* instilled by nineteenth-century mothers, the *omoiyari* instilled by Japanese mothers, and the *calm* instilled in Nso babies. Becoming part of a culture, any culture, means to have OURS emotions—not exclusively MINE.

Emotions remain OURS into adulthood. The fabric of our emotions is woven by interactions with others. These interactions account for how we feel and act. In the next few chapters, it will become clear that the course emotions run is different, depending on the episode or interaction, the relationship, and the culture of which they are part.

Chapter 4

. . . .

"RIGHT" AND "WRONG" EMOTIONS

WHEN I STARTED MY WORK ON EMOTIONS IN THE LATE '80s, the evidence for cultural differences appeared to be completely unsystematic. There were cultural differences (and similarities) in every aspect of emotions, but how could we ever hope to get a handle on this mosaic of differences? I now understand a logic to it: cultural differences in emotions are about the types of relationship changes that are either desirable and moral, or undesirable and despised. This logic is more apparent when starting from an OURS model of emotion, from what emotions *do* between people, than from a MINE model, or how emotions *feel*. Emotions change relationships.

We saw some examples of this in the last chapter. A proud child assumes a strong and independent position in a relationship. Pride is, therefore, encouraged and "right" in a culture that values relational autonomy. It is wrong in cultures that value harmony: a proud child is neither empathic nor deferent. In contrast, shame is "right" in the context of a strong cohesive social network, in which a child needs to fit in. In this context, a child who is ashamed acknowledges that their behavior failed to meet the norms, thus showing deference and assuming their proper place. Shame is "wrong" in a culture that focuses on building a child's autonomy and self-esteem, as it emphasizes the child's dependence on others' judgment and their failure to meet certain norms. Consistently, fear is "right" in a society that emphasizes authority as a basis for relationship, but detrimental when love and encouragement is the relational model. A fearful child is inhibited and avoids punishment (or danger in general), but fear simultaneously hampers the individual responsibility and initiative that is valued in many WEIRD cultures. Similarly, a child feeling *amae* yields to the care by others. This is "right" in a culture of close interdependence, but "immature" in a culture whose very developmental goal is to not depend on anybody. Finally, an angry child blames someone else for not giving them what they are entitled to. Anger is "right" (or at least condoned) in cultures (and situations) where children are raised to speak up for themselves, but "wrong" in cultures that teach their children the value of adjusting to the wishes and the activities of their community. In these latter cultures, anger is considered the most "immature" emotion of all.

In each culture, certain emotions are right and others are wrong. Right emotions help to foster relationships that are valued in the culture and wrong emotions support condemned forms of relating. Right emotions are culturally encouraged and rewarded, and wrong emotions are culturally avoided and punished. This is, very simply speaking, the logic of cultural differences in emotions. Cultural differences in emotions owe their logic to an OURS model of emotions—to what they do in our social and cultural worlds.

The remainder of this chapter is devoted to two emotions: anger and shame. Both are considered "right" in some cultures (or positions), but "wrong" in others. These emotions, associated as they are with dominance and avoiding exclusion, respectively, allow us to see how emotions weave the social fabric of our relationships, but also how they become part of, and are shaped by, the relationship in which they occur. By the end of this chapter, you will understand that anger and shame may run many different courses, depending on whether they are considered right or wrong in your culture (and for your position)— that is, depending on how others respond to them. And what, might you ask, does this mean for the universality of anger and shame? Are the same anger and the same shame hidden behind the different ways in which these emotions unfold? Stay tuned.

Anger

Rather than being merely an internal force that prods an individual, an emotion is a taking of a stance in a relationship. To illustrate this, let's stay close to home. Suppose I am angry that my husband is late for dinner: I cooked us a special meal, one that I know he likes, and he did not bother to let me know he was going to be late. Perhaps I am angry that dinner is getting cold, or more likely I feel my efforts went unappreciated. When my husband eventually does come home, I give him an earful. It is not hard to see how *this* could change our relationship, at least momentarily. But the point I want to make is slightly more subtle than that anger comes with behavior that affects your relationship. Anger *itself* takes a stance in your relationship: By getting angry, I take the position that what my husband did—disrespecting me when I made an effort—is not okay. I demand and expect better treatment.

The majority of emotions take place in unfolding social interactions. What happens to my anger—the stance I initially take—is dependent on its reception. Does my husband express regret, does he promise change, does he tread more carefully around me than he usually does and try to please me? Or, to the contrary, does he contest my version of the reality and replace it with his own? If my husband legitimizes my anger by being receptive to it, it may first flare up. However, once I feel seen, and my goals—at least for the future—seem to be met, my anger will fade away. If my husband contests my anger by yelling back, and saying that *he* is the one to be angry, that this is no way to come home, that my whining drives him mad as well as making him angry, I may have to choose another stance: swallow my anger, apologize. Over time, my husband's responses to my anger will also predict whether I become angry in similar situations in the future.

In my cultural context, being angry is acceptable under these circumstances. Communicating to my husband that I am angry may not be pleasant in the moment, but it tells him to respect me, and ultimately may result in a more honest and satisfying relationship between us, one in which both of us get our needs met. The act of nonacceptance can be "right" when the relationship goal is that both partners express their own needs, and that each makes sure that their individual goals are met.

Anger is considered a useful and normal, if not pleasant, emotion in many Western European and American contexts. In adolescence, anger and conflict are often accepted as necessary steps towards the important developmental goal of independence (see chapter 3). Even beyond adolescence, anger has a good role to play in a variety of relationships, private and public: it sets clear boundaries in both. It is the "normal" response to goal-blockage or frustration: a representative study of middle-aged U.S. Americans reportedly acted angry more often, the more frustration they met.

Anger has not always been an acceptable emotion, not even in the United States. In the nineteenth-century Victorian era, women's selfless love was the cornerstone of marriage. Had I been a Victorian woman, I would have shouldered the inconvenience of my husband being late without ever becoming angry. My dignity would have consisted of meeting my role obligations and serving my husband selflessly. I would have had no reason, but also no justification, for being angry. And the slightest reference to anger might have prompted condemnation.

Before the end of the seventeenth century, Western diarists had difficulty describing themselves as angry; they lacked the entitlement that is foundational to anger. Roger Lowe, a seventeenth-century shopkeeping apprentice who kept a diary, described many situations that were noxious and arousing, but he never described himself as angry. Some of his most difficult interactions were with his master, who did not do much to teach him the art of shopkeeping: "I thought it sad for me to be ingaged 9 yeares . . . to sell my Master's ware . . . and get no knowledge." When his master promises and then refuses to give him a new set of clothes, he also describes his feelings as grief: "soe I would have none and parted with grieve." Grief is also his go-to emotion in situations with equals: A woman starts some malicious gossip about him, and he is "in some greefe" about it. Lowe does not see himself as angry, because anger was not "right." God could be angry, but ordinary citizens could not. Entitlement and nonacceptance were not acceptable relationship acts. Instead, Roger Lowe and his contemporaries pray to the Lord to help them "walk humbly."

In many contemporary cultures remote from our own, especially in tightly knit communities and societies, anger is also considered "wrong." It would be nearly impossible to play the anger card if you were an Utku Inuit, a Buddhist Tibetan, an Ifaluk, or even a Japanese individual. In these cultures, communal and relational harmony prevail over individual goals and rights. Entitlement and nonacceptance conflict with the central goals of keeping relationships smooth. Anger is barely seen in any of these cultures, and also much less reported. The Utku Inuit, the same who were "never in anger," valued equanimity and generosity, and disruptions thereof were considered childish and dangerous (see chapter 3). Similarly, Buddhist Tibetans consider *lung lang* (roughly translated as "being angry") to be an extremely destructive emotion, harmful to both self and others. Anger is motivated by a desire to harm another sentient being, and therefore at odds with the Buddhist emphasis on compassion and the ethical code of speaking, acting, and living in non-harmful ways. The Ifaluk, the Polynesian group that hosted anthropologist Catherine Lutz, also condemned anger in their everyday lives. The irritability that accompanies sickness, the frustration that builds up over the succession of minor unwanted things, or the annoyance at relatives not living up to their obligations: all of these varieties of anger were perceived to be immoral and undignified. When relational harmony is prioritized over individual autonomy, entitlement and nonacceptance are wrong. As a result, interpersonal anger is not much seen.

Philosopher Owen Flanagan contrasts the acceptance of many types of anger in Western traditions to the complete condemnation of anger by, for instance, Buddhist and Stoic traditions. In Buddhist psychology *anger* (that I do not get what I want) is a poison in human nature—as despicable as the *illusion* that I am entitled to get what I want and that the world ought to give it to me (from which *anger* springs). In this worldview, anger harms others, but is equally harmful to the self, because it chains you to worldly attachments and delusions that cause your suffering.

When anger is "right" it is more prevalent in everyday life; when anger is wrong it is rare. Survey research finds that U.S. American college students have more anger in their daily lives than their Japanese counterparts—so do middle-aged American men and women, compared to middle-aged Japanese counterparts. When caught in a traffic jam, overloaded with schoolwork, or having problems with family members, U.S. Americans are more readily angered than Japanese in similar situations. When circumstances frustrate the ideal, U.S. Americans find blame and unfairness, whereas Japanese are more reflective of their own shortcomings, and try to overcome difficulties. Anger as nonacceptance is woven into a general view on life.

Anger and the Legitimacy of Power

If anger is a relational act of nonacceptance, then others will either yield to the angry person or resist. In the case of anger, much has to do with the question of legitimacy. In one study, Larissa Tiedens, Phoebe Ellsworth, and I asked U.S. business students to read a vignette in which a boss and an employee formed a sales team whose mission failed. It was not clear from the description whose fault this was, yet the students assumed that the boss was angry, and the employee felt either sadness or guilt. Emotions were simply derived from the power hierarchy: anger was associated with a higher rank, and sadness and guilt were associated with a lower rank. This tells us at minimum that the students in our sample were more exposed to angry bosses than to angry employees. Power or status is associated with anger.

Even in some cultures that condemn anger-like emotions generally, a type of legitimate anger occurs that is reserved to individuals in a position of power or authority. Among the Ifaluk, there is a special word for the kind of anger that is exempt from condemnation: *song* ("justifiable anger"). *Song* is typically claimed by powerful members of Ifaluk society, and a response to rule or value violations. Similarly, in everyday Japanese life, anger is generally considered "immature," but individuals with higher educational and professional status, who have the authority to take decisions, do report angry behaviors. When it is the privilege of the powerful, anger may take on a slightly different meaning as setting or guarding group norms, rather than responding to individual frustration. There is some indication that the powerful anger that is found in Japan is of a healthy kind, whereas anger in the United States (the kind associated with frustration) is unhealthy.

In a series of well-designed studies, Larissa Tiedens showed that anger as a power move may pay off. Her research was sparked by the impeachment hearings of President Bill Clinton; she observed the president being ostensibly angry some times and sad at other times. Would he earn more credit being angry than being sad?, she wondered. In an experiment, Tiedens asked college students to watch short clippings of the impeachment hearings that she selected to show the president either angry or sad. Independent of their political affiliation, Tiedens's respondents supported impeachment more when they had seen the sad rather than the angry Clinton. Apparently, Clinton's move of nonacceptance and entitlement convinced the students.

Starting with this lively but specific example, Tiedens found time and again that anger was rewarded in the U.S. context. In a study with an unknown politician (played by an actor), American students judged the angry (as compared to sad) politician more competent and worthy of their vote. In another study, she found that angry employees were more likely to be promoted in a tech company. And in yet another study, angry job applicants (again as played by actors) were more likely to be hired, and to be offered both a better job and a better salary than sad job applicants, even if all other qualities were the same. And remember who got the better business deal? The angry person who moves to not accept the deal if they do not get what they see as fair. Voters, managers, job committee members, and business negotiators seem to honor the power moves of the angry individuals (in the polls, in the hierarchy of the company, and at the negotiation table).

There is an important caveat, however. Anger will only work if others yield to your claims: when anger is contested, you lose control of the direction in which the relationship changes. Anger may backfire. I referred above to women in the Victorian era. Their role of providing selfless love to their children and spouses was in direct contradiction with claims of entitlement and nonacceptance. A good wife maintained her temper even as her husband lost his, and a good mother loved her children, and was both calm and cheerful. Anger, the opposite, "showed bad character, pure and simple." Similarly, in many cultures anger is so demonized that even the mildest sign of arousal may be met with disapproval.

But in many other cases, anger is negotiated—not always successfully. Let's start with contemporary examples. Larissa Tiedens's research had focused on male politicians and male job candidates. But some ten years later, two of her colleagues, Victoria Brescoll and Eric Uhlmann, were struck by the fate of another Clinton. Hillary Clinton was in a bind. As one opinion maker put it: If she seemed angry, she was "a witch and a shrew"; if she did not, she looked "timid and girly."

This observation spurred a series of studies, comparing angry expressions in men and women. In one study, Brescoll and Uhlmann literally replicated Tiedens's study with job applicants, this time including both male and female job applicants. They replicated her findings for male job applicants who fared better if they expressed anger than not, but not for female job applicants who did not benefit from an angry expression at all. Anger did not successfully claim entitlement for women; there is an emotional glass ceiling.

Black Americans suffer the same fate, or worse. The legitimacy of their anger is often challenged, and any anger is held against them. In a 2020 Op-Ed in the *New York Times,* political scientist Davin Phoenix makes this point precisely:

> . . . America has very different standards for who gets the privilege of expressing anger and defiance, without fear of grave consequence. Angry white agitators can be labeled good people, patriots and revolutionaries, while angry black agitators are labeled identity extremists, thugs and violent opportunists.

Anger is about entitlement, and if others deny you that entitlement, it may turn against you.

If anger is associated with a position of power, being angry can be a gamble. Will others accept your power claim? In a classic ethnography, anthropologist Edward Schieffelin describes how anger among the Kaluli in Papua New Guinea is a power move: "A man whose expectations have been frustrated or who has suffered wrong at the hands of others does not usually suppress his annoyance. Rather he is likely to orchestrate his anger into a splendid rage . . ." Thus showing anger is a claim for compensation. The person who is angry expresses their entitlement and conveys their expectation that others will make up for their suffering and support them. Yet, Kaluli often prevent angry claims before they gain rhetorical force. They do so by questioning their legitimacy. In everyday contexts, anger is countered by shaming. For instance, rather than either granting a child the food that they angrily claim, and also rather than refusing it, the parent will ask: "Is it yours?" Of course, shaming a more powerful opponent is risky, because they will override shame, and dominate the interaction by intimidation. They will just repeat and amplify the original relational acts of anger.

There are also cultures and situations where anger is a claim to legitimacy, without which you would loose position in a fragile hierarchy. This is the case in so-called honor cultures. Honor in these cultures is as much a claim to precedence as it is a virtue. As a claim to precedence, honor is a scarce resource in the social world to be defended by anger.

In the 1990s, cultural psychologists Dov Cohen and Richard Nisbett studied honor in the southern United States. "A key aspect of the culture of honor is the importance placed on the insult and the necessity to respond to it. An insult implies that the target is weak enough to be bullied," they write. In an experiment that cultural psychologists have come to refer to as "the asshole experiment," male college students were insulted as they squeezed by a research assistant who was just opening a drawer cabinet in a narrow hallway. Compared to those from the North, male students from the southern part of the United States were more readily angered when insulted. Anger was essential if they wanted to maintain their honor, as it calls a halt to the erosion of one's social position.

At least part of the way that anger operates in ongoing social interactions depends on its legitimacy, based on general ideas of morality, on the angry person's social position, age, or gender, and perhaps on the wiggle room perceived by someone else to challenge that legitimacy. Challenged anger may extinguish, legitimized anger will run its course. Woven into the emotion of anger are stories of morality: Is the emotion right or wrong? Who is supposed to have it, and who is not? Who can be their target? These contextualized stories are different across cultures.

THE COURSE OF ANGER

Once you see anger as acting between people, there are countless ways of being angry. The way I am angry at my child for not finishing their plate is different from the way I am angry at my human resources department for making a shortsighted decision, and different from the anger I felt at the Trump administration for separating children from their parents at the Mexican border. There are endless variations of anger.

But despite this variation within individuals and within cultures, it is also clear that the typical acts of anger differ between cultures (and between different positions within a culture), depending on what it means to be angry. When entitlement, blame, and nonacceptance are legitimate or even warranted, the course of anger will be different than when a stance of anger is seen as "selfish" or "childish." In the interview study my colleague Mayumi Karasawa and I conducted with American and Japanese college students and adults of the general population (chapter 2), anger seemed to run a very different course in these two cultural contexts. We asked our respondents to tell us about a situation in which they felt "offended or not taken seriously by someone else" as this represents a core theme of anger.

Our American respondents were recruited through churches and community centers in North Carolina, where I lived at the time. Jim, who had been accused by a co-worker of making rude sexual remarks, told us that the "young lady" "tried to get attention," that "she always wanted attention." He also accused her of being a liar and a cheater: "It turned out that she lies a lot. She was trying to get money out of the store." When American respondents told us about such situations, they focused on all the bad properties of their offender. Notice that blaming "the young lady" freed Jim himself of any blemish, leaving his self-esteem intact. "She found out that she and another guy were going to be fired. I think that is why she did this. She took it out on me." Jim was not the only one to tell us about the bad dispositions of their offenders, and the unjustness of their deeds.

Andrew, a supervisor of an electrical department for the state government, was called in to solve a problem in some public building. Against protocol, a security guard in the building demanded that Andrew justify his intervention for a fire report. Andrew declined, but the security guard insisted, and asked for Andrew's qualifications, which Andrew perceived as "overstepping his bounds."

> I was very angry . . . that anybody . . . would even question my ability. . . . And . . . to me [he] would be a subordinate . . . and so that seemed to be the worst that he was kind of on a lower level than me questioning me. I think he was trying to maybe get ahead, thinking that would help him in his job.

Andrew lashes out briefly, but then withdraws from the conversation. Bob, Andrew's friend and colleague, steps in on Andrew's behalf, and asks the guard for his ID. Andrew reports that, as a result,

> [The guard] ended up getting fired over it. . . . He ended up losing his job over it, . . . he was very aggressive, yeah.

Like Jim before, Andrew attributes improper motives ("he was trying to maybe get ahead") and norm-violating behavior ("he was very aggressive") to the security guard. These attributions justify his anger, while also eschewing challenges to his self-esteem. Our U.S. respondents often indicated that they did not think much good of the people who had offended them, and understandably, they distanced themselves (as did Jim), or took stance against the offender (as did Andrew).

On the Japanese side, anger looked very different. Remember that angry behavior is considered "immature" in Japan. The Japanese interviews referred to different situations, so a direct comparison of emotional episodes in the same circumstances is not possible. Yet, the gestalt of the Japanese "anger" episodes was really different. Emiko, a Japanese woman in her thirties, had been waiting at home for her sister to call and make final arrangements to go out for dinner with their father, but her sister did not call until the next morning. Emiko was clearly inconvenienced, and yes, offended:

> I thought she would be coming, and so I was stuck at the house and unable to make plans, but I did not hear from her all day . . . my father was coming to Tokyo, and the three of us had made a promise to eat out together. At the very least, she could have let us know if she was not coming but she did not. . . . I ended up going to the meeting place myself. If it had just been me waiting, that would have been bearable–I would have thought to myself "as usual"—but the promise included our father, so . . .

The sister apologized afterwards, but Emiko was not sure what it was worth, because this was her sibling's usual disregard. Yet, Emiko decided it was not worth complaining about too much: she knew that she and her sister had different perspectives.

> Even if I had told her: "I was waiting for you, and I was not able to plan my day without knowing what you were up to," she would have no doubt replied: "Why didn't you just go without waiting for me?" But the reason I stayed home was so that she could reach me, since neither of us have a cell phone and it's difficult to contact each other, but . . . (laugh) . . . (silence).

Emiko's response was not to take distance and vilify her sister, as many American respondents reported, but rather to come up with a solution: *I thought I want my sister to have a cell phone*, she answered when asked what she had felt like doing. The majority of the Japanese respondents analyzed the anger target's behavior, without vilifying them. They tried to understand the behavior of the person who had offended them, if not explain it away. Even Emiko's reflections that it was in her sister's nature to be lax can be understood as an attempt to explain or analyze the behavior. Our Japanese respondents sometimes went as far as to justify the behavior of their target of anger: Emiko pondered that it was hard for her sister to call, because she did not have a cell phone. This did not change her being offended by the behavior, but it did put it in perspective. Most Japanese respondents also reported "doing nothing at all," because any behavior would have been useless or counterproductive: Emiko thought her sister would not have been responsive to her complaints.

A pattern among the Japanese respondents emerged: they tried to adjust, and coped with the situation as best as they could. Emiko talked to her sister, but saw the solution in a cell phone. Hiroto, the Japanese man whom I introduced in chapter 2, similarly tried to understand the motives of the fellow committee member who criticized him. Hiroto felt "offended and annoyed" that this woman had started to annex his tasks, he thought she was wrong, he took some distance, but also sought to be cooperative in the committee. And Chiemi, the student whose grandparents criticized her for being late so often, even though she was usually home early, also focused on the relationship. She may have wanted to have more "fun until late at night," but she smiled away their criticism and made an effort to come home early after this exchange with her grandparents.

I have been asked if I was sure that what the Japanese felt was anger, and if their anger was "as intense" as the anger reported by the American respondents in our study. As you may remember, Japanese had trouble with the intensity question, but they did think these cases of offense were "important," and they did call them instances of *ikari*, the Japanese counterpart of anger. Is it possible that the episodes connected with "anger" and *ikari* are partially different, because life is different in the United States and Japan?

Perhaps the whole question of whether this is "the same emotion" originates from a MINE model: the idea that the real emotion is a mental state behind the episode of anger. What if anger *is* the way Jim, Emiko, Hiroto, and Chiemi take a stance in the relationship? What if, consistent with an OURS perspective, the emotion is what is going on between people? If we just stick with that idea for a moment, then what goes on between people is different in the Japanese and the American context. A typical Japanese scenario of anger is that I feel wronged by the other person and try to protect myself from their behavior, but in so doing I try to preserve the relationship, and not be selfish or childish. I might try to understand the target's perspective, and apologize for my part in what went wrong, or I do nothing at all. In a typical American scenario in a similar situation I would also feel wronged, I would think that I really do not deserve to be treated this badly, that actually my wrongdoer should have known better than to treat me unfairly, and that I'm not going to just take an insult. So I show my anger. Alternatively, I may wonder what is wrong with my wrongdoer to treat me this way, given that it is obviously wrong? Perhaps they have improper motives, or perhaps they just are that kind of person. In the latter case, I might decide to actively distance myself from the wrongdoer. Are these the *same emotions*? If you take an OURS model, no anger is exactly the same as any other. The angry episodes in Japan and the U.S. overlapped importantly in that they started with an offense, and were labeled "anger" and its Japanese translation *ikari*. Whether these are the same emotions becomes a question of less relevance when you are not assuming emotions are stable mental states. And why would you assume that the mental state is invariant if each angry episode is slightly different from the next?

Shame

In WEIRD cultures shame is "wrong." Shame is the experience of being a bad or inadequate person in the eyes of others; it has been described as feeling worthless, shrinking, small, powerless, exposed, and disapproved of by others. Shame means you imagine that others disapprove of you: it is the feeling of being evaluated by others and found to be deficient. People in WEIRD cultures do not *like* to imagine being dependent on others' judgment, least of all being disapproved of: they should be feeling good about themselves, independent from others. And because of this, shame becomes extremely uncomfortable.

When I conducted interview research in the United States—the same study we conducted in Japan—I found that shame was the hardest emotion to talk about for American respondents. Quite a few, especially in the non-student sample, told us that this type of event had never happened to them. And when these respondents did tell us about their experiences of shame, these were quite devastating; often these were instances from the more remote past that they could scarcely have forgotten.

For instance, Ryan (a married twenty-eight-year-old man) remembered how a car accident in his teens paralyzed his legs and made him fully dependent on his parents, until a successful surgery:

> When I had my car accident. . . . It was humiliating in a way because someone had to help you go to the bathroom or get dressed. . . . [I felt] Worthless. No one would want me: especially a woman who wants children. I blamed God and everyone else except the person who did it—me. . . . I had been very athletic before, and here I was, not able to walk or do anything . . . I just felt like I would not be any good to anyone. . . .

Dorothy, a sixty-five-year-old woman, remembered how she and her first husband had been refused as youth counselors for the church camp, because her husband was gay (and "he was not seen as someone that could be trusted with youth"):

> We were supposed to be youth advisors to a certain group at church . . . and everybody got their assignments but us. . . . I can remember sitting in the youth pastor's home that night and feeling that, through no action of my own, I was being lumped as somebody that was undesirable. . . . [The pastor and his wife] knew . . . how I would feel about it . . . , but it had to be done.

[I felt] a deep sense of loss . . . being exposed. A situation where you'd like to go somewhere and pull the lid over ya and not come out again. . . . [I felt like] avoiding going to church, but uh, I did go . . .

Ryan calls his feelings the strongest he ever had, and Dorothy says that if she had been suicidal, this would have been the time to end her life. Shame means to be criticized and rejected in a culture where you are supposed to feel good about yourself and be loved. Ryan literally falls short of the cultural ideal of independence, and Dorothy becomes "exposed" by what she holds to be the immorality of her husband's sexual preference; in either case, they fall short of a positive identity they value. Both are rejected (not qualifying as camp counselor), or at least imagine being rejected ("No one would want me: especially a woman who wants children") for reasons they agree with, and that are collectively valued. Ryan thinks he is "worthless," and Dorothy thinks that her and her husband's being barred from the youth camp "had to be done." Shame is "wrong" because it shows you are worthless or bad, but in addition, it may be "wrong" because it personifies withdrawal from social life. Ryan would "stay in bed," and would have liked to "just go away"; Dorothy felt like avoiding going to church. In both cases, shame interfered with their normal participation in social life.

That shame is socially debilitating is also clear from a study with salespeople in the financial sector, this time in the Netherlands. Marketing professors Richard Bagozzi, Willem Verbeke, and Jacinto Gavino developed shame stories that involved customers. For instance, the customer points out that the salesperson has neglected to fulfill a promise they previously made to the customer, or the salesperson discovers a mistake in their own presentation. Salespeople were asked to report the shame responses they had when something similar occurred to them. The Dutch salespeople felt what Dorothy called "exposed." They imagined that customers would be scrutinizing every one of their behaviors and seeing right through them. They also felt "worthless," the word Ryan used: they imagined that the customer knew that they were "an incomplete and inadequate person," and "a failure as an individual." And, finally, they felt the acute sense of shame, which neither Ryan nor Dorothy described because their stories were so far in the past. The salespeople imagined they would feel like "crawling in a hole," "suddenly shrinking," and "physically weak" and "tongue-tied." To the Dutch salespeople, shame meant feeling exposed, feeling a failure, and feeling small and weak.

Bagozzi and his colleagues were particularly interested in how shame would affect the relationship with customers. They reasoned that Dutch salespeople, coming from an individualist culture (similar to the U.S.), would "strive to be unique, to promote their own goals, to feel self-assured, and to compare themselves with others so as to surpass or achieve better achievement." When shamed, Dutch salespeople would become aware that their actions or accomplishments were negatively evaluated, and this would be a threat to how they wanted to feel. As they felt "denigrated and ridiculed," Bagozzi and colleagues reasoned, Dutch salespeople would be preoccupied trying to protect their self-esteem—so preoccupied, in fact, that they would not have the bandwidth to attend to their customer. This is what they found: Dutch salespeople who were ashamed became reluctant to take any chances in the relationship—they did not ask questions, they did not engage in small talk, and they did not make any business proposals. They became less effective communicators and they were no longer able to deliver appropriate service to the customer. Shame itself became a burden, and made the salespeople withdraw from their social engagements, as shame seemed to have done for Ryan and Dorothy.

It is possible that shame is so uncomfortable that we try to collectively avoid it? When was the last time you heard someone talk about being ashamed? In our own research, Michael Boiger asked U.S. and Japanese college students to rate situations that had elicited shame in previous groups of American and Japanese college students. The situations that Americans found most shameful were also the ones that they rated to be rare. One such situation was originally reported by an American college student named Elizabeth whose mother told her on her graduation that she was disappointed in her grades.

Shame is so damning that it comes with strong defenses. The one that received most attention is to deny one's own inadequacy, and instead blame someone else. Shame is often associated with anger or hostility. Ryan may have been more reflective than many a person experiencing shame, remembering: "I blamed God and everyone else except the person who did it—me. . . ." Psychoanalysts have called shame-turned-anger "humiliated fury." Humiliated fury appears to skip the painful experience of rejection and transforms it into aggression towards others. One way of understanding the benefits of humiliated fury is that ashamed individuals draw on anger as a resource to overcome the painful and paralyzing experience of shame, and to regain agency and control, though sometimes at a great cost to themselves and others. These costs become clear in a unique study on shame among American inmates who were followed from incarceration until after their release from prison. Inmates who felt shame about their crime often (though not always) suffered from humiliated fury, and it was humiliated fury that predicted the bleak future of recidivism. Inmates who reported shame-turned-anger were more likely to lapse into committing new crimes after they were released than inmates reporting shame without fury.

The bad rap of shame is also clear from the attention it has received among clinical psychologists, mostly psychoanalysts. Where the developing child is seen to be secure, happy, and full of self-esteem, the neurotic child is afraid of disapproval, and therefore, prone to shame. And at the root of the child's neurosis are detached or critical parents. These parents are doing the opposite of what is culturally valued: making their child feel bad (rather than good) about themselves. Not surprisingly, then, individuals who are easily ashamed are vulnerable to depression, anxiety, and somatic symptoms, always carrying the critical parent with them, and seeing everyone else as unescapably critical as well. The latter may be the reason for shame-turned-anger: a critical other is an easy scapegoat, and it is "a short step to attribute the cause of painful shame feelings to others who are perceived as disapproving." If the meaning of shame itself already interferes with the cultural ideals of self-esteem and being loved, then humiliated fury does not help its reputation. If anything, the hostility that is marshaled as a defense against shame helps to reinforce the idea that the shameful person is anti-social. But does shame have to be "wrong"?

In many cultures, shame or a mild form of shame, is omnipresent and "right." Remember, the Minangkabau and Taiwanese kids are raised to have shame, as a way to make them take their proper place in their networks. Showing shame is a virtue rather than a sign of weakness. When the primary cultural goal is to meet the social expectations for your role, showing an awareness of your violations is appreciated. Shame tells others that you know your place, that you are prepared to do what it takes to be accepted by them. Shame also means that you take others' perspective in the situation: How are you doing in their eyes? Are you meeting their expectations? Shame, in other words, indicates that you care about your bond with others.

In a *New York Times* Op-Ed with the title "An Admirable Culture of Shame," Nassrine Azimi, then senior advisor at the United Nations Institute for Training and Research (UNITAR), held a mirror to her American readers by describing exactly this kind of "right" shame for Akio Toyoda, the president of Toyota, a Japanese company:

> When in February of this year Akio Toyoda . . . testified before the U.S. Congress and took personal responsibility for the failures of his company, it was seen as a matter of course. But can one even imagine an American executive from Wall Street apologizing in the parliament of another country? Why would such an act of apology by an American be so unimaginable, whereas a Japanese doing this seems unsurprising?

To understand why the president of Toyota apologized to the U.S. Congress as a matter of course, we need to know that people in Japan habitually see themselves as incomplete, and are encouraged to be self-critical. Shame fits this focus on self-criticism, and on working hard to make up for the deficits you (as anybody) unavoidably have. Shame is not only rated as less unpleasant in Japanese than U.S. American contexts, but it helps to achieve a core cultural goal, that of maintaining harmonious social relationships and doing enough for the group.

The Japanese emotion *haji* (shame, embarrassment) fits the general Japanese ethos of perspective-taking and embodies a keen motivation not to burden others. Many of the emails I receive from my Japanese friends and colleagues start with, "I am sorry to trouble you." Apologizing is at the center of shame practices: it is an acknowledgment of burdening the other, and the wish that this could have been prevented.

When we conducted our interview studies, the same interviews that taught us that Japanese respondents were unsure what we meant by emotional intensity, we encountered another surprising fact: the Japanese interviewees felt most comfortable talking about situations of shame. In other cultures, we had saved shame episodes for the very last, and had started with a positive emotion, such as pride. But talking about moments of success, or standing out, risks jeopardizing the relationship with others in many Japanese contexts, and so it did not break the ice for our Japanese respondents. To the contrary, they were reticent to share prideful happiness situations. On Mayumi Karasawa's strong recommendation, we thus turned the order of the emotions around for the Japanese respondents. And much against my intuition, starting the interview by reporting an instance of shame broke the ice for Japanese respondents. When shame is a step towards remedying your shortcomings and mending a relationship in jeopardy, it is good to be talking about it. Shame was "right," and in our survey studies, Japanese respondents reported higher frequencies of shame than their U.S. counterparts.

If shame sets off a downward spiral in WEIRD cultures, it has the exact opposite effect in cultures where it is "right." In many of those cultures, it motivates you to invest in the relationship at stake, adding to its reputation as a socially beneficial emotion. In their study on shame, Bagozzi and his colleagues compared Dutch salespeople to their Filipino counterparts. Like the Dutch, the Filipino salespeople recognized shame as feeling exposed, a failure, and small and weak. But shame did not make the Filipino salespeople withdraw or stumble. To the contrary, shame signaled that they had to invest in the customer relationship that was not going well. Rather than making them want to hide, shame made them reach out to their customers. Separately, Filipino salespeople who felt shame reported better sales interactions and higher sales volumes—showing the yields of their investment in the customer relationship.

There are other cultures in which showing shame breeds acceptance. Among the Minangkabau and the Taiwanese, for example, the shameful child is a good child who saves their parents' face. Shame is shared by the members of the secure family network and gains them acceptance in the broader community. The Japanese friend or spouse expressing shame or self-criticism meets cultural expectations, and can count on their friend's or spouse's acceptance and support. And in fact, Japanese college students indicated that they encountered many situations eliciting strong shame—the opposite of their American counterparts. The Japanese students seem to seek out shame situations, rather than avoid them as the American students did. Shame means you know your place or your shortcomings, and in a culture where this does not change anything in the relationships, this is a good thing.

Yet, in other cultures where your position is less assured, and where social regard is subject to continuous negotiation, shame is the marker of losing ground. This is the case in honor cultures, when insults threaten the very thing that is important: the positive image that others have of you. Shame is "right" under these circumstances because it keeps you focused on your social position, but the social dynamics are very different from the cultures where your position is assured.

During the interviews in the Netherlands (chapter 2), it struck me that many Turkish participants reportedly ended the relationship with whomever offended them. A forty-seven-year-old Turkish college-educated man, Omer, told us how his friend Mehmet falsely accused him of having seized some of the valuable possessions of a recently deceased shared friend. In truth, Omer added, it was Mehmet himself who appropriated these possessions. Mehmet's accusations did not remain without consequences for Omer's social image: for a while, other people stopped trusting Omer. When Omer first learned about Mehmet's accusations, he was "sad" and his "confidence in his friend shocked." This happened back in Turkey and in the years since, he has remained "angry," and he never talked to Mehmet again.

Similarly, a fifty-year-old high-school-educated Turkish woman, Emine, stopped talking to her stepsister, Pelin, after the latter had eavesdropped on Emine's confidential conversation with her friend Duygu—all the while Pelin was pretending to sleep. After that happened, Emine's world collapsed: she felt so angry. If today Pelin would drop dead, Emine would not care; in Emine's eyes, Pelin was "nothing."

When they were offended by a close other, almost all Turkish respondents told us they ended the relationship, but even Turkish respondents who told us about insults by neighbors and colleagues reported to have been extremely angry, to the point of severing all contact. Aslan, a twenty-nine-year-old Turkish man who had moved to the Netherlands at the age of nineteen, reported that he was "the angriest [he] had ever been" when his Dutch neighbor threatened to hit his son. In response, Aslan hit the neighbor and also broke the neighbor's windows with his bare fists. Aslan's wife and friend witnessed it all, and tried to calm Aslan down, but to no avail. His wife ended up calling the police, who came and intervened between the two. Aslan describes the police as "very understanding that he was as angry as he was with the neighbor," even as they required him to reimburse the neighbor for the window —which he did. He hated to have to go to his neighbor and deliver the cash, but he refrained from beating the neighbor a second time. He never again talked to the neighbor. All Aslan's friends agreed that the neighbor's behavior was completely out of line.

Spontaneously, the Turkish interviewees reported that they were "angry"; they did not volunteer "shame." And yet, there is reason to suspect that it was shame that could explain why the the Turkish interviewees ended the relationships with whomever had insulted them. We did not ask them explicitly if they felt shame, but they spontaneously reported being very concerned with the impact of the event on the respect they, their family, or their ingroup received from others— concerns which in other honor cultures are highly connected with shame. In similar situations, the Dutch interviewees were hardly concerned with their social image. They too reported having been angry, but they painted very different endings. In most of the Dutch episodes, the anger had faded away: respondents had made up with the other person, got over the insult, etc.

Shame in honor culture is the awareness that your social image is exposed and threatened. However, as your social image is interconnected with the honor of your family and ingroup, honor attacking situations include close others. There is a ripple effect of shame such that your shame also affects the shame of your relatives and friends whose honor is equally attacked. Psychologist Patricia Rodriguez Mosquera and her colleagues specifically studied family honor; they compared Pakistani college students in Pakistan with white American students from the East Coast. They asked students to remember "a situation in which a member of your family did or said something that devalued your family." If family honor is shared, argues Mosquera, then every family member must avoid disrespecting the family, everyone is responsible for every other family member's behavior and must try to keep them from disrespecting or devaluing the family, and every family member is charged with protecting the family from insults and other devaluations inflicted by outsiders. Failing to meet any of those charges exposes you and elicits shame.

The Pakistani students did indeed find the situation in which a relative desecrated the family very shameful, more so than the American students. Moreover, among the Pakistani students, but not the American students, most shame was reported by those who perceived the highest threat to the family honor. So big was shame in those situations, that Pakistani students often reported distancing themselves from the relationship with the relative—just like my Turkish respondents in the Netherlands had done. When someone you are close to disrespects your shared honor, you have no choice other than to severe ties. An offense, particularly by someone who is supposed to share the burden of your honor, is deeply shameful, as it exposes the erosion of your social position. The Turkish interviews in my research show that this erosion is real: Omer's other friends no longer trusted him after Mehmet spread the lie that Omer seized valuable possessions, and Aslan's neighbor showed a clear disrespect for all to be seen by threatening to hit Aslan's son—in Aslan's presence, no less. Omer's and Aslan's ending the relationship with their respective offenders was not a result of anger per se, but of anger rooted in shame: anger as a way to restore the shameful situation, to rid yourself of any connection to a person with whom you can impossibly share honor.

Remember Emine's devastation when she found out her stepsister Pelin knew about her secrets? Emine severed her relationship with Pelin, to the extent possible within a family. Yet, the interviewer was the only person to whom she ever mentioned the incident. She did not even confide in her friend Duygu, because she did not want to harm Pelin's reputation; she "saved Pelin from the criticism of others." Was it a way to protect family honor, and thereby her own as well? It is very possible.

Ending the relationship with their offender was not the only way in which our participants tried to protect their social image. When possible, they also tried to convince others that they were in the right, sometimes by proving the offender wrong. Aslan convinced the police that he had reason to hit his neighbor, and he got his friends to agree with him that no person in their right mind would behave the way the neighbor had. Psychologist Ayse Uskul reasons that if honor is easily lost in honor cultures, then individuals are socialized to avoid the painful consequences. Convincing others that your offender is unworthy, particularly if you can distance yourself from them, is one way of avoiding them.

If shame in WEIRD cultures is "wrong" because it marks your own failure clearly visible to others, shame in honor cultures is "right," even as it is deeply disturbing. Shame is right because it tracks threats to your and your family's (group's) social position, which shows you share the central cultural concern of honor. Shame is everywhere in honor cultures. And when shame is recognized, it leads you to take action to protect your own and your family's honor. Often this is done by showing your strength—anger is a good, but not the only, way to restore your honor; some psychologists claim that it is not even the most important one. In any case, you must act in a way that claims your honor, or else you will lose your position—fragile as it is.

Is the shame-turned-anger in honor cultures different from humiliated fury? I would argue it is, for two reasons. First, as we have seen above, shame is the "right" response to extremely undesirable events in honor cultures, whereas in WEIRD cultures it is "wrong." Importantly, shame in honor cultures helps to achieve the important task of protecting honor; shame in WEIRD cultures, though certainly marking an awareness that others' acceptance is at stake, does nothing to achieve important cultural tasks. Second, shame-turned-anger takes place in the social world as a negotiation of positions (it is primarily OURS), whereas humiliated fury is a shift of the individual's attributions of unhappy outcomes—from self to other (it is primarily MINE).

Under some circumstances, shame in honor cultures may also consist of the awareness of *potential* threats to honor, and the behavior warding them off. Shame in this latter sense protects feminine honor: the (sexual) modesty of the female relatives, on which the family honor depends. Among the Egyptian Bedouins, *hasham* (roughly translated as "shame") is a dignified way for women, considered weak and dependent, to achieve respect and honor. *Hasham* is *part* of the modesty code that individuals adopt as matter of self-respect and pride, rather than an obligation. Shame, and the deferent behaviors associated (e.g., veiling, avoiding contact), are moral in this context. They mitigate any negative consequences that modesty breaches might bring for the less powerful. This shame is perhaps closer to the shame seen in cultures with a fixed hierarchy of positions, and in fact there may be a fixed hierarchy between men and women in honor cultures.

THE COURSE OF SHAME

Whenever I present cultural differences in shame, colleagues have asked me if "exotic" examples of shame are really the same emotion. Was Akio Toyoda, Toyota's CEO, really ashamed, as Dorothy was? Could Toyoda's apologies have been an expression of embarrassment, or could he have been merely polite? Was Aslan's aggression an "expression" of the anger following his shame rather than of shame "itself"? And did the Egyptian Bedouin women have an emotion at all, or were they merely rule-abiding? Do people in other cultures not mislabel their emotions? Are we talking about the same shame in all these cases?

Shame, like anger, is part of a relationship. Depending on the (projected) responses of others, shame runs a very different course. "Right" shame is successful at performing the act of reintegration in the community; "wrong" shame further alienates the person who feels shame. Right shame may either be the relational act of propriety or modesty, or interestingly enough, the awareness that your social position is under threat and needs to be reclaimed; wrong shame may be the "wanting to dissolve into nothing," or perhaps, having lost honor irrecoverably. Right shame is an awareness of others' perspective, wrong shame is the realization that you fall short. For instance, Japanese college students reporting shame were on average more focused on being judged by others ("I focused on what the other(s) is/(are) thinking of me"), and U.S. college students were focused on falling short of the standard ("I blamed myself for the outcome of the situation"). Spanish students (from an honor culture) associated shame more with "public evaluations," while Dutch students associated shame more with "self-failure." There are perhaps some universal themes that run through shame episodes, such as a bid for acceptance, but there is no reason to think that shame is characterized by an invariant feeling, or that it runs the same course.

As with anger, the question about the "same shame" stems from a MINE perspective. Not only is it primarily concerned with the feeling of shame, but it also assumes that shame has an invariant essence. Once we take an OURS perspective, the question of what shame "really is" becomes moot. It is a collection of episodes in which the relational act can be recognized as some form of seeking social inclusion. Each episode of shame runs a different course, depending on its cultural significance, the projected or actual responses of others, the kinds of relationships in which they take place, and the collective ideals for personhood and relationships.

Emotions like anger and shame *do* something in the relationship with others. Anger is a claim for dominance, which is "right" in cultures that emphasize entitlement and individual autonomy, right in cultures where people compete for the scarce good of honor, but "wrong" in cultures that emphasize kindness for all living creatures or harmonious relationships. Shame is a bid for inclusion, typically (though not always) by submission. This is right in cultures valuing the interdependence of people, but wrong in cultures that value independence and assertion. Right shame can take the form of propriety, or it can come with assertive claims for respect and precedence; wrong shame can be marked by hiding from sight and hoping others won't notice you too much. Emotions are prevalent when they are right and rare when they are wrong.

Is anger a healthy ingredient of every relationship? Is shame a self-destructive emotion? The answer is: It depends. When the emotion is right by your culture, it is healthy; when it is wrong, it is often unhealthy. Not surprisingly, then, when psychologists study which emotions make individuals feel good in their lives, and be healthy, we find differences across cultures. Those emotions that help to achieve sociocultural goals are associated with higher subjective wellbeing and greater health. People who have emotions that are more typical for the average person in their culture also report greater subjective well-being. When we have emotions that support our cultural values, we feel better and we even *do* better.

The prevalence of anger and shame are different, their consequences are different, but can we conclude that anger and shame *exist* across cultures? We can, if we refer to the leanest of meanings—what philosopher Owen Flanagan refers to as "proto-anger" and "proto-shame": emotions associated with assertion and avoiding exclusion, respectively. What we experience and do when we have an anger-like emotion is very different in a culture protecting self-esteem than in a culture protecting the relationship or a culture competing for honor, and justified anger is different from anger denied. Similarly, shame is different when it is of the self-deflating kind, or alternatively, of the relationship-restoring kind. Even if some prototype, some core relational themes (dominance, avoiding exclusion) can be recognized, anger and shame run very different courses across cultures, situations, and positions. It may be more appropriate, then, to speak of the plural "angers" and "shames" than to speak of the singular "anger" and "shame." Yet is this phenomenon true only of "unpleasant" emotions? Wouldn't we universally welcome and want "pleasant" emotions, such as love and happiness? Next, we will turn to those emotions.

Chapter 5

BEING CONNECTED AND FEELING GOOD

WHO WOULD NOT WANT A LIFE FULL OF LOVE AND HAPPIness? We may assume these emotions are "right" in all cultures, yet the universality of the desire to love and be happy is more controversial than you may think. Lives in many cultures are not geared towards maximizing love and happiness—at least not if we define love and happiness in the ways they are typically used in middle-class American, or other WEIRD, contexts. Instead, love and happiness are irrelevant, even "wrong." For all the progress "positive psychology" research has made in understanding flourishing, it has missed out on culture; the enterprise has been WEIRD.

Where positive emotions were traditionally not seen as doing anything in particular, psychologists have now started to ask, how do positive emotions act? Psychologist Barbara Fredrickson describes their role as "broadening and building." For "broadening," think of the energy that *happiness* infuses, making you want to "play and get involved," or alternatively, of "the urge to explore to learn, to immerse oneself in . . . novelty" that is inherent to *interest*. For "building," think of emotions such as *gratitude* and *love*, and the role they play in building the most important resource of all: the social connection with others.

In this chapter, we will explore the role of two such positive emotions, love and happiness. We'll see that "being connected" and "feeling good" are universal themes of flourishing, but just as how angers and shames operate within the bounds of the relationships in which they occur, we will see that loves and happinesses are tailored to interactions and relationships in particular cultural contexts.

Love

Love is a staple of Western cultures. In a U.S. American study from the late 1980s, college students recognized love as "the best example" of an emotion. In a Canadian study around the same time, students agreed that love "is one of the most important human emotions" and that "in our culture, we learn about love from childhood on." The Canadian students distinguished at least 123 different types of love, but found maternal, paternal, friendship, sibling, and romantic love the best examples of love.

What does love do? A person who loves someone else fully engages in a close relationship with a particular other, or tries to build one. For the most part love is felt for people who offer something we want, need, or like; who are psychologically or physically attractive; and who need, love, or appreciate us back. In other words, loved ones are special to us, and we are special to them—so special, in fact, that we spend lots of time with them and share special moments. We feel love when the relationship is secure and trusting, and when we enjoy open communication. Love means giving attention to your loved one—sometimes at the expense of attention for other things—wanting to be close to them, expressing your positive feelings for them, to hug, hold, cuddle, touch, pet (if it is an animal), kiss, and, in case of a romantic relationship, have sex with them. Love, especially the reciprocal kind, gives you self-confidence and makes you positive about life; having love makes you more secure and relaxed. Love is the basis for, and core of, important relationships in Western culture.

Love fits with a culture emphasizing the autonomy of individuals. As one U.S. American woman explained in an interview: "[Love] is a lot of sacrifice, a lot of work, a lot of giving, but it has to be something that is very free, freely given instead of you're forced to it." Love recognizes simultaneously that individuals are free to not connect, and yet have chosen to connect to this particular individual. Implicit in love is that the loved one's unique qualities invite a connection.

Love is "right" in WEIRD cultures, because it individuates and elevates the loved one. This is most obviously true for romantic love, but it can also be true for maternal love. I remember loving my firstborn so much that I pitied the other mothers in the pediatrician's waiting room for not having been as lucky with their babies. In my eyes, my little Oliver was the brightest and the most beautiful baby. It was only years later that I considered the possibility that my perception was part of the great love I felt for him. Love singles out and elevates one particular individual. In a culture that so dearly values the individual, love achieves the ultimate goal for individuals: to be united in mutual admiration, attraction, or longing. In these ways, love as we know it fits the cultural ethos of individualism that prevails in many Western cultural contexts.

Tenderness, empathy, and intimacy have always existed. But love as a private feeling for a unique person, love as a choice to be together, love as a source of self-esteem—that type of love may be a modern and Western invention.

WHERE WEIRD CULTURES VALUE AND foreground the autonomy of the individual, prioritizing their goals over the goals of the collective, many other cultures prioritize relationship and group goals over those of the individual. Where marriages are arranged, if love exists between partners (it often does), it follows rather than precedes marriage. It is less a matter of choice, and more of growing appreciation. But, you may ask, how can you really love someone who is not the partner of your choosing?

To give this some perspective, and to show how much love by choice is a cultural product, consider that love marriages—marriages by individual choice—are likewise ridiculed by people who have grown up with the idea of arranged marriage. In one news show an Indian woman giggled at the idea of young people choosing their own spouses, based on "love": "Physical attraction? That is not a big thing" she said. In that same show, a young Indian man explained: "My parents know me better than anyone else in the world. So they know what is the best for me. I think the same for her." In many communities of the world—such as rural communities in Afghanistan, Pakistan, Iran, Iraq, and China, but also some Jewish communities that strictly abide by the Torah—the idea is that marriage partners are best selected by your family or parents. Marriage is seen not only as a marriage between two people but as a joining of two extended families. Marriage partners are the sons and daughters of other, known families, or selected from families of similar ethnicity, religion, and socioeconomic status.

When love occurs outside of marriage, it may be drenched in sadness. In the 1980s Chinese respondents who sorted emotion words on similarity understood love as "sad," and categorized it as part of the negative rather than the positive emotion family. In the country of Filial Piety, love had the potential to break down the proper respect and deference that children owed their parents. This may be one of the reasons that romantic love was devalued; interestingly, Chinese respondents describe love using more negative features such as pain, sadness, sacrifice, and loneliness than American respondents.

When I teach about cultural differences in emotions, my students often think that love should be more pronounced in collectivist contexts. If the ties between people are strong in collectivist contexts, then wouldn't this be because individuals feel lots of love for each other? Wouldn't interdependence between people be achieved by individuals consistently seeking intimacy? The answer to both questions is a resounding "no"; in fact, nothing could be further from the truth. In truly collective cultures, relationships are either a given or chosen in close consultation with the group (the latter being the case in arranged marriages). In these cultures, relationships are not so much organized around admiration or attraction (love), but rather around the needs of others (empathy/compassion). The "right" emotions in many cultures are not about idealization and choice, but rather about need and the unavoidable connection between people.

Take the Japanese emotion of *amae*. Like love, this is an emotion that centers on caring and dependence, but it is very different from *love*. The prototype of an *amae* relationship is that between mother and child. As we have seen in chapter 3, Japanese mothers accept and indulge the childish behavior of their toddlers and kindergartners. They do not curtail this behavior, and show empathy and understanding. When the preschooler Nao (also introduced in chapter 3) clung to her mother's leg, she was acting younger than her age. She did not take control in the situation, and waited till someone else did. Another preschooler not yet introduced, Maki, became the nurturing partner and in so doing accepted an *amae* relationship. She approached Nao and convinced her to play with her. Maki thus accepted Nao's inappropriate demeanor and offered what Nao needed. *Amae* not only presupposes, but also—importantly—created an interdependent relationship between the girls. Therefore, *amae*, a central emotion in Japanese close relationships, achieves interdependence, rather than mutual admiration, attraction, and longing. *Amae* is certainly not restricted to childhood. You grant your close friends or your romantic partners what they need even, or especially, if it is unreasonable. *Amae* is based on need and indulgence, rather than idealization or elevation of the partner.

In her book *Unnatural Emotions,* anthropologist Catherine Lutz describes a central Ifaluk emotion of closeness and dependence: *fago*. One of the translations of *fago* is "love." However, unlike U.S. American love, which shares features with joy, *fago* shares features with sadness and compassion. *Fago* is "right" in Ifaluk society. It is a mature person's response to the suffering of others: the readiness to take care of other people in need. *Fago* is typically felt for someone who is sick, dying, or without family, but it also occurs in a more pleasant context, as is apparent from an example involving Tamalekar. A young man from another island came to visit him by ship. The visit was appropriate, because the young man shared a clan affiliation with Tamalekar.

> They and the rest of Tamalekar's family spent the evening in quiet talk, with the [. . .] man speaking with respect and politeness. The visitor had distinguished himself by bringing

a gift of a carton of cigarettes. The evening wore on past the point at which the family usually retired, and when the young man stepped out for a moment [. . .], Tamalekar said to his family, "We *fago* this one because he is calm. Even though we are sleepy, we'll stay up and talk with him."

Later Tamalekar gave the man one of his valued possessions. The meaning of *fago* as taking care of someone does not change, but this time the nurturing is prompted by a man, who through his calm and kind behavior (not through his needs), demonstrates having compassion himself. Compassion meets compassion and nurturing; in this case, the act of *fago* is more reciprocal.

Whereas *love* seeks joyful closeness between autonomous individuals who find each other special, *fago* is nurturing a person with whom a connection already exists, or else has come to be felt. Typically, *fago* is an unavoidable response to another person's needs, whereas love is seeking closeness to another person of your *choice,* one who has special qualities and who is particularly appreciative of you. To be sure, loving partners will take care of each other in case of need, and *fago*-ing individuals may find joy in each other (as when the young man from the other island came to visit Tamalekar's family). Yet the central acts of these two emotions differ, with love achieving mutual admiration, attraction, or longing, and *fago* achieving the nurturing of connected others in need. Each emotion is "right" because it achieves the most valued relationship goals in the culture.

Remember that the Chinese word for love was categorized as a negative emotion, a form of sadness by Chinese participants? One reason may be that Chinese love simply runs a different course—one including the awareness of another person's suffering, the sadness when life is hard on them, and the effort that goes into need satisfaction, rather than merely describing the bliss of connecting with a special individual. The bad always comes with the good.

In cultures where individuals are part of given and durable interdependent relationships, love may be less central. One way of understanding this is that individuals in these cultures are close to others already, and love as an emotion that discriminates between those who are worthy of your caring and those who are not is not as useful. You have to take care of the people with whom you are interdependent. Emotions of closeness or caring in those cultures, such as *amae* and *fago*, focus on meeting the needs of others, rather than seeking out contact with those who are worthy. *Amae* and *fago* are less about having fun with someone who makes you feel good, and more about helping others, and making sure that they do not suffer too much.

OTHER EMOTIONS IN CLOSE AND DEPENDENT RELATIONSHIPS

Contrary to the intuition of many a student (and colleague), it is also not the case that individuals from so-called collectivist cultures seek *more intimacy* in relationships. To the contrary, individuals in tightly connected, interdependent relationship networks are more concerned about limiting the burdens of such interdependence than about seeking more intimacy and love.

Take an example from Ghana, where cultural psychologist Glenn Adams was struck by the caution about friends found in slogans, poems, and stories. A Ghanaian poem sounded:

Beware of friends.
Some are snakes under grass;
Some are lions in sheep's clothing;
Some are jealousies behind their façades of praises;
Some are just no good;
Beware of friends.

Bumper stickers would carry such slogans as "Beware of bad friends." And when random Ghanaian and U.S. American participants in public places (markets, parks) were asked by interviewers about their friendships, Ghanaian participants considered it normal to be cautious, or even suspicious about friends. In sharp contrast with American respondents, Ghanaians also declared the person having *many friends* to be foolish or naïve.

Why would Ghanaians not seek as many good friends as they could? The majority of Ghanaians (versus a small minority of Americans) understand friendships to mean that you offer material and practical support. This expectation from friends may be a liability against the background of resource poverty. Moreover, in a Ghanaian context, you need not seek friends to keep you company—company is always assured. And finally, there is always the possibility that friends take advantage of you or are not to be trusted.

How different were Ghanaian views on friendship from American ones? Having friends was a good thing for Americans, who reported more trust in friendship relationships than did Ghanaians. Consistently, more American than Ghanaian participants reported that they had *many friends*, and the majority of Americans interviewed claimed that they had more friends than other people (only a minority of Ghanaian participants did so). Americans also described their friendships as closer than did Ghanaians. Friendship in American contexts meant emotional support and shared interest (spending a lot of time) first, and was also characterized by trust and respect. If having friends is good in American contexts, then not having friends is a sad thing. Americans thought that a person without any friends would be lonely and regrettable. In contrast, Ghanaians thought a person without friends was bad and wrong, not sad or regrettable. If friendship is about material support, then a person without friends is stingy and selfish.

In other words, individuals from Ghana were not as much concerned with assuring themselves of company (which they had already) as they were with being exploited, or with being harmed by kin. Again, this is not to say that close relationships are less valued, just that the "right" emotions focus on limiting the burdens of such relationships, rather than enhancing mutual affirmation, admiration, and belonging.

Closeness may also be limited in order to avoid burdening the other person, as is apparent from research on social support. My colleagues, psychologists Heejung Kim, David Sherman, and Shelley Taylor, tried to answer the question of whether individuals in interdependent cultures have and seek more social support, that is, confirmation from others that they are "loved and cared for, esteemed and valued, and part of a network of communication and mutual obligations." They found that Asian American and Latinx college students reported seeking less, not more, social support than their white American counterparts when dealing with stress, the reason being that they did not want to bother others with their own problems. The partner's needs, rather than their own, figured centrally into the calculation of approaching the partner for social support. When their partner seemed more available, more social support was sought. For example, Asian American romantic couples engaged in more social sharing with their partners, when these partners were trying to solve an easy rather than a hard puzzle. The point is: in non-WEIRD cultural contexts where individuals tend to prioritize relationship needs over their own, individuals hesitate to ask for "love" or reassurance. Under normal circumstances, they are reluctant to burden the relationship.

In one experiment, white American and Asian Americans were given three minutes to prepare a speech on why they would be a good administrative assistant in the Psychology department. All participants then were asked to count backward from 2,083 by thirteens for five minutes, while the experimenter urged them to go faster. Then they delivered their speech. Stressful, right? It was.

In the middle of this stressful procedure—right after preparing the speech—some participants wrote a letter to someone they felt close to, seeking social support for the upcoming tasks. This helped the white American individuals—their stress levels went down—but it did not reduce stress in Asian American individuals. Was there anything else that could reduce the stress of the Asian American participants? Yes, there was, but it was not seeking closeness or social support. Instead, their stress went down when they thought about "a group that they were close to" and wrote "about the aspects of that group that were important to them." In Asian American contexts, people do not seek active affirmation from others, but they still find it good to know that they are part of a group when the going gets tough.

What can we learn from these and like-minded studies? Love is an invention of societies that are organized around autonomous individuals; it is needed less in societies where the relationship networks are unquestioned and permanent. It is no coincidence that love is so central in modern child-rearing: in WEIRD cultures where we raise our children for independence, we need to assure them that we as parents stay close, because they are so special. As indispensable as it now seems to healthy child development, it has not always been the "right" emotion in the relationship between parents and children.

"I love you" is a fairly modern invention, but human relationships are not. No human being lives by themselves: we all need and value social relationships. But the "right" emotions, the emotions that regulate those relationships to the needs of the social context, are different. *Love* is right in an individualist culture, where autonomous individuals seek to connect. *Amae* and *fago* may be the right emotions in collectivist cultures where relationship partners seek to meet each other's needs. In cultures where strong ties exist and people are inherently interconnected, individuals may be more focused on limiting the burden on themselves, or avoiding the burden on others. It cannot be ruled out that some form of love occurs in these cultures as well, but love is not "right" in the same way as it is in WEIRD cultures.

There are many kinds of "love," all of which spin the connection between people. Nobody would confuse romantic love with parental love (and if they did, we would strongly condemn this confusion). But it is even more true when we look at collectivist cultures: emotions of connection do many different things, ranging from helping another person in need to making another person feel unique, from maintaining existing connections to procuring new ones, from providing another person with material resources to cherishing time together. Which emotion is "right" depends on the context.

Happiness

If you're reading this book in the United States, you probably value happiness. Happy people are healthier, more successful, and better liked.

Linguist Anna Wierzbicka, describing middle-class white American social life, points to "important norms of interaction, with great emphasis being placed on being liked and approved of, on being perceived as friendly and *cheerful*. . . ." Happiness American-style is omnipresent and "right." The reason may be that it helps to uphold three pillars of contemporary American life: success, being in control, and choice.

In one study, my colleagues Yukiko Uchida and Shinobu Kitayama asked white American and Japanese college students to list "features" of happiness. Nearly all features generated by the American college students were positive. Importantly, American college students associated the good features of feeling happiness (e.g., joy, smiling) with personal achievement (e.g., feeling good about myself, getting what I want). This is what Kitayama, Mayumi Karasawa, and I found too: American college students—predominantly white—rated themselves as happy, when they were "proud," felt "on top of the world" and "superior," and had "self-esteem." In yet another study by psychologist Phil Shaver and his colleagues, American college students who described experiences of happiness from the past—either their own or someone else's—also noted feeling both good and successful. In the U.S., then, an essential aspect of happiness is feeling good about yourself and your own achievements.

White American college students describing instances of happiness characterize the emotion as outgoing, energetic, and approach-oriented. They describe happy people as being courteous and friendly, hugging other people, doing nice things for other people, and seeking to communicate and share their good feelings. Moreover, happiness is portrayed as energetic, active, and bouncy—to the point of being "hyper" and jumping up and down. Happy people laugh, smile, talk enthusiastically. The most commonly used psychological measures capture "happiness" as an active and approach-oriented emotion. Happiness is paraphrased as "enthusiastic," "interested," "determined," "excited," and "inspired."

Energetic, active, and bouncy happiness serves you particularly well when you want to make things go your way. In one experimental study, psychologist Jeanne Tsai found that individuals who were told they would be "influencers" in an interactive task chose to be excited. This was true for "influencers" from very different cultures. Tsai argues that the white American preference for a happiness with energetic overtones stems from a culture in which individuals encounter many opportunities to influence and exert control over their environment.

This kind of happiness is ingrained in Americans from an early age. American mothers stimulate their babies by repositioning, playing, and chatting with them, thus planting the seeds for bouncy happiness. American parents are strongly encouraged to ensure a level of entertainment for their children, in this way eliciting activated happiness as well. Children should have fun (high arousal), rather than being bored (low arousal). They are kept busy and excited with innumerable toys, a variety of extracurricular activities, trips to amusement parks, and other forms of entertainment.

As adults, Americans continue to seek this energized happiness. One of Tsai's studies found that, on their vacations, white Americans wanted to "explore and do exciting things" rather than go to a place where they could totally relax. They also preferred coffee over chamomile tea. And finally, those using illicit drugs preferred stimulants (such as cocaine and amphetamines) over narcotics (heroin). All of these preferences can be interpreted as ways to promote an excited (i.e., outgoing, active, energetic, approach-oriented) kind of happiness that helps you take control.

Happiness is also important because it informs choice, a third cultural pillar of American culture. Happiness has not always served choice. Psychologist Shige Oishi and his colleagues tracked the changing meanings of "happiness" in State of the Union addresses and books from around 1800 onwards, and found that the use of happiness to describe an individual, rather than the nation, is recent. Happiness came to describe the satisfaction of desire and self-expression just around the time consumer culture was on the rise—in the 1920s. It was then advertisements started to show smiling people, promising a product would give you pleasure. Happiness became a compass for choice: what you choose is who you are.

FIGURE 5.1 Happiness as the standard of good choice; an ad from 1949.
(Image courtesy of Candy Hoover Group, SRL)

In one study, white American students were more likely to choose to play basketball over throwing darts when they remembered that playing basketball two weeks earlier had gone well, and had made them happy. "Do what will make you happy." This advice reflects the options open to a segment of contemporary society, but would have been ill-suited (and irrelevant) in a time where children took over the family business, or had no choice but to work in the nearest factory, or serve the nearest rich family.

Happiness is so interwoven with the pillars of the American Dream—success, control, and choice—that it is a "right" emotion. It shows an individual's perception of self-worth, and reflects a desirable status quo. Happiness marks individual initiative and provides direction. As ingrained as this version of happiness likely is for most readers, modern happiness has not always existed, and, incredibly, does not exist everywhere. In many places, it is not a desirable emotion; in some places, it is "wrong."

WHO WOULD NOT WANT TO BE HAPPY?

Robin Wang, a Chinese philosopher and Daoist, taught her two American-born daughters to stick to "mama Wang's rules," which were simple enough: Eat well, exercise daily, get plenty of sleep, and do well in school. One of her daughters inquired: "What about being happy?" "No," she answered her daughter, "being happy is not important."

Happiness is not an end in the Daoist tradition. If there were an end, it would be to be flexible enough to adjust to any turn of events. Life is constantly changing, and happy events may turn out to have a dark side or miserable consequences. As one traditional Chinese text reads: "For misery, happiness is leaning against it; for happiness, misery is hiding in it."

The views of our foreparents in the United States may have been closer to the Daoist perspective than to ours. The 1850 *Webster's Dictionary* reads that "perfect happiness, or pleasure unalloyed with pain, is not attainable in this life." The same dictionary recognizes that happiness occurs against the background of unhappiness: "Happiness is comparative. To the person distressed with pain, relief from that pain affords happiness." A century later (in 1961), the definition of "happiness" has changed to include: "a state of wellbeing characterized by relative permanence . . . and by a natural desire for its continuation." An undilutedly positive state became defining of happiness.

In many cultures, though, the model is closer to Wang's and the Daoist definition: happiness and unhappiness are intimately connected. My friend, the psychologist Mayumi Karasawa, told me that, growing up, her parents and teachers warned her against showing happiness about a good grade, because it would have disrupted her relationships with her classmates. Happiness, especially the proud and excited happiness that is so common among white Americans, does not serve the Japanese goal of maintaining good relationships, and is considered harmful. In the study described before, Japanese psychologists Yukiko Uchida and Shinobu Kitayama compared U.S. with Japanese conceptions of happiness and found that, in contrast to U.S. students, who saw their happiness as exclusively positive, Japanese college students routinely listed negative features of happiness: Happiness is "elusive," because it never lasts, it is hard to put your finger on, and it is deceptive (distracting from reality). Happiness is "socially disruptive," because it makes people inattentive to their environment and their obligations, and because it risks eliciting the envy or jealousy of others.

Negative interpersonal consequences make happiness an undesirable emotion elsewhere as well. I remember my own mother admonishing me that I should be acting normal, which in her words was "crazy enough." Excited happiness was not valued in Amsterdam of the '60s. My upbringing has seeped into the way I experience happiness as an adult. When my son Oliver's baseball team played well (or the other team made mistakes in the his team's favor), the happiness of the other mothers at the sideline seemed strong and undiluted. They cheered and celebrated without reservation. I too felt happy when my son's team played well, but I would never have cheered in the same way, and in fact, I was concerned about hurting the feelings of the six- and seven-year-old boys on the other team, who also tried to play their best. My happiness was less blissful, and I was more reticent to cheer. This is just to say that we do not need to go to "exotic" cultures to find a different attitude towards—and a different experience of—happiness.

And if Amsterdam still sounds exotic, then author Barbara Ehrenreich's description of American settlers may bring home that happiness has not always been, and is not universally, sought out. The predecessor of America's present culture of happiness was nothing short of an unhappiness culture:

> The Calvinism brought by white settlers to New England could be described as a system of socially imposed depression. Its God was "utterly lawless" . . . , an all-powerful entity who "reveals his hatred of his creatures, not his love for them. . . ." The task for the living was to constantly examine "the loathsome abominations that lie in his bosom," seeking to uproot the sinful thoughts that are a sure sign of damnation. Calvinism offered only one form of relief from this anxious work of self-examination, and that was another form of labor—clearing,

planting, stitching, building up farms and business. Anything other than labor of either industrious or spiritual sort—idleness or pleasure seeking—was a contemptible sin.

We were not there to measure the everyday happiness of American settlers, but we have been able to compare everyday feelings of happiness in East Asian and contemporary white American cultures. To this end, psychologists have used a method called experience sampling, where they ask people several times a day how they are feeling. Using this method, we have found that Japanese and Asian American college students consistently report less happiness (and more unhappiness) than their white American counterparts. They experience happiness less often, and when they experience happiness, it is less intense. Clearly, then, the value attached to happiness has an effect on its prevalence in everyday life.

But even if happiness is not cherished to the same extent, would it not be universally motivating? The answer is no. If happiness informs and facilitates action in WEIRD cultures, in the majority of the world's cultures, people act according to their societal roles as well as the decisions and desires of others, rather than pursuing their own individual happiness.

In psychological experiments, Japanese and Asian Americans appeared to be more motivated to work on a task when they had failed it than when they had done well on it. Very different from white Americans who liked to do puzzles, or play a sports game when they had found they were good at it, East Asian participants thought it important to improve their skills when they had found they were bad at it. The East Asian participants did not *like* to persist on these tasks—they did not expect working on these tasks would make them happy—and yet they chose to spend time on them. The pursuit of happiness is just not as central. Just like the Daoist Robin Wang, the East Asian college students participating in the experiments valued working hard and doing well, but not being happy.

In fact, individuals in East Asian contexts may not believe that happiness helps their task performance, as white Americans do seem to believe. White American college students savored the happiness from an unrelated previous task when they knew they would face a cognitively challenging task next; East Asian college students (both in Asia and in the United States) did so to a much lower extent. To them, happiness was neither an end in itself, nor a means to successful task performance. It did not need to be cultivated.

So, it turns out happiness American-style is not as universally desirable as some might believe it to be. There is far less value attached to it in many cultures remote (and not so remote) in place and time. But if the emotion is differently valued in some cultures, may it not still exist? Even if it occurs less, or co-occurs with unhappiness or concern, even if its expression may be regulated, would the "emotion itself" not be the same? Good feelings have existed across all times and places, but American happiness is a modern, local invention in the same way love or anger are. The unique way WEIRD cultures, and particularly middle-class white Americans, understand and experience happiness, is tied to this epoch. Feeling good comes in many different shapes, depending on its role in relationships. It is certainly not always an energetic, action-oriented kind of happiness, and neither does it have to be tied to success and self-esteem.

OTHER WAYS OF FEELING GOOD: CALM

A centuries-old story in Daoism is about the way the legendary Daygu managed a flood. Daygu did not try to stop the water; he did not build dikes as my Dutch ancestors did. Rather, he yielded to the natural force of the water, redirecting the flow by dredging new channels. He "adjusted to the flow" of the water.

Psychologist Jeanne Tsai has found that calm and connected emotions are valued in many East Asian contexts. Hong Kong Chinese, and even Chinese Americans, reported that they would "ideally" like to feel calm, at rest, relaxed, and serene rather than the excited kinds of happiness, and these preferred feelings were related to their actual feelings. How do we know that this calm happiness relates to "adjusting to the flow"? In the same experimental task where some participants became influencers, Tsai told other participants that they would become "matchers." The leader decided on the order of twelve tangram cards (cards with different geometrical figures), and the matcher tried to put the cards in the same order as the leader. A matcher's task was to closely follow the instructions of the leader while trying "to think about the Leader's frame of mind." Matchers across cultures preferred to be calm and connected over energetic emotions. Calm and connected emotions presumably helped them be oriented to the leader, and adjust to their flow.

Everyday East Asian practices produce calm happiness. Much like the Cameroon mothers described in chapter 3, Japanese and Chinese mothers soothe and quiet their babies, by rocking them, lulling them, having constant body contact, and producing soothing vocalizations. Bestselling children's books in Taiwan (for ages four to eight) show many more protagonists with calm smiles and fewer protagonists with excited smiles than bestselling children's books in the United States (for a similar age range). Taiwanese children's books also describe fewer arousing activities than American storybooks. Very early on, children in East Asian contexts prefer calm over excited emotions. When asked which smile was happier, a calm or an excited smile, preschool children in Taiwan pointed to the calm smile.

"Calm happiness" remains favorite among adults too. I still remember having an excellent dinner with my friend Mayumi Karasawa when she closed her eyes and seemed to doze off, all the while saying, "It is so good!" I had to remind myself that being completely relaxed was good, and not the result of my failure to entertain her in spirited conversation. The goal was calm, yes even sleepy, happiness—not energized excitement.

In the early days of Tsai's research program, I remember her being challenged at professional conferences. "Should *calm* and being *at peace* be considered real emotions?" many a colleague wondered aloud. Remember, some of the most commonly used psychological scales of emotions focus exclusively on excited happiness. My (Belgian) master's students similarly mistook the Japanese preference for "calmness" to be a desire to "be rational" and contrasted this desire with the Belgian acceptance of emotions. Turning the temperature down was seen by my Belgian students as being rational, not as being calm. The cultural emphasis on excited happiness may have blinded psychologists in general to the importance of calm happiness (as *an emotion*)—which, even in WEIRD cultures, may play a bigger role than we realize.

Psychologists and health researchers now find health and well-being associated with culturally valued feelings. You may remember that taking a bath, rather than feeling excited, predicted health in Japan. Calm activities are healthy in Japan; energetic happiness is not only less desired, but also considered not particularly healthy in Japan. Conversely, depression among Hong Kong Chinese meant not being calm enough, whereas among white Americans it meant a lack of excitement. Ill-being was related to lacking the happiness that is *culturally valued*.

There is also strong evidence that, when calm is culturally valued, people prefer others who seem to have "calm feelings." Tsai and her colleagues found over and again that individuals better liked, trusted, and treated others who had the "right" emotions, compared to others

FIGURE 5.2 "Excited" and "calm" smiles. Smiles were coded for facial action units. AU6=arched eyes, AU12=corners mouth up; AU25+26=lips parted (teeth possibly showing) and jaw drop. (Copyright © 2016, American Psychological Association)

who had not. Here too the findings suggest that the preference for calm happiness goes beyond lip service. As a case in point, the publicly posted pictures of business leaders, university presidents, and political leaders—people entrusted with responsibility—showed smiles that corresponded with the "right" positive affect in their respective countries. If calm happiness was culturally preferred, then the smiles of its leaders were "calm" and closed; if excited happiness was preferred, then the smiles of leaders in those countries were "excited" or open. Differences could not be explained by higher GDPs per capita, level of democracy, or development.

Tsai's team also found that Korean students who played a computer game with an avatar (supposedly representing a real-life playmate), trusted an avatar with a calm smile more and gave them more money than an avatar with an excited smile; for white American students, it was the reverse. Interestingly, the intensity of their smiles, but not the gender or ethnicity of the avatars, determined how trustworthy the students felt them to be. These experiments made use of avatars generated by a computer. They are not exactly modeling natural interactions, and yet, it is because of their artificiality that we can conclude that the subtle facial cues from which we infer emotions play an important role in whose faces we find trustworthy, and to whom we give money. Korean students preferred the calm faces.

OTHER WAYS OF FEELING GOOD: CONNECTED

Emotion research was saturated with East Asia–North American comparisons when I started studying emotions in Latinx in the United States and Mexicans in Mexico. If I thought that all *collectivist* cultures were alike—less happy than white Americans—I was in for a big surprise. Judging by survey research, the happiest people in my studies were the Latinx in the U.S. and the Mexicans in Mexico; they reported more happiness even than white American samples. Together with several gifted master's students at Wake Forest University, and my colleague Hilda Fernandez de Ortega, now at the Universidad de las Américas Puebla in Mexico, I collected data on happiness in the early 2000s. We ended up not publishing them, in part because we found it hard at the time to make sense of them. What did it mean that the first-generation Mexican community samples in North Carolina and the Mexican students in Mexico were so happy? Did they put less emphasis on connectedness than the Japanese? That seemed unlikely.

I would now say that happiness figures prominently in achieving the connectedness and *familísmo* that is so central in Latin culture. Happiness is part of a strong sense of attachment, loyalty, reciprocity, and solidarity among members of the nuclear and extended family, and it plays an important role in the pleasant relationships, or *simpatía*, that governs Latinx and Mexican social life more broadly. *Simpatía* means to be happy and positive in positive situations, and to de-emphasize negative feelings and behaviors in negative situations. A *simpático/simpática* person is happy, polite, and agreeable, and avoids being stressed or losing their temper. Therefore, where happiness in some East Asian contexts can be a threat to connectedness, connectedness in Latin contexts—within the family and outside—is the whole reason for happiness.

Interviews with first-generation Mexican immigrants to North Carolina pointed to the connectedness of happiness as well. We asked Mexican American working-class men and women to describe a situation in which they felt happy. And many of them described their happiness in terms of connections. Carmen, a twenty-two-year-old housekeeper who had come to the United States six years prior, told us about a surprise party that her girlfriends organized for her birthday.

I felt happiness and wanted to cry, cause like I say . . . that had never happened to me. . . . I felt like hugging them all at once. Truly, cause I was so happy right then that I didn't just feel like hugging one, but all of them at once time. (laughter). I cried for joy.

And Juan, a twenty-seven-year-old restaurant worker who had been in the United States for eight years, was happy that, four years earlier, he had been able to help his wife getting through the birth of their first son:

> My presence counted a lot at the time my son was born and my wife was kind of nervous since it was her first baby. My presence was important so everything would turn out right. . . . "Keep going" was all I said for the time being, but she would answer: "I can't". . . . Some of my friends had already told me about the situation I was going to be in. Right? I tried to do things correctly, to be calm and to keep motivating my wife during those moments . . . and that is how it happened. At the time, what we were going through . . . there were not enough translators . . . and it was not our language . . . I did the best I could with what I knew . . . I felt [different] things at the same time, I felt bad but later on . . . something very . . . great happiness. What I felt like doing at that time was to be near my family; be with them, and I did that.

Juan is happy because he was able to support his wife; his happiness is about connectedness. In fact, when the Latinx interviewer asks Juan if the situation increased his self-esteem, Juan replies he does not understand the question very well. Only when the interviewer highlights the connection with his wife, does Juan understand:

> **Interviewer:** The fact that you were there during that difficult time with your wife, does it make you feel more respect for yourself, where you feel more . . .
>
> **Juan:** Yes, because I think that it is nice to know that you are important to other people.

Even happiness about your own achievement is about earning respect in the eyes of others. The esteem from others is what simultaneously makes you feel good in general, and makes you feel good about yourself. Luisa, a forty-two-year-old farmworker who had come to the United States eight years earlier, managed to repair the tractor that she used to sow the fields.

> Some of the men were not able to do the job, and so I had to do it. . . . The boss congratulated me, and said it would be great if he had other people like me. I told my husband what he had said, and so he congratulated me too, he said, "this is my old lady." And that made me feel good.

In another study, psychologist Krishna Savani and colleagues (one of them being me) asked Mexican college students (in Mexico) and their white American counterparts to describe situations in which they "felt good." Mexican students described more connected happiness, using words like "affection," "gratitude," and "sympathy." These are emotions that create a positive link between yourself and another person. For example, one Mexican student reported:

> My newborn nephew opened his eyes after sleeping and he fixated a look on my face for 15 seconds. I felt affection and harmony [between unequals].

White American college students reported as many situations that made them feel good, but they did not report as much connected happiness. Instead, they reported self-esteem-related happiness, using such terms as "pride," "superior," and "confident" to describe their good feelings.

Not only did Mexican college students report more good feelings that connected them to others, these positive connections also motivated them. In a follow-up study, Krishna Savani and colleagues asked Mexican students in Mexico and white American students to write about a time when they experienced good feelings either towards another person (connected happiness) or about themselves (self-confident happiness). Next, they asked them to solve anagrams. Mexican college students were more motivated to solve the anagrams after recalling a time when they felt connected happiness towards another person: It is important to do well for your family. Therefore, it is not just that Latinx or Mexicans experience more happiness in the context of connectedness, but this kind of happiness (and not the happiness that is tied to high self-esteem and high activation) is what motivates them in task pursuit.

In Latinx contexts, feeling good is feeling connected. It is a happiness that comes with connecting behaviors: to want to be with others or hug them. The "right" happiness is not the happiness in which self-esteem figures prominently. Connected happiness is right and motivating.

Feeling good is of all times and all places, but *happiness* is not. Happiness American-style is a contemporary, local emotion. Happy people may also reach out to others, but first and foremost, they shine and stand out—the ideals of middle-class white Americans. In many East Asian contexts, feeling good is being calm, as calm happiness optimally prepares you to adjust to social and situational requirement. Not surprisingly, calm activities are healthy. And in East Asian contexts, you choose activities in function of being prepared to the point where you *can* be calm, and no longer worried. Immediate pleasure is sacrificed to calmness in the long run.

Loves and Happinesses

Love and happiness *do* something in the relationship with others. American-style love seeks connection with desirable others and elevates them. It is an emotion much needed in a culture emphasizing the autonomy of individuals and the voluntary nature of relationships, but this type of love is not focal (and not particularly right) in a culture with inalienable bonds that come with demanding obligations. Happiness of the kind that marks self-worth is energizing, motivating, and "right" in cultures where individuals are responsible for initiating the right action, choosing direction, and influencing the outcomes of their lives. It is less important, or even "wrong," in cultures where individuals are expected to meet their role requirements or to flexibly adjust to the conditions. In these cultures, being calm, balanced, flexible, and ready for adjustment (or alternatively, feeling connected) are more important goals.

But aren't love and happiness universal feelings *deep down*? Is it possible that people around the world feel love and happiness American-style, but have to suppress these feelings, because of the norms of their culture? Does the eloping couple in a traditional culture of arranged marriage not show us that passionate love as we know it is natural? And does the child who is excitedly happy but gets reprimanded show that the natural way of happiness is ours, but that cultural norms prescribe emotion suppression?

No.

If you think of emotions as part of relationships—if you consider them as episodes that evolve in tandem with the emotions of others—then romantic love will be very different depending on whether it is "right," "wrong," or "irrelevant" in your culture. Similarly, the bubbly, bouncy kid who gets stimulated and encouraged will ultimately live a very different cultural episode than the excitedly happy child who gets frowned upon. We should move away from a model of culture as something outside ourselves that imposes norms on the natural emotions that we have. Instead, we should recognize how we constantly enact culture in our everyday interactions, and how these interactions scaffold our emotional lives.

As for positive psychology: we simply cannot assume that we know which emotions constitute flourishing in other cultures. Flourishing in Ghana may be better served by limiting love and establishing boundaries. Flourishing in Japan may be better served by self-improvement than by happiness. Flourishing among the Ifaluk may be better served by *fago* than by love. The emotions that contribute to flourishing differ by culture (and by position), depending on the relationships goals. And even if some form of love and some form of happiness are part of flourishing in some or most cultures, the modal types of love and happiness run very different courses. It may be better to speak of *loves* and *happinesses* in plural rather than love and happiness in singular.

Chapter 6

WHAT'S IN
A WORD?

WHEN BARA PARENTS ON MADAGASCAR TELL THEIR CHILDREN to show *tahotsy*, or label their children's behavior as *tahotsy*, they introduce their children to the cultural goal of obedience in the hierarchy. When an Ifaluk mother calls on her young son to show *fago*, she introduces him to the emotion that is marked by taking care of another person; she implies that throwing a piece of coral rubble at your two-year-old cousin is incompatible with *fago*. Similarly, when European American or German parents label their own or their children's behavior as *angry*, they introduce their children to concepts of blame, personal accountability, fairness, and also to the goal of defending your autonomous rights. Once their children show some maturity, Japanese parents teach them *omoiyari* (roughly, empathy): episodes of *omoiyari* will be highlighted, or carved out, in everyday life.

A child's learning of an emotion word is not so much starting to recognize their own deep mental states, to which a caregiver does not have access after all, as it is to connect a cultural concept—*tahotsy*, *angry*—to an unfolding episode. Parents constantly provide their children with emotion concepts to disambiguate what is going on. Especially towards the second year, when children start using emotion concepts themselves, parents use emotion words very often. In one study, urban Japanese mothers used an emotion word between once and twice per *minute* during interactions with their two-year-old sons. The more emotion words caregivers use, the more emotion words their children learn.

Parents point out when the child is angry, warn them when they are angry or are about to get angry, or describe a protagonist in the book as looking angry. Imagine an emotion concept such as anger as a container of particular types of emotional episodes. Once this container is in place, your parents and others point out different instances of anger. Eventually, you may understand instances of anger all by yourself. All these particular instances will then be stored as part of the container of episodes that "anger" is. With every new experience—every episode of "anger" that you encounter—the particular emotion concept of anger gets an update. In the end, anger will be filled with experiences you sample during your life. This means that the anger category, even within a culture or within an individual, is not homogenous. It does not refer to a single state. Rather, it consists of many different episodes: "angry" when your mom challenged you in a rough-and-tumble fight, and you lost against her; "angry" when your friend took your toy and you pushed him to get it back; "angry" as your mom was scolding you for treating her with disrespect. "Angry" becomes the container of the many episodes that, in your culture, count as anger.

Psychologist Lisa Feldman Barrett, in describing exactly this process of concept learning, points out that emotion concepts make connections between different emotional episodes that, on the surface, have little to do with each other. Minangkabau parents using the word *malu* (roughly translated as "shame") draw the connections between "being-shy-as-a-stranger-approaches-you," "feeling-bad-about-not-obeying-your-mom," and "being-publicly-mocked-for-improper-behavior," even though these episodes may feel different, look different, and have different antecedents, and behaviors attached to them. By categorizing them as *malu,* the child learns to connect a large range of situations that urge deferent behavior. Similarly, American parents teach their children that "happy-about-getting-praise-for-turning-the-book-right-side-up," "happy-about-winning-a-game," "proud-about-being-a-good-student" all belong to the same category of "pride" (colloquially referred to as "feeling good about yourself"), even though these instances of "pride" arise in different situations, call for different action, and probably "feel" different to some extent. By teaching our child emotion concepts, parents attach culturally shared meanings and goals to these episodes. By naming an episode *malu*, parents imply that deference is called for; by suggesting that the child should "feel good about themselves," they indicate that individual pleasure and being in control are of utmost importance. By learning what "emotion" they have, children become aligned with their parents' (and their cultures') meanings and goals.

But that is not all: as a member of your culture, you get a jump start. Early in life, when you start learning the emotion words in your language, these words are containers partly stocked. It is not that every child, with the help of their parents, needs to start all over again assembling instances of "anger" or *malu*. Emotion words come with the emotional episodes from your culture's collective memory as well as collective insights about these emotions. You learn them by talking to others, by hearing the collective wisdom about these emotions, and by observing how they are used in public life. It is this collective knowledge that scaffolds your own experiences.

Emotion Words

The emotion concepts of your language structure your experience. They are the tools that your parents use to help you make sense of ongoing events, including your own responses. They also prompt appropriate behavior. What if the emotion concepts vary across languages? And to what extent do we know this to be the case?

The first thing to know is that not all languages have a word for "emotion" itself. The category, as we think we know it, is historically new, and geographically unique. This is a problem, because it makes it harder to even know what concepts to compare across cultures. In some languages emotions are grouped with other sensations such as

fatigue or pain, in others they are grouped with behaviors. The Turkish respondents in my word-listing study were an example of the latter,
listing as emotions such behaviors as crying, laughing, helping, and
yelling. The Himba in Maria Gendron's research are another example
of a community where behaviors are included in the category of emotions; they saw the communality of emotional faces in terms of behaviors (not mental states): "all laughing." In deciding which emotions
are different across cultures, it is important to realize that there is no
universally shared way of drawing the boundaries around the domain
of emotions. This makes the comparison across cultures all the more
complicated.

Even without considering the difficulty of deciding what exactly
counts as an emotion concept, it is clear from the outset that not all
English words will have translations in other languages. Emotion
vocabularies in some languages—such as Chewong in Malaysia—
count as few as seven emotion words, and other languages count in
the thousands, with English containing more than two thousand emotion words. There is no question, therefore, that languages organize
the domain very differently, and make both different kinds as well as
different numbers of distinctions.

Can we find good translations for the most important categories of
emotion? Many languages fail to make the distinctions that seem obvious in English, such as those between anger, sadness, love, and shame.
Some of the most central emotion concepts (as we distinguish them in
English) share a word in other languages: for example, native speakers of Luganda, a language spoken in Uganda, use the same word,
okusunguwala, for "anger" and "sadness." Native Luganda interpreters
had a hard time making the distinction between anger and sadness
in English. Similar blends of anger and sadness are found in other
languages. Turkish-minority respondents in my research in the Netherlands used *kızmak* to describe an anger that was permeated with
sadness, and that typically occurred in intimate relationships in which
high expectations had been disappointed. *Kızmak* does not come with
aggression, but rather with ignoring or avoiding the other person.

In Indonesia, the Nias do not clearly distinguish between anger and envy. The expression *afökho dödö* (literally, "pain-hearted"), a focal emotion word among the Nias, refers to a range of emotions, including offended, spite, resentment, envy, malice, and ill will. It also refers both to "acts of spite and the sentiment." Another blurred distinction is the one between sadness, love, and empathy. The central Ifaluk emotion *fago* is translated as "love," yet shares features with sadness and compassion. The word for "love" in Samoan, *alofa,* also means sympathy, pity, and liking. My Turkish respondents used *üzüntü* not only for their own ill fate but also for the ill fate of close others. By doing so, elements of empathy were mixed in with sadness. Thus *üzüntü* prompted reaching out and being kind to others, in addition to crying, the inability to do anything, and wanting to be helped. My informants told me it is a celebrated emotion in Turkey, and this makes sense from the point of view of the sociality of the emotion.

Many languages lump shame and embarrassment together. The Japanese word *haji* refers to both shame or embarrassment, and does not clearly distinguish between the two. The Bedouins mentioned earlier use *hasham* to describe an even larger range of feelings: shame, embarrassment, shyness, and modesty or respectability. Among the Ilongot in the Philippines, *betang* similarly refers to shame, timidity, embarrassment, awe, obedience, shame, and respect.

Not all languages have words for emotion concepts which, in English, are considered important. A recent article in *Science* surveyed emotion lexicons in almost 2,500 languages grouped into six large language families. The researchers, psychologists Kristen Lindquist, Joshua Jackson, and their colleagues, focused on twenty-four English concepts—among them "anger," "love," "happy," "proud," and "grief." Cross-cultural similarity in emotion concepts would have minimally required that all languages (100 percent) had words that corresponded in a one-to-one fashion with the various emotion concepts that are so clearly distinguished in English. The only term that came close to 100 percent was *good* (feeling good): almost all languages had a distinct word for it. The percentage of languages having a distinct word corresponding to the other English words was much lower: *bad* (as in feeling bad) occurred in 70 percent of the languages, *love* in less than one-third, *happy* and *fear* in about 20 percent, and *anger* and *proud* in less than 15 percent of the languages. This in itself is an important finding that is supported by anecdotal evidence. The linguist and polyglot Anna Wierzbicka pointed to the absence of a word for *disgust* in Polish, her native language. Similarly, Tahitians seem to be lacking a word for *sadness*. Tahitians suffering a loss did not recognize themselves as sad, but used "a variety of other terms all referring to a generally troubled or subdued bodily state" that could also have been used to describe fatigue or illness.

Even when translations for English emotion words *are* available, the emotion categories to which they refer appear to be different across cultures. The same article in *Science* shows that if you learned a new language, especially a language from a different family than English (an Indo-European language), you would have much more trouble understanding the new emotion terms than you would have, say, understanding the color terms of that language. And even colors are not the same in all languages. Did you know, for instance, that some languages use the same word for pink and red? Or that there are languages that fail to make the distinction between green and blue? If differences in the conceptualization of colors surprise you, the differences in emotion lexicons are much larger. Emotion words in different languages do not neatly map onto each other. As may have been clear from the previous chapters, you cannot assume you understand an emotion from another culture, just because there is a translation of the English emotion word. And if you did, you would risk projecting the English-language version of the emotion, rather than understanding the local emotion category represented by the word.

The research reported in *Science* looked at different patterns of word-sharing across languages. Take my example above: "sad" and "angry" share the word *okusunguwala* in Luganda, and "embarrassment" and "shame" share the word *haji* in Japanese. The linguistic reasoning is that emotions sharing a word are not distinguished in the language. Word-sharing occurred for all different emotion concepts that the researchers distinguished at the outset of their study. Even though almost all languages had a word for "good," the same word was used in a quarter of the cases to describe other emotion categories that the researchers had distinguished at the outset of their research. "Happy," "want," "merry," "like," "love," and "hope" are examples of emotion categories that share a word with "good." The researchers themselves point to the word sharing of "anger" with "envy" in some language families, and with "hate," "bad," and "proud" in other languages. Imagine how different anger might be when it is indistinguishable from envy, or pride. As another example, "pity" is expressed by the same word as "grief" and "regret" in some languages, but by the same word as "love" in others. Again, how different is pity when compounded with regret from pity when compounded with compassion? Note that not a single emotion concept was similarly bounded across all language families. It is fair to say, then, that the ways in which languages conceptualize emotions is different.

The big study published in *Science* only included concepts that involved "a mental state that could be felt (e.g., to feel good, to feel grief, to feel angry, to feel pity)" and that "had some precedent in past literature on emotion." This means that terms like "crying" or "laughing," considered good examples of emotion in some but not in all languages, were not considered in the study. Crying is not a mental state ("I felt crying" is not a common expression), and it has not been treated as "an emotion" in emotion literature. Given that "crying" and "laughing" are commonly mentioned as emotion words in some languages, omitting them may have underestimated the cultural differences in emotion lexicons.

The study in *Science* also disregarded such culture-specific concepts as *fago* (among the Ifaluk), *gezellig* (in my native language, Dutch), and *amae* (in Japanese) that cannot be translated by a single word in English, but yet are central in the culture of origin. As we have seen before, *fago* is the feeling of wanting to take care of a person with whom you have a strong relationship. Interestingly, *fago* combines instances of emotion that in English do not form one category: the love or empathy felt when this person is suffering; the sadness (vulnerability) felt upon separation from this loved one.

Gezellig too would require more than one word to translate into

English. It combines aspects of the situation—the fireplace, a living room, some hot drinks, a couch—and feelings of closeness to others, security, and relaxation. Having been trained as a psychologist, I might not list it as an emotion, but my Dutch respondents many years ago did.

Amae is a final example of a culture-specific emotion. It refers to one's "inclination to depend on or accept another's nurturant indulgence, including one's dependency wish, typically applied to the mother-child relationship": the mother represents authority but at the same time acts as a servant. In an *amae* relationship, the dependent partner fully submits to the nurturing partner, giving up control; the nurturing partner is focused on meeting the needs of the dependent partner, without ever judging these needs; they just empathize. Receiving *amae* (i.e., being the dependent partner) is a bit like letting yourself fall backwards trusting that others will catch you: the nurturing partner catches the trusting, dependent one. *Amae* is so ingrained as an emotion concept in Japan that when Japanese psychiatrist Takeo Doi told one of his colleagues that there was no translation for this word in English, the colleague responded in astonishment: "Why, even puppies do it!"

Leaving out these central emotion words in other languages may have led to an underestimation of the cultural differences in emotion lexicons as well. As illustrated by Doi's astonished colleague, these words are at the very basis of emotional experience in other cultures, but were not in the list included in the *Science* article as they did not make it to the WEIRD agendas of emotion researchers.

Emotion words play an important role in the socialization of emotions. Although emotion concepts are not limited to a word, emotion lexicons are good starting places to look for cultural differences in emotions. All we know points to the conclusion that different languages conceptualize the emotion domain differently. The category of emotion itself is differently understood across cultures, but moreover, emotion lexicons from different languages do not neatly map. This is one of the reasons that children in different cultures do not come to understand emotions in similar ways.

Cultural Episodes

What emotion concepts come to mean for children depends on the episodes to which these words become attached. My son Oliver's concept of pride will include the experiences of his parents praising him for turning a book right side up, or for the many baseball games he won and the cheering as a result of those wins. His "pride" includes the "best student" awards, and the story of "the little engine that could," one of his favorite children's books describing a train engine that had all reason to feel good about himself because of his determination. Similarly, Didi's shame experiences include all instances where his mom was ashamed of him because he disobeyed her, and probably also of instances where his sister behaved shamefully, and perhaps the adventures of some children's books' protagonists. Minangkabau toddlers' *malu malu* ("baby-shame") includes the occasions where their parents point out their behavior towards strangers. Ultimately, then, what an emotion concept comes to mean is largely dependent on common encounters within the culture, or on the encounters that receive attention.

How emotion concepts come to incorporate children's experiences within their communities is nicely illustrated by developmental psychologist Michael Mascolo and his colleagues who, based on the available evidence, described different types of experiences that may become part of the pride and shame concepts of European American and Chinese children. The most rudimentary experience that parents might label *pride* occurs within the first six months of life when babies smile at the result of their actions, for example a ball dropping as a result of the infant releasing their grip. When infants visibly notice caregivers' responses—Mascolo estimates this to be the case when they are about a year old—parents may also peg this as pride. My son Oliver would look up to us after he did his trick of turning the book right side up, and so he must have noticed our approval; we certainly took this to be pride. While experiences at this basic level of "achieving something by your own doing" and "gaining approval for something you do" may be part of the pride concepts of many cultures, there are cultural differences in the types of episodes that babies experience even then. For instance, one-year-old white American infants are "proud" of self-selected activities (Oliver one day just happened to turn the book right side up, without any encouragement on our side), whereas Chinese infants are proud of actions that their parent coaxed them into ("Give Grandma some candy!"). Also, white American children who feel good about themselves are more abundant in their behavior than Chinese children. The former show an erect posture, smile, seek direct eye contact with the parent, point at the outcome, applaud, or even give themselves a compliment, while the latter say something like "I gave candy to Grandma" or "I did what mama wanted." In both cultural contexts, parents acknowledge the outcome, but white American parents are more effusive in their praise than Chinese parents.

Cultural differences in the pride concepts may further increase at the end of the second year, when children become aware that it is *they* who are responsible for the action and the outcome. As children become socialized, and as their ability to grasp the divergent relational arrangements in their cultures grows, the meanings of pride and shame become increasingly cultured, reflecting the different cultural practices. As we saw before, middle-class white American parents work on their child's self-esteem, praising them for their achievements. Correspondingly, white American children interpret their accomplishment as a result of their own competence (I am good at it!).

The responses in Chinese families are more complicated. On the one hand, some opportunity is created for pride to happen. Mascolo writes that it is customary for children to display skills they learn in school to relatives and guests, who will be praising the child and their parents effusively. On the other hand, parents self-efface, because they are implicated in their children's performance. When a child performs a song, the parent will say, "He did all right, but he has to learn the song better!" This is the mirror image of the shame anecdotes in the Taiwanese children: the child's connection with their parents is foregrounded rather than the child's position in the outside world. The parents cannot be satisfied with the children too quickly, because they are responsible that the children keep up the work. Children may resonate with the sentiment, because they begin to show restraint in self-celebratory action upon success. The focus of pride for Chinese children is on practicing to keep up the good results.

Pride in white American children increasingly takes on the meaning of being *more* competent than others. In contrast, Chinese pride stories become increasingly about modesty and honor. The meaning of pride in the United States may shift to include valued identities, such as being proud to be an American. In contrast, Chinese pride stories grow out to be about honoring your parents by working hard and being successful.

The meaning of *shame* in white American and Chinese children similarly includes a simple, and possibly universal, story—a caregiver's disapproval and the child's feelings of inadequacy—as well as complex and cross-culturally different stories. American children come to associate shame with episodes in which they are lacking in valued general traits, and Chinese children's shame episodes are about the failure to fulfill their social roles and obligations, and about dishonoring their parents. The initial story associated with shame may be as simple as the parent not smiling when you expected them to, but later scenarios differ commensurate to differences in the culturally habitual relationship goals, and the role children play in fulfilling or falling short of those goals.

What these examples seek to illustrate is that emotion concepts derive meaning from the socialization contexts in which they occur. Chinese pride (shame) simply refers to a different set of episodes than American pride (shame), and that becomes true very early in life. Do the concepts of pride and shame occur in both Mandarin Chinese and English? Yes, there are words for pride and shame in each culture, and they share the rudimentary scenarios—doing something that bears the approval of others in the case of pride, and the disapproval in the case of shame. Yet, if you were familiar with Chinese pride, it would probably be hard to predict when Americans feel pride, how they act in pride, how others respond to pride, and perhaps even what they feel exactly. The reverse would be true as well: American pride does not help you navigate the experiences typical of Chinese pride. The most common elements of pride differ across cultures: the antecedents, the actions, the reactions from others, the consequences, and arguably the associated feelings.

It may be possible to come up with rudimentary scenarios for many other emotions: anger may start with distress or frustration (and not giving up in the face of obstacles), love may start with feeling good in someone's presence (and perhaps wanting to be in someone's presence), and happiness starts with feeling good, and so on. But the episodes that give happiness, anger, or love their ultimate meaning appear to differ across cultures, resulting in different emotion concepts across cultures.

In reality, an emotion concept in one language does not correspond with *one* typical episode; it refers to a set of many different situations of pride or shame or anger or any other emotion. The sets of different languages do overlap. Not all instances of American pride differ from all instances of Chinese pride. It is possible that a European American child feels pride because they managed to meet their mom's expectations, and occasionally a Chinese child may feel smarter than their friend. The child's responses of pride need not be completely distinct either. Occasionally, a white American child may be modest, while a Chinese child may be gleeful. My point is that the *sets* of emotion episodes that are brought online by the concept differ.

To illustrate this, let us follow the events of the day for Motoko, a sales representative at a pharmaceutical company in Japan, and Heather, her American counterpart. On this particular day, both women encountered several instances of anger. In the morning, they gave a team presentation about the proposed sales strategy for the new season. A young colleague who had just started their job at the company started ranting about the proposal, claiming it was the wrong strategy altogether. Both Motoko and Heather felt frustrated with the colleague's interruption and struggled to focus during the remainder of their presentation; however, whereas Heather wondered what she could have done to make her presentation more convincing, Motoko was appalled by her junior's lack of respect. A few hours later, when Heather and Motoko were getting ready to visit a medical center where they had an appointment, they each walked back to their cars which had been parked at a spot reserved for company vans (because no other spot had been available early on). Each found that one of the company vans was parked right behind them, and was blocking their car. Heather cursed the driver of the van: Did he not see that no other parking spot was available? Why had he not taken the spot right next to her? She would have liked to give him a piece of her mind. In contrast, Motoko told herself she should have known better than to park in an unofficial spot, keeping her frustration to herself.

Even if Heather and Motoko agreed on the instances that counted as anger, would their angers have looked the same? In one study, my collaborator Michael Boiger and I looked at anger instances across different kinds of situations, and we considered the meaning of the situation and action tendencies associated with it. In this particular study, we examined different experiences of anger and shame *across situations*. We wanted to know if the *sets* of anger and shame experiences in the United States, Japan, and Belgium differ. Students from each culture (almost one thousand in total) read hypothetical scenarios that were chosen to span the full range of anger and shame situations in all cultures. I say "hypothetical" because the students in this study might not have encountered situations exactly like the ones described in the survey, but actually these situations had been reported by other students from all three cultures in previous research. In that sense they were not hypothetical at all: they were the actual situations in which students in their cultures had felt either anger or shame.

Each participant read scenarios of protagonists whose names were matched on self-reported gender and culture. American, male students would read situations about Joshua, Matthew, Anthony, and Richard, for example. American, Japanese, and Belgian students of either gender read the very same scenarios. Four very different anger scenarios read as follows:

Joshua and his friend had agreed to meet right after school. Joshua took off as soon as school had ended and hurried to his friend's place. After 20 minutes of waiting, his friend had still not arrived.

Matthew went to university away from home and came to see his family during the holidays. Whenever Matthew talked about something he felt proud of, his father changed the topic to his younger brother's football career.

Anthony and his friend were going upstairs in a restaurant, when a large group of people squeezed by on their way down. One of them hollered to Anthony and his friend: "Hey, stop pushing us!"

Richard shared a room with another student. One night Richard came home to a big mess. His roommate had invited a bunch of people to their room. They had been drinking but obviously failed to clean up after themselves.

After they read a vignette, the respondents answered how they would appraise these situations, had they been Joshua, Matthew, Anthony, or Richard (or any of the other protagonists, names matched by culture and gender), and what they would have felt like doing. They also told us how angry (or ashamed) they would have been. There was agreement among participants that anger does not feel the same whether you walk in Joshua, Matthew's, Anthony's, or Richard's shoes. But how exactly individuals described these differ-ent instances of anger varied across two sets. Interestingly, the same sets did occur in all cultures, but cultures differed with respect to the most common sets. For shame we found three sets, and here too, shame sets occurred in all three cultures, but their respective preva-lence was different.

The first *set* of anger experiences was reported by the great majority of Japanese students, and only by a small part of U.S. and Belgian stu-dents. It was characterized by blaming distant others most. For exam-ple, individuals in this set thought that Richard's roommate's behavior was much more inappropriate and unfair than were Joshua's friend's and Matthew's dad's. Furthermore, individuals in this first set were not so preoccupied when friends or relatives were offensive, especially not when friends or relatives had acted intentionally, such as was the case for Matthew's dad.

The second set of anger was most common in the U.S. and Belgium. It was characterized by blaming close others who did not meet relational norms. In this set, individuals blamed Joshua's friend and Matthew's dad more than Richard's roommate. The friend and the dad were seen to be more unfair and behaving more inappropriately than a group of strangers. These same individuals reported that they would be very preoccupied in Joshua's or in Matthew's situation, where it involved a friend or a relative, but much less when strangers were either inconsiderate or purposefully offensive, as was the case for Anthony and Richard, respectively. In Joshua's and Matthew's place only, would they feel unable to concentrate on anything else and paralyzed. This second set of anger instances was found in the majority of American and Belgian students, but only in a very small minority of Japanese students.

The different sets appear to be consistent with the dominant cultural concerns: whereas Japanese are primarily concerned with protecting their close relationships (and thus refrain from other-blame in these instances), Americans and Western Europeans are more concerned with protecting their autonomy, and this concern plays a more central role in close relationships, where relational norms ensure good treatment while allowing for autonomy.

At one point in my career I would have told you that people's emotional lives are different, but emotions themselves are the same. But what would it mean that emotions are the same? What if the episodes of emotions *are* the emotions? What if we are talking about different, though somewhat overlapping, categories? If emotion concepts each store collections of episodes, then no community—and also no individual—would have exactly the same emotion concepts as any other. Perhaps, then, the whole idea that *ikari* (Japanese), *anger* (English), and *kwaadheid* (Dutch) are "the same emotion" originates from a MINE model: the idea that the real emotion is a mental state behind the story of anger. If emotion concepts refer to sets of episodes of an emotional community, then translating "anger" into *ikari* is stepping into the encounters of another world.

Similar Emotion Concepts?

Some might argue that many languages have words for happy, calm, pride, love, angry, shame, fear, grief, disgust, envy, and perhaps a few other emotions. They are right. So, why would this be the case if emotion concepts refer to sets of cultural episodes? For one, the conditions of human lives are very similar in basic ways. As anthropologist Andrew Beatty concludes: "Because loving, getting, wanting and losing figure among any group of human beings, cradle to grave."

An additional reason is that, given these human conditions, the logical possibilities of acting are limited. You can move towards or away from another human being or a group. Western scholars have proposed taxonomies in which "love," "esteem," "happiness," and "interest" represent *moves towards* others (or as it may be, towards objects in the world), and "fear," "contempt," and "disgust" as *moves away*. College students from all over the world associate "joy" and its translations with *moving towards* and "shame," "guilt," and "disgust" with *moving*

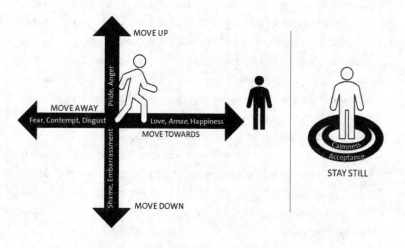

FIGURE 6.1 Example emotions in the space of logical possibilities. *Caveat:* Not all instances of a given emotion concept need to take the same direction.

away. Emotion concepts may signify who does the moving. "Love" has been understood to mean moving towards another person. The Japanese emotion word of *amae* is (wanting) another person to move to you (though it is not *just* that). "Anger" has been understood as moving someone else away from you, and "fear" as you moving away from the other.

You can also be dominant (*move up*) or submissive (*move down*): anger (and its translations) signals you are up. Getting angry at my husband for being late is a power move; it shows I am "strong" (relative to what I could have been had I been sad, for instance). Pride also means you are up. Western adults (including some psychologists) turn this around, and infer pride from strong and dominant posturing in a situation of success. That inference is not universally justified. *Fago* comes with the acknowledgment that other people are weak, and need your protection. Shame, embarrassment, and perhaps sadness, mean you are down in the relationship. These concepts come with submission, or with the acknowledgment of being weak, at least relative to the other person in the relationship. Awe is another emotion where you are down in the relationship, this time by mere awareness of how small you are compared to a particular other, or to the environment at large. For awe, think of being in the audience of an extremely inspiring concert, or listening to a charismatic teacher or leader.

You can move closer or further away, be up or down. Yet another option is that you stay where you are. Some emotions describe just that: acceptance and calmness are examples, but so is depression. There are many reasons for not moving: You can be at ease with the environment (calm), open to anything that has, or would, come your way (acceptance), or not know where to move, even if you wanted to (depressed, hopeless). You can also "keep calm and carry on," as the British say. But the movement is staying where you were, and the result is no immediate change in the environment—at least, no change that is initiated by you.

It does not take a scientist to come up with these emotional moves: they are the basic moves to be found in any relationship, and at this basic level, they will occur in all human societies and in other animals that live in groups (e.g., apes). Finding emotion concepts across the world that refer to these basic moves (or basic "episodes," as I have labeled them above) should not surprise, because these are the logical possibilities of aligning oneself with the environment—in other words, this is how we live. Yet, even if we share these logical possibilities of relating to the world, we do not share universal emotion concepts.

Words in Action

As an Egyptian Bedouin woman, I would feel uncomfortable encountering a man my own age. Knowing this to be an instance of *hasham* directly makes sense of the situation, and tells me what to do: I cast down my eyes, I avoid any contact, and I disappear, if possible. And in doing so I know that this is the right response. As a Japanese mother, I would perceive my unreasonable and loud toddler to *amaeru,* which tells me that I am to *amayakasu*: to accept my child's unwelcome behavior. This is what good mothers do. Should I be a German mother, having *Ärger* (annoyance or anger) at my disposal, I might perceive my equally unreasonable and loud toddler as disobedient. I would not accept my child's unwelcome behavior, I might hold them accountable, and set them straight. Once again, I would allow the concept to help me write the story. Characteristic of emotion stories is that there is an urge to act; *not* responding is not an option. The way you make sense of your feelings depends on the emotion concepts that are available in your culture; these concepts are shared within your social community. The emotion concepts that I have available afford certain ways of "writing" the emotion story, and make alternative endings of the story unlikely.

Emotion concepts also help us make sense of the behavior of our interaction partners. Applying the "wrong" concept is at a cost. Marie, a U.S. American student in psychologist Phillip Shaver's research, reports being confused because her boyfriend was "so mad" at her, when all she had done was be a little late. Following the lead of "mad," Marie was looking for the behavior that had merited her boyfriend's rage. Why was she looking into her own behavior? Because anger suggests there is a reason—anger is justified. She might have had an easier time making sense, had she seen his behavior as "jealous." It turns out he was outraged because he thought she had an affair, and was late for her appointment with him because of it.

Applying an emotion concept, either to oneself or to others, disambiguates the meaning of an ongoing emotional episode. It does so by focusing attention on certain aspects of the situation, and ignoring others; by making meaning of the event in a certain way, and by privileging a certain type of action. A similar situation (a disobedient child) taken as an instance of *amae*, shifts the focus on your child's immaturity and needs, but taken as an instance of *Ärger* will focus on your frustration as a parent, and will lead you to emphasize the ill intentions behind the behavior of your child. You as a mother engage the situation differently, depending on your interpretation: empathic coaxing in the case of *amae,* and annoyed punishment in the case of *Ärger.* Recognizing an emotion (among other emotions) is inserting your knowledge of a particular set of episodes. It means that you bring online everything you know about your emotional episodes in comparable situations, plus all the cultural knowledge that is implicit in the set. There is good reason to assume that without a concept, there is no emotion as we know it.

Woven into the emotion concepts are sets of cultural episodes with outcomes that are either desirable or undesirable, given the context and the position of the person. In the language of this book: "right" emotions are episodes with desired endings, "wrong" emotions are stories with endings that you would like to avoid.

As we have seen in chapter 4, "anger" is considered a useful, if often unpleasant, emotion in U.S. contexts; it has desirable endings. In close relationships, it is thought to help individuals protect their needs and expectations, and in work settings, it sets clear boundaries. In puberty, it helps the adolescent to gain independence. And it may also highlight societal wrongdoings, sparking movements for justice (nonacceptance of the current situation). Measured anger is considered right and healthy in European American contexts. This is not true everywhere. Especially in tightly knit communities, anger is often considered wrong (examples were described in more length in chapter 4). Utku Inuit shared with Jean Briggs that anger is a dangerous emotion that threatens equanimity and generosity—valued qualities. Similarly, Buddhist Tibetans regard *lung lang* ("being angry") as "a fundamentally destructive sentiment, equally harmful to self and others . . . as arising from an intrinsically flawed motivational state (a desire to harm another sentient being) and generative of ultimately bad results." The Ifaluk, the Polynesian group that hosted anthropologist Catherine Lutz, also condemned everyday anger. The irritability that accompanies sickness, frustration building up over the succession of minor unwanted things, or the annoyance at relatives not living up to their obligations, all of these varieties of anger were perceived to be immoral and undignified. Similarly, anger in Japan is considered a destructive emotion, better to be avoided. Where relational harmony is prioritized over individual autonomy, anger is considered wrong.

Importantly, where the concept of *anger* has undesired outcomes, it may have helped to write emotion stories as well—away from anger. Some languages have concepts that seem to be in place for the very reason of retaining some elements of anger without having to engage in the whole story: concepts that re-route the urge of action. The Samoan emotion of *musu* "expresses a person's reluctance to do what is required of him or her," but without blaming anyone. It is typically reported in the context of unreasonable demands made by one's parents, and semantic similarity tests confirm a close association between *musu* and the word for anger in Samoan, *ita*. The word allows actions of non-acceptance without implying the unthinkable of criticizing the parents' demands.

Something analogous may be true for *shame* in Western cultures. Sociologist Thomas Scheff suggests that shame in contemporary American society is taboo, as it stands for real and/or imagined rejection by others. And, if acknowledged as shame, such rejection would end in low self-esteem, shrinking, and withdrawing from contact. But since these acts are all undesirable in a culture where self-esteem is key and the goal is to be independent from others, shame is avoided. Rather than "writing" the episode of shame, people may use the more favorable endings that concepts such as "awkward" or "funny" suggest; neither concept requires any action at all.

Lacking a Concept

So, what if your own language does not have a word for an emotion concept? Would a Polish person not be able to understand *disgust*, if you told them it is what you feel when you smell rotten food or when you encounter rotten behavior? Although the relationship between words and experience is complex, and much debated, the availability of a word clearly makes a difference in the encoding of emotions. The Luganda-English interpreters who translated "to get sad" as *okusunguwala* (the word for "to get angry") did not think they had made a mistake, even if they were "corrected"; they simply did not encode the difference between angry and sad. Not having a separate concept available masks any distinction. Similarly, not having a word for sadness in Tahitian, French-Tahitian bilingual speakers did not understand that the French word *triste* (in its sense of "sorrowful, mournful, sad, melancholic, dejected") was anything else than "fatigued" or "gentle." They lacked the concept, not only the word, for "sad." Finally, psychologist Lisa Feldman Barrett and her team have clearly shown that without a word available, it is also harder to perceive emotions in the face. Emotion lexicons organize our experiences; it is a fair hypothesis that culturally different lexicons constitute your emotional experience differently.

This is not to say that it is impossible to imagine having a feeling for which another culture, but not yours, has a word. My American friends seem to relate pretty well to the Dutch word *gezellig*. They like it, even. Similarly, native speakers of English resonate with *amae*, *fago*, and *hasham*. In one study, despite not having a word for *amae*, American college students recognized *amae* situations, and interpreted them in similar ways as Japanese students. American respondents considered *amae* situations such as "a good friend calling late at night to ask for help with computer problems" as inconsiderate, yet acceptable—in line with the Japanese definition of *amae*. And similar to their Japanese counterparts, American college students also thought the inconsiderate request would make them feel closer to their friend.

Yet, learning about *gezellig* or *amae* as a native speaker of English may be a bit like a toddler's first encounter with an emotion concept: You do not know about all the different ways which the emotion can feel or look; you only have a skeleton. You have an outline of an emotion, and most likely only one facet. In the *amae* study American college students were only asked about the role of the caretaker, *amayakasu*, and there were differences in the way they perceived this role from how the Japanese perceived it. American college students said they would feel control in this role, whereas Japanese respondents did not. Arguably, American respondents were more focused on themselves and their individual agency than the Japanese respondents who were merely focused on the relationship. But even disregarding the difference in perspective, it can be argued that *amae* was not the same for the American students as it was for the Japanese. American students did recognize these situations in which they were called on to nurture their friends, but most likely they did not have the associations that any Japanese person would have based on their lifelong experiences with all the different facets of an *amae* relationship. Did I say that *gezellig* also refers to Dutch winters where it is dark outside and cold, but you are all together warming yourselves at the fire, with no need to go outside anymore? I am sure you could not have guessed that from the description of *gezellig* as "being snug in a warm and homely place surrounded by friends" that *gezellig* is for winters.

There is a big gap between recognizing *amae* or *gezellig* in a neatly carved-out emblem or in one situation where your friend points out what the emotion is, and having a lifelong stock of stories. Research with second-language speakers suggests just this. English speakers learning Russian did not have any trouble learning the meaning of the verb *perezhivat*: to experience something keenly, to worry, to suffer things through. Yet they failed to use the term in places where Russian natives did, in part because they "were not sure about its range of reference and the contexts to which it might apply." Even if you get a sense of the concept, you do not live that emotion without having had the experiences to furnish the concept.

It is easier to recognize that your grasp of exotic emotion words falls short than it is for emotion words that *do* have translations in your own language—and yet your concept falls short there too. *Ker* (Ifaluk) can be translated as "happy," but the emotion of *ker* is despised among Ifaluk, whereas happy is a desirable emotion in English. Very different cultural episodes are associated with these concepts. *Ikari* and *haji* in Japanese can be translated as "anger" and "shame," respectively, in English, but that does not mean that they come with the same stories. So, even if there is a good translation of an emotion word in your own language, it does not mean that you share either a history, or the cultural lore of an emotion concept. We make sense of our emotions differently, we connect them to, and furnish them with different cultural episodes. I would once have said that the emotions are the same, even if the stories are not. But what are the emotions if not their stories? Even considering a MINE model of emotions, the feeling of (despised) *ker* can hardly be said to be the same as the feeling of (desirable) *happiness*. And from an OURS perspective on emotions, "doing" *ker* is different from "doing" *happiness*. The stories or scripts are the emotions.

Influencing Others

Within a culture, emotion concepts enable you to communicate with other people in your culture: first your parents, and then a widening circle of people. By naming my emotion, I am invoking the cultural episodes that go with that emotion, as we all know them, to influence you and our relationship. Which episodes will come online depends on our relationship and on the particular context, but by talking about my emotion, I am piggybacking on all the things you and I, and many other people in our culture, know about these emotions.

In my culture, telling my husband I am mad that he is late for dinner is a way of warning him that I won't accept his behavior, that I blame him, and that I think I am right, and in the position to expect him to treat me better. By saying I am angry, I am taking a stance in the relationship. Psychologist Brian Parkinson makes the interesting suggestion that saying I am mad is even more powerful than just saying that I don't accept his behavior, because anger "sends the message that I may not be able to stop myself from following through if the situation does not change, that my action impulse has a momentum of its own." Thus, "my angry warning of aggression may constitute a compelling threat." Of course, anger episodes may have many different endings, but if in your culture, or within your relationship, aggression is a likely ending of the anger story, then saying you are angry may add some force. The urge to act is an indisputable characteristic of the emotion story. Others may indeed infer that *not* acting is no option.

Similarly, *hasham* does not only help an Egyptian Bedouin woman to "write" the story, but also to communicate it to others. And in doing so, it helps to achieve the very goal of *hasham*: to convey that you defer. Saying you are *hasham* may be just as powerful as casting your eyes down, avoiding any contact, or disappearing. And again, saying you are *hasham* is particularly useful because it communicates what we all know to be the right response.

There are many other examples. When I tell my partner I feel *guilty* about something I have done (or not done) that caused them distress, I convey the very script of feeling guilt: my commitment to the relationship, and my preparedness to make up for my wrongdoings. When I tell someone I love them, the very act of saying it works towards the script of romantic love: to give them attention, and to seek closeness. Of course, we can feel guilt and love without saying it, but saying it *is* "acting": saying it is working towards the goal of the emotion, which in the case of both love and guilt is (re)commitment to the relationship.

There are also times when saying you feel an emotion is nothing more than acting. Saying "Mommy is angry" is primarily an effective way of conveying your nonacceptance. It does not rule out you have angry feelings, but whether or not you do is inconsequential. The same with expressing guilt or regret in friendships. You may say you feel guilty, merely referring to your preparedness to act, even when you do not have the feeling. "I cannot believe I forgot. I feel so *bad*," is expressing a wish I had remembered, or that I could have made my act undone. It may, but does not have to describe, a *feeling*.

In cultures with OURS emotions, there are many examples of people using emotion words without necessarily feeling the emotion. Inauthentic? Not necessarily. If the most important part of emotion is what happens between people, then inner feelings become irrelevant—implied, but not necessary. Anthropologist Andrew Beatty describes the use of emotion concepts on Nias, an Indonesian island, as mostly limited to public events. The people living on Nias are "among the poorest in Indonesia, but they marry expensively, a contradiction certain to generate passions and passionate words." The bride's family is responsible for the grand reception of the groom's family, but the groom's is expected to pay a dowry that weighs up against the "gift of life": the bride's fertility and labor force. It is in the context of the public and theatrical negotiations of the dowry, where the families are gathered around, that emotion concepts are used most. These negotiations are not conducted by the people most involved, the bride's or groom's parents themselves, but rather by orators who represent each side. In one instance, the groom's family complained about the welcome they have received upon arrival, possibly in an effort to bring the dowry down, and says: "If I accepted it I'd be ashamed, mocked by my own children. . . ." The bride's side makes it known that they are concerned with the groom's reproach, and disappointed with the dowry. On both sides, emotions are proclaimed, but as Beatty notes, it is doubtful that the orators actually feel every emotion they express. And yet, emotions articulated by the orators perform their interpersonal role. They influence others, and in doing so, promote their goal. In going back and forth, "[p]eople sum up their position or mark where the debate has got to by referring to their hearts, each claim to frustration or resentment pegging their progress and forcing the other onto the back foot."

Labeling emotions may also directly appeal to *other people's* emotions. This is the case when caregivers encourage their children to have the culturally right emotions, or not have the culturally wrong emotions. Utku Inuit told their children not to *cry*, or "you'll make your pants wet and then you will freeze." Javanese kids were told to have *isin*, shame, in front of elders. Ifaluk mothers admonished their children to *fago*, "as a way of promoting gentle (as well as generous) behavior."

Adults may do the same. Tamalekar, the Ifaluk man who had "adopted" anthropologist Catherine Lutz, tells his family that they should *fago* a young man who visits from another island. And closer to home, my mentor and friend Hazel Markus told me on many an occasion *"You should feel good about yourself!"* thus socializing me to have emotions American-style. She encouraged me to enjoy a moment of success, to shine and take my spot. In doing so, her suggestion was to replace my Dutch, hesitant and shy response, which came from my concept of Dutch "success stories" that looked very different from the middle-class American concept. My mom always told me that "acting normal was special enough." And my grandmother warned me against boasting. Over the years, Hazel's encouragement and that by other American friends did add to my reservoir of American pride stories, from which I can now take direction.

Stories in the World

When I tell interested friends, acquaintances, or journalists that I study culture and emotions, they invariably ask me the same question: Which emotions are different? I have never been sure how to answer that question, because it requires backtracking many assumptions. It is a bit like answering the question if Joy or Fear in a similar Japanese movie would have the same colors as in the Pixar movie *Inside Out*, when you don't even know if Joy or Fear had been cast.

The MINE model of emotions would have it that if you lifted the skull of individuals, metaphorically speaking, you would find the emotion figurines living there. Emotion words should tell us about these figurines. Cultural differences in emotion words could mean that in some cultures people have faulty information about the "actual" emotions. When English lacks a word for *amae*, U.S. Americans may still be able to feel *amae,* despite the fact that the language does not correctly encode it. Alternatively, a MINE model of emotions may suggest that differences in emotion lexicons reflect the emotions "living inside" people from different cultures. Following that track of thought, the Ifaluk may have a figurine for *fago* (love, sadness, compassion), and the Japanese a figurine for *amae,* which U.S. Americans lack. And Polish speakers may lack a figurine for disgust that English speakers have. But how plausible is this idea of figurines living in our metaphorical skull?

This chapter suggests an entirely different way of thinking about emotion concepts—one much closer to the OURS model of emotions. Emotion concepts are sets of cultural episodes that we have experienced, directly or by observation, supplemented with the cultural lore of an emotion category. And to the extent that people's emotion lexicons and experiences differ across cultures, so will the emotional experiences that they distinguish. This is not a radically constructionist view: cultures cannot invent people's emotions from the ground up. This is because all our emotions are situated within relationships between people, who themselves are confined by the bodies that make them up. Human relationships and human bodies have a lot in common across cultures, but they also allow for much variation.

If emotion concepts are sets of cultural episodes, which by definition vary across cultures, groups, and individuals, then this also has implications for the original "face recognition" studies, paradigmatic of the field when I started my research on emotion. Remember, the claim at the time was that people around the world match a number of facial configurations with particular emotion concepts, such as anger, disgust, and joy. But how would this claim be affected when the translations of anger, disgust, and joy in other languages are only partially overlapping—when emotion lexicons poorly map onto each other? Something may be similar in those emotional faces—after all, they were associated with translation equivalents—but that something may not be an invariant emotion. In fact, this is what the newest research suggests.

If emotions do not refer to mental states, but rather to stories in the world, then our emotions differ because the worlds in which we live differ. That we can talk about emotions across cultures is owing to the fact that some things are stable: people in all cultures have emotions about other people they care about, challenges of their social position, the success of their group, and about what they consider to be good, beautiful, and moral.

Chapter 7

. . . .

LEARNING THE WALTZ

WHEN I FIRST MOVED TO THE UNITED STATES, I PREPARED myself for the hurdles of learning a new language, establishing myself in a new economy, and becoming familiar with new people and new customs. It is much harder to realize that a move will challenge the very assumptions we have held since childhood about how to do emotions.

Like partners in a dance, your emotions and those of others complement and steer each other to form the interaction. And shared cultural knowledge, in the form of language and practices, orchestrates the ways in which different individuals do emotions together. It is like dancing the tango at the rhythm of tango music, together with a partner who knows their dance steps, as you know yours. The dance emerges from everyone knowing their moves, and from the moves being in sync with the music. Doing your emotions in a way that fits with the relationships in your culture, and with your position in those relationships, is akin to having the right dance steps.

So, what happens when people move to another culture? If doing emotions is like dancing the tango, is doing emotions in another culture like dancing the tango with a partner who has never learned the tango steps? The metaphor holds in that you think you are producing the right dance steps—you expect your steps will merge with the other person's steps to form the dance—but they end up being out of sync, and possibly result in stepping on each other's toes. And there is more to doing emotions than just you and a partner doing a private dance: doing emotions in another culture, at least initially, is dancing the tango when everybody else in the ballroom dances to the music of a waltz.

Some individuals never get beyond the stage of noticing that other people perform a different dance than they were used to in their culture of origin. By her own admission, the anthropologist Jean Briggs had great difficulty understanding the emotions of Utku Inuit. At first, she did not understand when and why her hosts were angry, and she had difficulty identifying anger expressions when they occurred. Her ethnography shows an understanding of the emotion norms in the end, but she never internalized those norms. As linguist Aneta Pavlenko astutely conjectures, the very fact that Briggs considered her own way of doing emotions "natural" prevented her from ever completely fitting into her new emotional community. Briggs might have been unable, and perhaps unwilling, to do so, perhaps because she never saw herself as permanently living in the Utku community.

At the other end of the spectrum are immigrants who end up clearly mastering the dance to the new music. In her autobiography *Lost in Translation*, Eva Hoffman describes how she gradually adopted new ways of doing emotions after moving at the age of thirteen from Poland to the United States:

> Eventually, the voices enter me; by assuming them, I gradually make them mine. I am being remade, fragment by fragment, like a patchwork quilt; there are more colors in the world than I ever knew.

Hoffman may have been temporarily "lost in translation" but in the end she managed to become part of the new emotion culture. Immigrants *can* learn to dance the waltz, but how much or how often do they? And which are the conditions under which they do?

Much of the research I will cover in this chapter was the result of a heart-to-heart conversation between Heejung Kim, an immigrant from Korea, and me, an immigrant from the Netherlands. At the time we had this conversation (in fluent English), we both taught psychology at U.S. universities, we were married to (white) American husbands, and we raised our respective children in the U.S. We lived American lives: We celebrated Thanksgiving and the Fourth of July, watched *Saturday Night Live* and read the *New York Times*. We held barbeques and pot-lucks, went to baseball games in the summer, and threw Super Bowl parties in the winter. We were fully immersed in U.S. culture, and yet we confessed to each other that our feelings were not fully "American." Even after all these years, we were no naturals at dancing the "emotion" waltz. We felt that "doing emotions" may be one of the hardest things to learn when you move to another culture.

Kim and I were interested in knowing if immigrants, on average, were more like Jean Briggs, more like Eva Hoffman, or more like the two of us, which was probably someplace in between. We also wondered what would make emotions change: What are the conditions under which immigrants learn to dance the waltz? Finally, we wondered if learning to dance the waltz means that you lose your tango skills. Does it mean that new "colors" replace the old ones, or does it mean to learn "more colors in the world than [you] ever knew"?

A MINE model of emotions does not explain why emotions would be slow to adjust. If emotions are hardwired, they would be just as unlikely to change when you move to a new place as the color of your eyes. Psychologists have generally assumed that all a person needs to learn after moving to a new culture are the proper names of emotions in the new language, or perhaps their proper display. The self-observation that Kim and I had flew in the face of these assumptions.

In our research, we started from the idea that emotions are OURS. If emotions are tied to our contexts, then moving to another context requires more than learning new labels for existing figurines in the head. Linguist Aneta Pavlenko addresses exactly this issue when she describes the tasks awaiting a second-language (L2) learner:

To move beyond initial and often faulty assumptions and to understand the emotional world of their host community, L2 learners ... have to puzzle out unfamiliar behaviors, to identify what triggers which "emotions" and when, to learn how particular "emotions" may be managed and to discover what cues to pay attention to and how to interpret verbal and non-verbal "emotion displays."

If emotions are tied to our cultural contexts, then moving to another context involves learning a whole different way of "doing emotions" in interactions.

A New Culture

Honest authenticity is a Dutch virtue. This is well illustrated by the lyrics of a famous Dutch song (partially represented as):

Life is a wonderful thing
But spread your wings and don't get trapped in a cage
Have the courage to live life to the fullest . . .
Don't give a damn what others may think . . .
Be a prince on your own square meter!

By doing as you like and showing your true feelings, even if others may not like them or even if they cast you in an unfavorable light, you are true to yourself and honest in the relationship. I embodied this special Dutch form of "intellectual autonomy" when I left the Netherlands.

In the Netherlands, you do what you feel like, but you also dig in your heels when you do not like what is happening. By feeling and expressing indignation and anger, you go against the grain, but this does not mean that you are antisocial. To the contrary, anger and indignation provide the opportunity for "real" connection, as they show you authentically.

During my ten years in North Carolina, I gradually shed some of the "honest" anger and indignation. I shed them because they conflicted with the relationship goals of respect and politeness in my

North Carolinian environment. In a Southern culture of honor, anger and strong indignation marked discord and were reserved for occasions where others had challenged your reputation or had treated you without due respect. Being angry and indignant were a last resort to help you avoid becoming a laughingstock. They were not signs of being merely opinionated and authentic, as they had been in the Netherlands; they certainly did not help to authentically connect with others, as they had helped me back in Europe.

I also shed these emotions because no one else around me focused on self-expression the way I did, and because self-expression of this kind did not get positive responses. With help of subtle and not-so-subtle feedback, I came to see my Dutch way of self-expression as too forceful and unnecessarily impolite. There was the clearly written feedback on my teaching evaluations: "She is blunt at times" or "Professor Mesquita tried to impose her beliefs." But there must have been more subtle signs as well—from colleagues, friends, my children's schoolteachers—that I came to interpret as disapproval. A journalist from my university's monthly magazine nodded politely when, during an interview, I volunteered my criticism on the university's research policy. He seemed in a hurry to leave the topic behind us. My experience of sticking out like a sore thumb served as a cue to suppress my indignation or weaken it. At first, I tried to not express what I felt, or not as bluntly. But after a while, I lost my sense that it was natural to feel this way, and I traveled some distance towards learning emotional ways that were more effective and better understood in my new cultural environment. When I did show indignation or anger on occasion, as with the journalist from my university's magazine, I immediately realized that this was a relic from my time in the Netherlands. It did not feel "right" anymore, not in that context. My emotions came to serve respect and politeness rather than intellectual autonomy. The learning was not merely cosmetic; I *felt* less anger and indignation. I never became fully North Carolinian, but I do think my waltz became smoother over the years. Less stepping on other people's toes. In the same way my emotions had once allowed me to be part of a Dutch relationships, they now allowed me to grow more in sync with my North Carolinian environment.

My colleagues Heejung Kim, Jozefien De Leersnyder, Alba Jasini, and I have come to see similar changes in immigrant populations that we study. These changes are what we call in psychology jargon *emotional acculturation*: learning to do emotions in the new culture's ways. In much of our research, we studied emotional acculturation by comparing the emotions of immigrant minorities with those of the *average* majority respondent for a particular type of situation.

Suppose that Ayse, a second-generation Turkish Belgian student, was reprimanded by her teacher for talking, and then asked, in front of the whole class, to leave the room. Looking at Ayse's feelings (see figure 7.1), we can see that she was somewhat angry, but she also felt respect for the teacher, and ashamed because she should have paid the teacher more respect. Her "profile" was one of much anger, combined with quite a bit of shame and respect. We compared Ayse's profile with how her Belgian-majority peers on average felt in a similar situation. They were angry, but some also felt pride, perhaps questioning the teacher's intervention ("Why does she treat me like a three-year-old?"). The average profile for the Belgian students shows that, in this particular

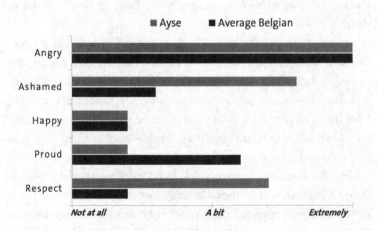

FIGURE 7.1 Illustration of Ayse's "emotion profile" with an example of an average majority profile

case, anger was important in the Belgian profile, as it was for Ayse, but shame and respect were not. Ayse's feelings did not "fit" the Belgian average—the norm—that well.

You might ask how it is that we can compare these emotion profiles, if meanings of the words for *anger*, *shame*, *pride*, and *respect* in different languages and cultures do not correspond. The answer to that question is that the meanings of these categories were *similar enough* that we knew something changed when a girl like Ayse would start reporting less shame and respect and more pride after they had spent more time in Belgium. We made sure that the Turkish and Belgian (or Korean and U.S. English) words took similar positions on certain dimensions of meaning: valence (positive versus negative feelings) and goals (protective of personal versus relational goals). If Ayse felt less shame and more pride after having spent some time in Belgium, it meant her "emotions" shifted from negative, relationship-protecting to positive, personal-goals protecting.

Using this method, we found in study after study that first-generation immigrants have the lowest fit with the average majority emotion profile; the cultural fit was a little higher with every next generation of immigrants. As you might expect, the emotions of the majority—either white Americans or white Belgians—were closest to the majority emotion norm.

In one of our studies, with a large number of students in a representative sample of middle schools in Belgium, we even found that half generations made a difference: the 2.5th generation of immigrants, with one first-generation and one second-generation parent, differed from the third generation. Not until the third generation was the emotion profile of immigrants indistinguishable from the majority. It is very clear that, *on average*, it takes more than a lifetime for minorities to achieve the emotional fit comparable to majority members. Of course, some individuals will in their lifetime learn to waltz in a way that is indistinguishable from the majority—Eva Hoffman, for example—but this is not true for most. It is good to keep this in mind when we think about the reality of minoritized people from immigrant populations.

During the last two decades, particularly in many Northern European countries, the formal expectation has become that minorities fully participate in the new culture within five years of arrival. In my native country, the Netherlands, an "integration test" was introduced. The discussion around this test has overtones of assimilation: if "they" want to stay here, they need to become part of our lifestyle. I will return to this expectation in chapter 8, but it suffices to say here that five years is almost certainly not enough for "emotional acculturation"; any expectation to the contrary would be psychologically naïve. My dad once reflected that it took our Sephardic Jewish ancestors more than a century to get acclimatized to Amsterdam, their new home, after they had fled from the Spanish Inquisition in the first half of the seventeenth century. "How can we expect new immigrants to do it in five years?," he wondered. Our research proves him right: when it comes to emotions, only the third generation of immigrants becomes indistinguishable from the majority.

Lest you think this would not hold true in the big "melting pot" of the United States, we started our research there, and we have no reason to assume that the process of emotional fit is fundamentally different. Studies with first-generation Korean American adults in the United States show very similar patterns to the ones obtained with the representative sample of Belgian middle schools; on average, first-generation immigrants do not achieve an emotional fit with the white American norm, but later generations do.

Doing emotions in a different culture can be learned but, for most people, it will take more than a lifetime. This may also be true when it comes to emotion perception. Psychologists Hillary Elfenbein and Nalini Ambady found that individuals agree more with the standard emotional interpretations when the facial displays come from their own than from another culture. They studied four groups of participants with varying levels of exposure to both the United States and China: Americans of non-Asian descent, Chinese Americans, Chinese students living in the United States, and Chinese students living in China. All participants viewed pictures of Caucasian faces originally developed by Ekman and Friesen to "display" six emotions, as well as pictures of Chinese faces developed to match the original face set. Pictures appeared on a screen one by one, each time followed by a list of six emotion words. Participants checked the "emotion" that described the face best. Elfenbein and Ambady found that participants more often checked the intended emotion to the extent they were familiar with the poser. American students of non-Asian descent more readily perceived emotions as intended for a white American than a Chinese face set. For their Chinese peers in China, it was the other way around. Importantly, the more time Chinese immigrant groups had spent in the U.S., the closer their performance on the white American face set was to the non-Asian American students. Chinese Americans had more "ingroup advantage" for the perception of the European American facial displays than did Chinese students temporarily residing in the U.S., and the latter had an advantage over the Chinese students in China. Even within the Chinese American sample, exposure mattered: later generations showed more ingroup advantage for the European American face set than earlier generations; conversely, earlier generations showed more ingroup advantage for the Chinese face set than later generations. While the classic paradigm of linking emotion words to static displays is not tremendously helpful in describing the daily emotional interactions of immigrants or later generations of immigrant minorities, it does help to make the case that all aspects of doing emotions are subject to cultural learning—even the ones that were originally claimed to be universal. Remember how our Japanese respondents thought Jon or Taro were happier if a happy-looking Jon was surrounded by people who also looked happy, rather than looking angry, sad, or neutral?

Remember also how North Americans, when asked to judge Jon's happiness, *only* focused on Jon without considering the affective context? I used this finding as one example of North Americans perceiving MINE, and Japanese perceiving OURS emotions. Taka Masuda, himself Japanese-born and now a professor at the University of Alberta, set out to study whether the perceptive lens of Japanese immigrant populations would change from OURS to MINE. Tweaking our original research a bit, he found it did.

White Canadians judged Jon's emotions without regard for the affective context; they just looked at Jon's face. As immigrants became part of North American social life, their emotion model gradually seemed to shift from OURS to MINE. Though both Asian Canadian and Asian international students in Canada relied too on the emotional displays of the surrounding people when they were asked to judge how happy, angry, or sad Jon was, their emotion judgments became *less* reliant on the emotions of the surrounding people with increased exposure to North American culture. The eye-tracking data show even Asian international students, who had spent relatively little time in Canada, focused on the central person's emotions more than the Japanese students in Japan; yet not even the Asian Canadians had bridged the gap with the European Canadians.

Describing changes in emotional lives as a result of immigrating to another culture is no easy task, and the available research only scratches the surface. With exposure to another culture, emotional lives presumably change in many different ways: we may learn to feel and perceive emotions differently, and to act and interact differently with others. There are many new steps immigrants or sojourners learn, and it is not so clear which are the most essential for dancing with the majority. What is clear is that most immigrants do not learn all these new dance steps in their lifetime, but at the same time even a relatively brief exposure to another culture affects the way we do emotions.

Learning Emotions

It may have taken my Sephardic Jewish ancestors a full century to get attuned to the emotions of the rest of Amsterdam because for the longest time they were completely segregated: They had their own schools, their own governing board, their own jurisdiction, their own social and cultural events, and they married among themselves. They seldom interacted with majority others, and if they did, it was primarily to do business, a very narrow context for doing emotions.

In the late '70s, social psychologist Yasuko Minoura followed more than seventy Japanese-born school-aged children whose parents' jobs took them temporarily to the United States. She interviewed them extensively, and found most emotional learning took place in children whose social lives had become American. The children who were comfortable articulating their own strengths ("pride"), made their wishes clear (i.e., made clear what made them "happy"), and took their own decisions (i.e., they pursued what made them "happy") had spent more time in the United States, had the largest number of American friends, and also were more proficient in English—all suggesting that they were more immersed in U.S. culture.

At the time of Minoura's research, some scholars believed that moving cultures any time after early socialization would leave one poorly attuned to the emotional ways of another culture. Early socialization practices were thought to be responsible for putting emotion practices in place once and for all. Minoura's observations confirmed that the feelings of some of the Japanese parents did not change much upon their move, but it was different for their schoolgoing, mingling children. The "emotions" of these Japanese-born youth continued to align to their new social and cultural environments.

Several of our own studies converged with Minoura's findings. The larger the proportion of life that immigrant minorities spent in their majority (versus minority) culture, the higher their emotional fit. This means you are never too old to learn, but that the same exposure to a culture may not have the same effect on your emotions. I spent about a quarter of my life (or fifteen years) in the United States. My children spent roughly the same number of years in the U.S., but for them these years constitute a higher proportion of their lives. According to our studies, having spent a higher proportion of life in the U.S. should make their emotions more Americanized than mine. Age of immigration plays a role, but mostly because arriving late makes it harder to gain as much experience in the new culture as you had in your heritage culture. No person is too old to learn from experience, but no person gets to erase their past either.

Of course, being in a country is not enough to learn the culture's way of doing emotions: you have to take part in its social life. In our large Belgian middle-school study, we found that having close majority friends really helped to have "Belgian emotions." Each close majority friend helped towards the emotional fit, so that having more close friends helped more than having just one. Having friends also helped more than merely being surrounded by majority students. The emotions of minority students were more "Belgian" if a higher proportion of their classmates were majority students, if they generally spent more time with majority friends (during as well as outside of school), and if they spent less time speaking the language of the country of origin *during school breaks* (presumably leaving more time to speak Dutch). You learn to do emotions in the majority culture when you take part in interactions with majority others.

There is not much research on how we learn the emotions of another culture, but late-life socialization may not be fundamentally different from early-life socialization of emotions; it comes outside-in. One of my socializing experiences occurred when I first arrived at the University of Michigan. I attended a seminar on emotions where most of the other participants were graduate students; I was a postdoctoral student. In a general round of self-introductions, I stated I was interested in "culture and emotion." The senior professor supplemented my understated (Dutch) introduction, saying that I was one of the world experts on the topic of culture and emotions. In doing so, he created an opportunity for "pride." It was not much different from the way in which, many years later, Oliver's father and I created opportunity for his feeling pride, or Didi's mother and sister created opportunity for shame.

If not literally *create*, others may also *categorize* emotional episodes in the new culture's way. As an immigrant you learn new emotions, because others in the new culture categorize emotional events according to shared emotion concepts. Again, this is not so different from the way children learn to do "emotions."

Other people also show and tell you *how* to do emotions. I remember that same first time with the senior professor, I looked down in embarrassment, and mumbled that "expert" was a big word. I did not know how to take my place in this emotional interaction that was creating an occasion for "pride." Rather than joining my host in his effort by being pleased and thanking him—the American scenario, I later learned—I reciprocated with a Dutch scenario, showing myself "no better than anybody else." I danced the tango, when my interaction partner invited me to the waltz that was common in the my new (North American) environment. Gradually, by observing others gracefully taking their place to shine, I learned to take opportunities to feel pride when they were offered.

Taking part in majority contexts also teaches you when interactions are smooth. I learned because, clearly, interactions were less awkward if I did American-style "pride." Similarly, noticing that my indignation was not shared, and my anger ignored in the American South, made me express (and ultimately feel) less of these emotions. If others consistently make waltz steps, the music that is playing is waltz music, and your tango steps are not reciprocated, you learn to waltz; your "emotions" get calibrated, though not all at once, and not flawlessly.

Immigrants learn emotions when others create opportunities for them to feel "the right" emotions, when others eagerly categorize emotional episodes in terms of those "right" emotions, or when others model how to feel the "right" emotions in similar situations. As with socialization of emotions in young children, socialization later in life is outside-in. As we have seen before, this does not mean that the emotions are any less real. During my years in the United States, "feeling good about myself" American-style increasingly became part of me, and I think that what this means is that after many iterations of looking at myself and my achievements as important, worth noticing, and worth being singled out for, I did start seeing them as such. It was more than *acting*; it was doing emotions in the right way, truly incorporating the concept of "feeling good about myself." Rather than being socialized early in life once and for all, we keep changing and adjusting to new social—and cultural—challenges.

New Concepts

As a student of emotions, still in the Netherlands, I remember that the word "distress" confused me. The term was often used in English-language psychological research on emotion, and I understood distress was not a happy state, but I had trouble pinpointing its meaning. Was "distress" closer to the Dutch *angst* ("anxious/afraid"), or closer to the Dutch *verdriet/wanhoop* ("sadness/despair")? At the time I surely did not know distress as an emotion. After having spent considerable time in the United States, I now no longer draw a blank when the word is used. I know both *when* distress is felt, and *what* the experience of distress can feel like. Distress has become an "emotion" to me.

Sofia, an English-Greek bilingual speaker who had lived in Cyprus for over seven years, reported something similar for the Greek word *stenahoria*—literally, "constricted space." *Stenahoria* does not have a linguistic equivalent in English. Sofia knew approximately *when sten-ahoria* was used. But despite knowing the word, and some of the conditions under which it was used, Sofia has real trouble describing the emotion behind *stenahoria*. The word was "used by old people" only, never by her Greek husband. Sofia had not been part of the cultural episodes or interactions that could have fully furnished the Greek word *stenahoria* with its meaning. Learning to speak a language is learning not only new words, but also acquiring new emotions. The process can be slow, and research confirms that immigrants learn the words in a new language before they learn the associated emotions.

I knew that I did not know under what circumstances distress occurred, how it felt, and what you would do when distressed. I knew that I did not know if distress made you a bad person, or what responses it elicited in others. Similarly, Sofia had no trouble recognizing her unfamiliarity with *stenahoria*. It is much harder to become aware that you have to learn the emotions associated with words for which your native language *does* provide a linguistic equivalent. Yet, learning *these* "emotions" is not necessarily any faster or easier than learning culture-specific emotion words. In fact, second language learners who are not immersed in the new culture simply attach the new language's emotion words to the concepts from their native culture. This is what happens in classroom learning of a second language—the way I started to learn English: we learn the labels of the new language, but without learning their actual meaning.

The linguist Howard Grabois nicely illustrates this point in a study on Spanish second-language learning. To chart the respective meanings of words for love, fear, and happiness in Spanish and in English, he compared the word associations that Spanish native speakers had with these concepts with the associations that English native speakers have. There were differences in these association networks. For instance, the English *fear* was more closely associated with fear responses ("anxiety," "nervous," "stress," "sweat," "scream," "shaking"), whereas its Spanish counterpart, *miedo*, was associated with words for loneliness and aloneness. Interestingly, foreign-language learners who had never lived in a Spanish-speaking environment, or not for very long, learned the Spanish words but without acquiring the Spanish associations; they simply glued a new word (e.g., *miedo*) to an existing concept (e.g., associations with "anxiety," "nervous," "stress," "sweat," "scream," "shaking"). Only when second-language speakers of Spanish had lived in the country for some time would they start to make the Spanish word associations; they could be said to have learned the "emotions"—i.e., a new set of episodes—rather than merely the labels. Not until you personally experience, or watch, the new culture's emotional interactions do you learn what it means to have the emotions of a new culture. Until then, the new words are empty vessels, or rather, vessels filled with old baggage.

When I learned English, I never suspected that *anger* was different from the Dutch *boos*. I just used them interchangeably; I attached my old experiences to the new word. I now know (from research) that these words are different, if only somewhat. *Anger* words in English (e.g., "angry") are more closely associated with aggression (e.g., "yell," "argue," "hit") than *anger* words in Dutch (e.g., *boos*, *kwaad*). In turn, Dutch *anger* words have a stronger association with distancing yourself from the situation (e.g., "leave," "ignore," "forget") than English *anger* words. This may be so because the *angry* and *boos* episodes in the respective cultures are different. It is not until you experience a lot of those episodes that you come to learn the "emotion" in the new culture.

By merely including emotion concepts that were similar on the dimensions of valence and goals, and by exclusively focusing on these dimensions, our research with emotion profiles steered clear from the way immigrant individuals learn new emotion concepts. However, in some cases, linguistic equivalents in Turkish and (Belgian) Dutch were different, even with respect to the two basic dimensions of meaning we considered. The Turkish words for "resigned" and "embarrassed" were positive, but the Belgian Dutch words were negative; the Turkish word for "jealousy" was relationship-protecting, but its Belgian Dutch equivalent was protective of personal goals. For a Turkish immigrant, there may be a point where they do not only learn Dutch words, but also learn the associated meanings. "Resigned" will become an emotion that marks the lack of personal control, rather than accepting one's place in the world. "Embarrassment" will become an emotion that underlines the dependence on others' judgment, rather than the awareness of one's modest social position. And "jealousy" will become selfish, rather than a justified response to threats to the relationship. These concepts take on new meaning, because the social realities they reflect are different.

Ironically, it may be the difficulty of recognizing that linguistic equivalents do not refer to the same "emotions" that clouds our understanding of the emotions of a person from another culture. Having translations available, even imperfect ones, may seduce us to think that deep inside people from other cultures have the "same emotions." It is this same difficulty that may account for the reluctance of many scientists to recognize cultural differences in emotions.

The Tango and the Waltz

Some of the children of Japanese descent in Minoura's study—after having spent considerable time in the U.S. because of their parents' jobs, experienced difficulty reentering Japanese culture. One of them, seventeen-year-old Jiro, tells Minoura: "I had to make a Japanese out of myself. . . ." Jiro's "emotions" had become Americanized at the expense of being Japanese. Other Japanese-born teens also noted they had adopted the American way of doing emotion to the exclusion of the Japanese way. They had a hard time conforming and communicating in the indirect ways that are normative in Japan; some actually went as far as to feel "disgusted" with the Japanese ways.

Jiro's experience may reflect the fate of many immigrants, as a study by my colleague Jozefien De Leersnyder suggests. De Leersnyder took our emotion profile questionnaire to Turkey and Korea, and established the Turkish and Korean emotion "norms" for the different situation types. In a situation like the one Ayse reported about the teacher publicly reprimanding her, the Turkish profile might have primarily consisted of shame and respect. When De Leersnyder compared the emotion profiles of immigrant populations with the normative emotions of their culture of origin, she found that the immigrant groups had lost some of their original emotional culture. On average, the emotions of second-generation Turkish Belgians were not Turkish anymore—no more "Turkish" than those of a Belgian-majority sample. Similarly, the emotions of Korean Americans were not "Korean" anymore: no more "Korean" than the emotions of their European American counterparts. Only the first-generation Turkish Belgians still experienced "Turkish" emotions: they were just as "Turkish" as the emotions in the Turkish sample. As you will remember, the emotions of the first-generation Belgian Turks were hardly aligned with the Belgian ways of doing emotions yet.

But does the learning of a new way of doing emotions necessarily replace the old way? The story of Jiro, the Japanese teen in Minoura's study, suggests that it does not. Three years after his return to Japan, he finds an opportunity to go back to the U.S., where he reflects on both cultures' ways of doing emotions, and now also recognizes the advantages of the Japanese system of conformity and *amae*. Jiro is aware that the relational goals in the US and Japan are different, and he can relate to them both:

> In Japan you will not be acceptable unless you keep up with others. In the US there is a lot of diversity [in choices, behaviors]. It is all right as long as you are happy with it. When I returned to the United States [after having been in Japan for a while] I

felt relieved. I thought that now I could assert myself without worrying about conforming to others. But on the other hand, it was difficult. Here you have to make decisions yourself . . . you should be alert and support yourself, or you drop out. . . . Being taken care of in the Japanese way isn't so bad as I used to think. After all, you enjoy more a feeling of security.

Although individuals from immigrant groups may come to spend more time dancing the waltz, many of them still remember how to dance the tango; they are familiar with the emotions of two (or more) cultures. I still remember how stunned I was when, fresh upon my arrival back in Europe, the newly elected chair of my department accepted his position by saying that he would accept this time-consuming job, even though his wife was surely not going to be happy with the news. He assured the department that he would work hard on its behalf, and would try his best. He was no slacker, but in his acceptance speech had no trace of the honor of having been elected, and no reference to pride or happiness. He did not express his happiness that this wonderful department gave him their trust, and made no mention of the great department that he was going to make greater. His acceptance speech was humble, not exhilarated. I was surprised because I had expected the North American waltz. Yet, I also instantly remembered that I was back in the country of tango. My own ways of doing emotions had changed. At the same time, my more than thirty years of experiences in the Netherlands kept an indelible influence. I was able to shift gears right away.

What Jiro and I had in common was that we sparsely interacted with people from our own heritage culture while we lived in the U.S. This may have been the case for the *average* second-generation Turkish Belgian and Korean American respondent: On average, the emotion profiles of the second-generation immigrants in De Leersnyder's study were not very "Turkish" or "Korean." Yet, some individuals formed an exception in that their emotional profiles were "Turkish" or "Korean." What these individuals had in common was that they had Turkish and Korean *friends* in their everyday lives. The reality of having a "Turkish" or a "Korean" friend trumped anything else when it came to emotions. You can be quite attached to your heritage traditions, you can feel identified with the heritage culture, and you may *wish* you were surrounded by friends of your heritage culture, but unless you also have heritage friends, these are not enough to preserve your heritage way of doing emotions. Not participating in the relationships makes you lose a culture's ways of doing emotions pretty quickly, although perhaps not permanently.

My friend psychologist Shinobu Kitayama is Japanese American bicultural. He grew up in Japan with an OURS model of emotions. Coming to the U.S. for him meant a shift from an OURS to a MINE model of emotions. In Japan, "emotions" were out in the world. Throughout the many years he lived in the U.S., he learned to think about his emotions as mental states. Yet, whenever he comes back to the U.S., after having spent some time in Japan, he at first has trouble answering the simple question of "How are you feeling?" It is as if he needs to zoom back into his insides again, shifting his focus outward-in. He goes through this small adjustment each time again.

An equally telling example is the fact that the feelings of excitement and pride that I experience in American contexts are not sustained in the same way in European everyday life. Whenever I spend a lot of time on the European continent, my excitement and pride peter out, and are replaced by feelings more appropriate as well as better attuned to that European context.

It is possible to phase in and out of a certain way of doing emotions, and to draw on the "right" emotions for each context. The adjustment to either context can be effortful, as has been the case for both Kitayama and me, but it is never as hard as learning to "do emotions" in that culture for the first time. Also, it is possible that the switching itself can be trained. Shinobu Kitayama and I may not be typical biculturals: we take airplanes to switch between our cultural contexts. Many biculturals switch between their cultures on an everyday basis. Our migrant middle school students in Belgium in many cases were from immigrant families, spoke the heritage culture at home, yet went to Belgian schools, where some of them had white Belgian friends.

They are part of the majority culture, and at the same time, they spend a substantial part of their time in immigrant communities.

It is possible that biculturals who often switch between two (or more) cultures are no longer aware that they do. With practice, we may dance the waltz to waltz music, and tune in to the tango music when it is playing; we may do so without noticeable effort. For instance, some Japanese Americans may adopt a MINE model when interacting in majority American contexts, and an OURS model of emotions in their Japanese homes. Engaging in the relationships that are situated in one cultural context or the other may prompt the associated ways of doing emotions. There is some research suggesting that biculturals do the "right" emotions in the right context.

Remember that happiness and unhappiness are intimately connected in many East Asian cultures? Individuals in East Asian contexts often report the co-occurrence of the two. This is not so in European American culture, where by default, happiness means that you are not unhappy. In one study, East Asian Canadian undergraduate students were found to report different patterns of emotions depending on whether they identified more with Western culture, or more with Asian culture. The study monitored these students' emotions for ten consecutive days. In situations where the East Asian Canadian students felt Western (or spoke English), they felt happiness at the expense of unhappiness; however, when they identified Asian (or spoke an Asian language), happiness and unhappiness co-occurred. Overall, the students were no less unhappy in situations where they identified as Western than in situations where they identified as Asian, but the co-occurrence patterns of happy and unhappy feelings did differ depending on their identification.

Research with Korean American and Turkish Belgian immigrants by Jozefien De Leersnyder, Heejung Kim, and I similarly showed that immigrant emotions are more acculturated in public spaces that are likely associated with Western culture than in the private space which tends to be non-Western. The emotion profiles of the immigrant groups were more similar to the respective majority groups at work or school than at home. Emotion profiles differed by cultural context.

It is possible that the emotion profiles differed because immigrants encountered different types of interpersonal situations in public spaces versus at home. If they were more happy in public spaces, perhaps the reason was they encountered more (or fewer) situations that elicited happiness. For example, I might have been more "happy" after I immigrated to the U.S., because people in the U.S. create so many opportunities for happiness by celebrating you and giving you compliments. Alternatively, if the kinds of situations were no different, immigrants might have switched to a different frame of doing emotions (much like I started to do less "opinionated indignation" in North Carolina, just because the relational goals there were different than they had been in my native Holland). Both explanations may hold, but my colleague Jozefien De Leersnyder and I wanted to see if we could detect frame-switching in emotions, even if biculturals encountered the same kinds of interpersonal situations.

So we designed a study to test this. We asked bicultural Turkish Belgians to collaborate with a "neighbor" on designing their ideal neighborhood. Their task was to jointly come up with a plan, helped by a map of the neighborhood, pictures of such things that they might want to have in their neighborhood (such as playgrounds and trees), pens, glue, etc. We created two cultural contexts. Half of the biculturals were invited to the social room of the Turkish neighborhood mosque, where they interacted with a Turkish "neighbor" and a Turkish experimenter, and spoke Turkish throughout the interaction. The other half of the biculturals were invited to the community center in the neighborhood that was funded by the local (Belgian) government, they interacted with a Belgian majority neighbor and a Belgian experimenter, and they spoke Dutch (the language spoken in this part of Belgium) throughout the experiment. Our main question was whether the emotional responses of the Turkish Belgian biculturals in the Turkish condition would be more "Turkish," and in the majority Belgian condition more "Belgian"? Would the dance be different, depending on dance partners and music playing in the background?

We made sure that the biculturals encountered the same interpersonal situations, whether they were in the Turkish or the Belgian context. The "new neighbor" was in all cases a confederate who would conduct themselves poorly several times throughout the collaborative task; these misdemeanors were carefully scripted. So, we recorded the emotional responses of biculturals to the same interpersonal situations, but in different cultural contexts. For example, one misdemeanor occurred towards the end, when the plan for the ideal neighborhood was taking shape. The experimenter entered the room to check on the progress, upon which the "new neighbor" jumped up to explain the plan, volunteering right away that they had practically come up with the whole thing by themselves (with the clear implication that the participant had not made any useful contribution). Our bicultural participants responded noticeably to this infraction in both conditions, but differently in the Turkish and the Belgian context. Biculturals in the Turkish context more often responded to the neighbor's claim in disbelief that anybody could be so disloyal: they scanned their neighbor from top to toe, and they widened their eyes. We interpreted these behaviors as *contempt*. In contrast, the biculturals in the Belgian context showed more behaviors, such as frowning and frustration in the voice, which we interpreted as *anger* about the neighbor's unfair judgment.

Importantly, depending on the cultural context, the same group of biculturals responded differently to the same emotional events (e.g., the neighbor telling the experimenter that they did the task practically by themselves). Cultural context mattered, and this is yet another way in which emotions are outside-in. The cultural context in which the interaction takes place was the music to which our biculturals danced.

Do We All Negotiate Different Contexts?

I distinctly remember a meeting in my department in which new positions were being divided between the different research areas. In our area, the department had neglected to fill the positions of several retired faculty in the preceding few years. Moreover, there had been a promise of more hires if we lived up to the high expectations that the department held for our newly formed research group. We had outperformed those expectations in the past few years. Yet, in the proposal that the board sent around, none of the new positions to be filled would come to us. As the area chair, I of course defended my group's interests at the meeting where the proposal was discussed, but in the process I started crying. The reactions afterwards were not subtle, and it was very clear that my crying was not considered the right emotional response in this male-dominated environment. One colleague reminded me a couple of weeks later by saying I probably "did not remember what had been decided," given I had been "emotional" at the meeting. Another colleague was heard to say that he never wanted to have another meeting like this, suggesting this was the ultimate sign that the meeting had strayed.

In retrospect, the problem was that my emotions were not "right" in this context. Crying belongs to the context of close relationships where people take care of each other, but does not belong in a professional meeting in, what still is, an environment governed by male gender roles. Mind you, I was not the only person to be emotional at the meeting, but my male colleagues did do their emotions very differently: the debate was heated, and people raised their voices and claimed that parts of the proposal were ill-conceived and unacceptable. This way of doing emotions was meant to not cede control to each other. My crying in the moment did not fit that logic but instead appealed to others' understanding and help, which my colleagues in the meeting clearly resisted. I ceded some responsibility for my well-being to my colleagues. I was dancing the tango when everybody else was dancing the waltz.

This is only one person's experience—mine—but it would not surprise me if many women in a male professional environments have had to learn to feel, express, and manage emotions to be acceptable and effective in these latter environments, pretty much like people in minoritized positions acculturating to majority emotions. The relational goals governing these contexts are different. It may equally be true that female gender roles for emotions are still rewarding and acceptable at home, even if they are not in traditionally male professional environments. If they are, then many women would be switching emotional cultures in their everyday lives, just like people in minoritized positions switch emotions when moving from majority to heritage cultural contexts.

Context-switching may not be exclusive to women and minorities either. Perhaps everyone who moves across different spheres of life will have cultivated (slightly) different emotional understandings, expressions, and management strategies for these different contexts. The close relationship expert Margaret Clark gives the following example:

> Imagine you are dining out with your romantic partner. You spill your wine all over the table and your partner harshly ridicules you for having done so. You're likely to feel hurt, perhaps angry, perhaps both. But what if the person who ridiculed you is a total stranger sitting at a nearby table? You're very <u>un</u>likely to feel hurt; you may feel angry, or you may just think the stranger is a jerk and brush him off as irrelevant. Our point is that the emotions you experience (or do not experience) in the face of identical ridicule will almost certainly differ if the ridicule comes from a close partner compared to coming from a stranger.

Why would this be? Your hurt feelings, says Clark, are instrumental in the mending the relationship. They not only communicate to your partner that the relationship is not going well, but also that you are interested in them repairing it. Ideally your hurt feelings elicit your partner's guilt, and a desire to repair the relationship. Anger is different, in that it "cedes no control to the other person." Anger does not ask the other person to mend the relationship (though it may be used to steer a relationship in a desired direction also). Spilling wine in a restaurant is obviously a particular cultural environment to begin with. But within this narrow niche, your emotions will differ by type of relationship. In a close relationship you would be after relational repair, but when the ridicule comes from the nearby table, you would likely stand your ground, or just ignore it. In a close relationship you may experience hurt feelings (and possibly cry); you are more likely to lash out at the stranger sitting at the nearby table, or completely ignore them. In a close relationship, your partner may feel guilt and try to make up for their insensitive behavior, but your relationship with the person at the nearby table is not likely to improve after you lash out. Or, as Clark and colleagues put it:

> Our point is simple, whether you experience emotion at all, as well as the form the experience takes, will depend on the extent to which and the ways in which you are (and/or wish to be) interdependent with another person.

The rules of engagement are different in close relationships than with strangers, and the emotional interactions between partners will follow these different rules. It is not just that my partner ridiculing me in public has a different emotional meaning than a stranger doing the same. It is also that my own emotions have a different meaning: I would feel guilty after I lashed out at my partner. My partner's emotions may have a different effect on them; they would likely feel bad after ridiculing me. If I experienced anger, it would feel different in a close relationship—it may be penetrated with hurt or desperation, for instance. And so how we would feel, act, and interact would all be tied to this particular relationship, with its particular relational goals.

Close relationships are not the only contexts that define how we do emotions in our everyday lives. A power position grants us anger, and makes others more likely to yield to the claims of the angry person. The powerful will not have to second-guess or regulate their anger in the way the less powerful have to. And anyway, lacking that position of power may render you less likely to be angry in the first place, be more tentative and circumspect in your demands, and on top of it, make you less likely to have your claims met (chapter 4).

The inescapable conclusion is that doing emotions differs by context. Just like my anger and indignation from a Dutch context did not translate well to North Carolina, my anger as a boss does not mean the same as my anger as a partner in a close relationship. Crossing cultural and linguistic boundaries may render the transitions between contexts more distinct, but even without these boundaries, we may cross back and forth between different emotional contexts every day. Biculturals, in other words, may provide a clear model for the OUtside-in nature of emotions that holds for all of us: our emotions are attuned to specific situations whether defined by culture, gender, type of relationship, or something else.

This OUtside-in perspective of emotions challenges the idea that our "own nature" limits what we can feel. Given what we now know, we are constantly attuning our emotions to the interactions in which they occur—not perfectly, as illustrated both by my anger and indignation in the North Carolinian context and by my crying in a professional meeting, but practice makes better.

Practice makes better, and this is not merely the case for immigrants. It is possible for anybody to learn and become attuned to other contexts. We can learn from each other and understand. This, I will argue in the next chapter, is the future of the multicultural societies in which we live. Emotional cultures are ever-changing, and we can contribute to changes that are inclusive.

Chapter 8

. . . .

EMOTIONS IN A
MULTICULTURAL
WORLD

IN A 2015 INTERVIEW WITH TERRY GROSS, AUTHOR AND JOUR-
nalist Ta-Nehisi Coates describes how he threatened his ninth-grade
teacher when the latter shouted at him in front of the whole class. "I
said something like: 'If you say something like that again, I will knock
you out.' It was a physical threat. And in that moment it was not idle
either. . . ."

Coates, who grew up in a poor family in West Baltimore explained
to Gross that at that point in his life, all he had was his "dignity." The
teacher challenged that dignity by shouting at him. He explains:

"You cannot tolerate anybody to threaten your body. You must
respond with force. . . . I felt like he disrespected me. He yelled
at me in front of the class like really really loudly. And again,
this was the sort of thing that you could not really tolerate."

[Terry (laughing): This is like teachers do sometimes].

"I know, you are laughing, it is funny when you have never
been in the environment. . . . Teachers yell loudly at kids
from time to time, you are exactly right. But if you live in an
environment, if you are from a place where all you have is like
the basic, physical respect, you will talk to me in a respectful
way. You don't have anything else to lean on. . . ."

How much would you understand of this emotional episode if I only told you that the young Coates was "angry" or if you had perceived his face or body language to be "angry"?

You would not have known how deeply the teacher's shouting cut in the child Coates's very being. You would not understand how that shouting, given the poverty and racism to which Coates was subjected, threatened the only power he had—to be a dignified person in front of his peers. Just knowing (or seeing) that Coates was angry would not guarantee you appreciated his lack of options: if he wanted to keep the only thing he had, his dignity ("a basic physical respect"), Coates *had no choice but to* threaten the teacher with violence; he would have been laughable to his peers had he not responded this way. The broader cultural context, Coates's position in it, the immediate context of his onlooking peers, and the meaning of Coates's behavior given these different levels of reality may have been lost had I merely told you that Coates was "angry." If you had known that Coates was angry, or had seen his threats without knowing the context, would you have substituted Coates's reality with your own? Would you have ignored the difference between your sociocultural position and his?

Similarly, how much would you have understood about the emotional exchange between the Taiwanese toddler Didi and his mom (introduced in chapter 3)? Would you understand what it meant for his mom to say: "You never listen. I am going to spank you. You are a child who does not obey rules, and we don't want you. Look how ugly you are on tape. Shame on you." Or how much would you understand if I told you Didi felt *shame*? What if I told you that *shame* is a "right" emotion in the Taiwanese context, and Didi probably wanted to be the kind of person who feels *shame*? How much would you understand if I did not tell you that shame served to reinforce the bond with his mother, rather than alienate her? Unless I told you the full story, you may have substituted Didi's experience with your own notions of shame. And you might have missed how Didi's shameful behaviors brought him closer to his ideal self as well as closer to his mom, how they may have helped his mom save face in the presence of an outsider (the researcher), in spite of his poor behavior.

And how much did Ellen, a Belgian middle school teacher, understand when Ahmet, her student of Turkish descent, cast his eyes down, and was submissive and polite after she had expressed her suspicion that it was he who had left a mess in the school library? Ellen thought Ahmet's shameful behaviors confirmed that he had been up to no good. He had to be guilty of something, or he would have responded with indignation, she thinks. Would he not have protested if she had treated him unfairly? But Ahmet's shame-like behaviors were a way of paying respect to his teacher, rather than a form of penance, as Ellen assumed. Ahmet focused on protecting his relationship with Ellen, rather than asserting his right to be fairly treated (as perhaps a Belgian-majority kid would). Ahmet's frame of reference was diametrically opposed to Ellen's, leading to unfortunate inferences on her side that Ahmet was not to be trusted. Ironically, the boy's emotions had as their sole intention to restore the relationship with the teacher, but this intention was lost in the encounter between different cultures.

Coates's, Didi's, and Ahmet's *emotions* can only be fully understood from the respective roles these emotions play in *their* contexts. To grasp these emotions, it is not sufficient to know only what to call them; it is necessary to understand what they do in the context that serves as their frame of reference. Even Terry Gross, for many in the U.S. the cultural emblem of empathy, almost failed to grasp what it meant to the young Ta-Nehisi Coates when his teacher shouted at him in front of the class. Her remark that shouting is "something that teachers do," was the beginning of a suggestion that it was no big deal, and that intense feelings of *anger* might not be warranted. Maybe so, the adult Coates explains ("I know, you are laughing, it is funny when you have never been in the environment"), unless in your position, in your culture, that shouting takes away the very last thing that you were left with: your dignity. Maybe so, unless physical threats are the only way to regain at least part of your dignity: if you didn't vehemently respond to your teacher's shouting, your peers around you would have witnessed you being a pushover.

Similarly, anybody assuming that critical parents raise maladjusted children—that shaming a child is unhealthy—would miss the special meaning shame may have in a cultural context in which the relationship between parent and child is interdependent. When Didi feels shame, he likely feels good about himself, because everybody in the relationship feels good. Didi was raised as a perfectly adjusted little boy: adjusted to a cultural context in which the child's shame helps prevent their mom from losing face.

My point is: We cannot understand the emotions of others unless we try to adopt their frame of reference. We need to understand the emotions of the Ta-Nehisis, Didis, and Ahmets of this world, by considering them within *their* social and cultural environment, and the goals *they* have for their relationships. Stated differently, we can only understand their emotions when we understand them as OURS—following them OUtside, rather than INside.

Understanding the emotions of others is not merely a matter of intellectual curiosity. Emotions make you part of your group or culture, and unfortunately, the opposite can be true, too. Anthropologist Catherine Lutz, following middle-class American emotion norms, smiled encouragingly at an Ifaluk girl who appeared happy. She was fiercely reprimanded by her Ifaluk hosts, because she should have been "justifiably angry": happiness is wrong in the Ifaluk, as it leads people to neglect their obligations. Anthropologist Jean Briggs, by following her North American inclinations, "exploded" in anger when she perceived that *kaplunas* (white Canadians) were about to harm her Inuit hosts. The Inuit were mortified by her response, because to them anger is a dangerous emotion. By now, you'll remember Briggs was ostracized for months as a result.

Being emotionally out of sync may generally be a reason for alienation and exclusion. By following the emotion rules of the street, young Ta-Nehisi Coates got himself suspended from school. Ahmet's teacher, mistaking his shame for penance rather than as a form of respect, wrongly assumed that he was up to no good, when in fact his shame was conciliatory. We can only imagine the consequences of such mistrust. It is hard to belong when you do not do emotions like the people around you. When your emotions are tied to a different OURS than the emotions of the people around you, you may not be well attuned to your emotional dance partners, and you may step on each other's toes. This is true, whether you are an anthropologist during fieldwork, or a member of a minority group within a given context in your own society. The difference between anthropologists on one hand, and Ta-Nehisi Coates, Ahmet, and me on the other, is that anthropologists have another life on reserve. The rest of us are here to stay.

The reality of modern societies is that we come together as people from different cultural backgrounds (and different positions). We know that it takes more than a lifetime to grow new emotions—if that is even the goal. In the meantime, we coinhabit our organizations, our schools, and our neighborhoods. We meet as colleagues, neighbors, and citizens, but also as teachers and students, doctors and patients, therapists and clients, and bosses and employees. In all of these relationships, cultural differences in emotions may be the source of subtle misconceptions, even if we are not necessarily aware of them. In intercultural relationships, our emotions may act at cross-purposes, as when Ahmet tried to make peace when his teacher expected independent indignation. When some of us are in positions of power—as is the case with teachers, doctors, therapists, managers—our misunderstandings may hurt others' chances. In those cases, emotions become invisible gatekeepers. If we don't want that to happen, we need to look into ways of understanding emotions across cultures.

Beyond Empathy

In his book *The War for Kindness,* psychologist Jamil Zaki makes a case that, as a human species, we need kindness: we need each other's understanding and help, because only together, as families, groups, and societies, can we survive. Kindness has played a role in our evolutionary survival, but it is not merely a relic of the past. We still need it to flourish, as individuals and as a society.

Zaki assumes a big role for empathy. "Empathy is the mental super-

power that overcomes [the] distance" between people, he writes.
Where hate dehumanizes others and creates schisms, empathy human-
izes them and grows connection. Empathy has been key to our survival
as a species, because it inspires kindness towards each other. A culture
of empathy grows social cohesion: it shows the human face of students, employees, patients, and citizens, and in doing so, creates room
for development and well-being. Some of us may be endowed with a
higher "set point" of empathy than others, but each of us can decide
to become more empathic than we are. We can invest in becoming
more attuned to other people's feelings and experiences. So how do we
grow empathy? Zaki's answer is to try to imagine how another person
thinks or feels. Meditating on someone else's "motives, beliefs, and history . . . conjures an authentic inner world." Attend to another person,
grasp their circumstances, and know what they feel.

I hope you now understand that we can neither directly read emotions from other people's faces, nor simply "catch" the emotions of
other people. We can think we can, but our perception need not match
the interpretation of the target—even less so when they are from a different culture. It is challenging to "meditate on someone else's motives,
beliefs and history," as Zaki suggests we do, when the distance with
your own motives, beliefs, and history is large. *Just* imagining how *you*
would feel in a similar situation will not do the job. If you tried, *you*
would almost certainly make sense of a given situation in a way that
fits *your* culture's values and relationship goals. *You* would be likely
to have emotions that are "right" in *your* culture. *You* would interact
with others who draw from the same collective repertoire of emotional
episodes as you do. As Coates points out: "It is funny when you have
never been in that environment, but very serious when you don't have
anything else to lean on, if you are from a place where all you have is
like the basic, physical respect." Projecting your own feelings is of limited value when you try to understand emotions that are embedded in
another cultural reality.

I met Hazel Markus thirty years ago at a conference that she and
Shinobu Kitayama organized on the topic of culture and emotion. Neither of us knew at the time that Markus was to become my American

mentor, but right away I felt we meshed. When we ran into each other in the women's restroom, I showed my empathy, or so I thought: she had so much on her mind being one of the organizers—I had seen her really busy. So I looked at her warmly, and said: "You look a little tired." Upon which Hazel looked startled, turned to the mirror and confirmed that, yes, she needed to refresh her lipstick. I stumbled, and added that I did not mean to suggest she looked bad.

Research by psychologist Birgit Koopmann-Holm, herself of German descent and living in the United States, suggests that I was projecting the understanding of the situation that would have applied in my (then Dutch) cultural environment onto Hazel. In nicely controlled experiments, Koopman-Holm shows that Germans (and by extension Dutch) see more suffering in ambiguous materials than do their American counterparts. She finds Germans imagine that receiving sympathy focused on negative feelings would be more comforting after a bereavement than receiving sympathy that emphasizes the silver lining. Americans preferred to receive "sympathy" that focuses attention on positive aspects of the situation—cherishing the memories of the deceased. While none of Koopmann-Holm's studies focuses on conference organizers in a bathroom, it is a safe assumption that my empathizing with Hazel by projecting my own feelings (she must be tired), and focusing on her pain (or fatigue), was of limited value in making connection. I might have been more successful, had I emphasized the silver lining of her fatigue: "Wow, so much work, but the conference is going great!"

Mere empathy does not work, because it does not overcome the cultural gap. Yet there are ways of achieving more kindness, and growing closer, which do close the cultural or positional gap. The good news is that you can learn to bridge the cultural differences by unpacking the emotional episode. As a researcher of emotions and as an immigrant myself, I have made my share of mistakes: disbelieving what others told me about their emotions, misinterpreting their behaviors, and projecting my own feelings or interpretations on them. In the end, keeping an open (enough) mind, talking with friends, collaborating with valuable colleagues and informants, reading ethnographies of fieldwork, and living in other places have all helped me better appreciate—perhaps even predict and anticipate—how emotions in other cultural contexts are done. I arrived at this point by asking questions about (and observing) how individuals in other cultures interpreted what happened, what they "wanted" from their relationships, and which responses from the other people in their social worlds they expected or received to their emotions. And most important of all, I relinquished my own assumptions of what the (right) answers to these questions would be. Rather than trying to squeeze my own person under the skin of someone else, I tried to look at the social ripples of emotional episodes in the respective contexts in which they took place. Everyone who has emotional encounters across cultural, or ethnic, or gender boundaries can do the same.

It is what anthropologists do: the very experts on intercultural encounters set aside their own assumptions—as much as they can—and try to ask and observe. Christine Dureau describes her attempts to resonate with the maternal love of Simbo women living on one of the poorest of the Western Solomon Islands. Dureau was accompanied by her toddler daughter during her fieldwork, and this provided a starting point for her exchanges with some of the Simbo women on motherly love. Where Dureau started her fieldwork thinking that she could fully relate to the Simbo women's maternal love (*taru*)—after all, she herself was another woman with a small child—she soon realized that *taru* was different from the maternal love she had projected. *Taru* for the Simbo women meant "sadness" as much as it meant "love." Women who felt *taru* were compassionate with their children, and knowing their children's fate, this often involved sadness. As one woman rhetorically asked Dureau: "How can you have *taru* (*love*) without *sore* (*sadness*)? You love them; you think of all the awful things in their lives, all the hard times [they will experience]."

Simbo women did not always succeed in empathizing with Dureau, either. One time, Dureau's daughter Astrid, then three years old, was "persistently ill." Liza, a woman Dureau did not know very well, came and sat beside her on the doorstep, saying that she understood Dureau's anxiety because her own son had died of measles four years previously.

Upset by this story, Dureau expressed her sympathy, which prompted Liza to add, "Usually I don't think of him. If one of my [other] children is ill, I remember and quickly take them to the clinic." Liza had wanted to empathize, and comfort Dureau, perhaps simply seek connection, but she achieved the opposite effect. Dureau felt different: " . . . while I felt horrified sympathy, I only distantly understood Liza's sentiments, which spoke to profoundly different possibilities. Against her assertion about childhood mortality and her statement that her loss enabled her to feel empathy, I was aware that my worry was not her resigned foreknowledge." Dureau knows she would have had the monetary and cultural capital to get Astrid better medical care than had been available to Liza's son. Dureau would not have been resigned, or merely prayed to God, because her position in life afforded her to exercise more control. And she could not even begin to imagine resigning in the death of her child, let alone never thinking about her anymore. Liza and Christine Dureau had different emotions, because they lived in different realities.

The current wisdom in anthropology is that it is possible to approximate, or sometimes even share, the emotional experiences of individuals from other cultures, but also that you should not be too sure too soon that you do. As one anthropologist points out: "the problem with empathy is not that it involves feelings but that it assumes that first impressions are true."

Managing to understand other people's emotions is not the same as sharing their experiences. Interestingly, approximating others' feelings often means understanding how emotional episodes are tied to a context different from one's own. It means to be aware of the *incongruence* of your emotions with the emotions of someone else. Christine Dureau eventually gained insight into the motherly love among Simbo women, not by projecting her own notions of love, but by trying to grasp how their love was situated in the conditions of child mortality, poverty, and hardship on the island. Empathy in a cross-cultural setting is unpacking another person's emotions by tying them to their (social) realities.

Importantly, recognizing these differences allows you to see the similarities as well. Even as you realize that you may never experience or do emotions in the same way, there can be resonance with people from other cultures. This resonance means that you humanize another person, trying to find meaning in their emotions, and in this way bridge some of the distance.

From Cultural Competence to Humility

Joop de Jong is a Dutch transcultural psychiatrist who is one of the driving forces of rethinking the Dutch mental health system to accommodate an increasingly multicultural clientele. He knew of my early work on culture and emotions and asked me in the mid-1990s to contribute to a volume on cross-cultural psychiatry and psychotherapy. How did my work on cultural differences in emotions speak to the psychotherapy and mental health context? I did not know, but the question intrigued me. A flurry of books on migrants had saturated the Dutch market at the time, all telling their white Dutch readers how to understand, and talk to, a growing immigrant population.

Attention to diversity and inequality was much needed, then and now, both because of the demonstrated mental health disparities among racial and ethnic minorities, and because of the inadequacy of mental health provisions. In practice, however, what was known then as "cultural competence" consisted of bits of knowledge about the values, beliefs, and attitudes of ethnic groups. In the U.S., these were the ethno-racial blocs that had been created by the U.S. Census—African American, Asian American and Pacific Islanders, Latinx, American Indian and Alaska Native, and White. Clinicians learned to think about these "blocs" in relatively stable, essentializing terms. Cultural competence was treated as set of concrete skills for mental health workers—a domain of expertise to which I had wanted to contribute a fact sheet on emotions.

The "clarity" and "competence" that mental health workers once sought has since been replaced by "cultural humility." Rather than proliferating knowledge facts about the emotions and emotional disturbances of certain cultural groups as rigidly and narrowly defined by ethno-racial or national identities, mental health professionals have "embrace[d] uncertainty as a path to competence," to quote one of the founders of cultural psychiatry, Laurence Kirmayer. The knowledge that emotional episodes *can*, and systematically *do*, differ across cultures should make therapists inquisitive: you should be aware that you do not know how another person is feeling, but this is all the more reason to want to find out. Embracing the uncertainty and following its path is not unlike the "unpacking of emotional episodes" that is practice among anthropologists.

Kaat van Acker, a cross-cultural therapist with a practice in Brussels, describes an example of embracing uncertainty. She was seeing a war-traumatized Lebanese woman, Ramla. Ramla, incapacitated by pain, had quit her job, and she and her daughters lived on social welfare benefits. Of all the topics that could have been covered during therapy—Ramla's traumatic experiences, her inability to do paid work—the shame about her failure to fulfill her role as a daughter took center space in the therapy. During one session, Ramla told Van Acker that she had been unable to accompany her old and frail mother on her pilgrimage to Mecca. Tears ran down her face as Ramla recounted this. Was she sad? Van Acker kept herself from jumping to conclusions, instead asking Ramla what her tears meant. In so doing she unpacked what the emotional event meant to Ramla. Ramla tells Van Acker that she cries because she is deeply ashamed.

Following her own Western European emotional logic, Van Acker might have comforted Ramla, or talked her shame down. Instead, Van Acker explored what shame meant to Ramla in *her* cultural context. Ramla explains that her failure to meet her obligation as a daughter makes her less respectable (in the eyes of others). But there is more: To Ramla, feeling shame is "right," even if failing to be a good daughter is not. Shame shows Ramla's commitment to counteract her moral failure. To Van Acker's question what Ramla's *shame* "wants to do," Ramla answers it wants to hop on a plane, sit down next to her mother, hold her mother's hands, and not let go of them again. Shame thus connects Ramla with her mother. Perhaps then,

Van Acker concludes, Ramla's shame should not be talked down, but rather acknowledged. Van Acker's embrace of uncertainty allowed her to meet Ramla where she was. She unpacked Ramla's emotions by tying them to their social and cultural contexts; this way, Van Acker gained insight in her client's ailing. A therapist should not assume they know how their clients feel, but rather find common ground with their client.

Therapists trying to understand other people's emotions do well to examine the ways in which their own emotions are OURS. In the mirror of another "culture," therapists may find some blind spots they might not otherwise have discovered. The need to relinquish your own assumptions is all the more clear when the client does not share your cultural experiences.

Unpacking emotions may be helpful in therapeutic relationships across the traditional cultural boundaries, but it may be equally helpful to understand emotions from others who share your ethno-racial or national identity. No two people have experienced the very same episodes in their lives, and even if we speak the same language and share the same emotional concepts, our unique experiences may have colored those concepts differently.

A Toolbox for Unpacking Emotional Episodes

In our everyday lives, we can take from the insights of anthropology and the mental health field and unpack the emotional episodes of other people. The unpacking of emotions may also be helped by knowledge of where cultural differences in emotions occur (see figure 8.1). Each of these junctures provides an opportunity to dig further into the other person's experience. Each of these junctures leads us OUtside the person, to the Relationship, and the Situation.

First, find out "what people are up to, their multiple compelling concerns, and what is at stake for them." I choose to illustrate this by a delicate example from Europe: the Muhammed cartoons that appeared in a Danish newspaper in September 2005, and that were

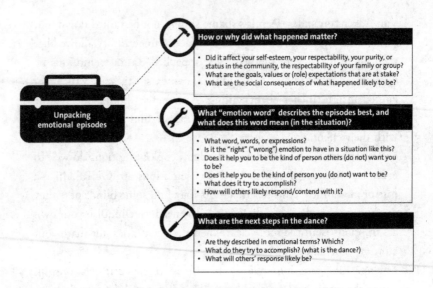

FIGURE 8.1 Unpacking emotional episodes: A toolkit

reprinted and presented in many other European news outlets. These cartoons depicted the Prophet Muhammed and his followers. What was at stake for many Muslims? First, illustrations of human beings—no less the most important religious prophet—are considered blasphemous by many Muslims (as they are by some Jews). Second, the illustrations were compromising for the Prophet Muhammed and for Muslims as a group. As if this weren't enough, the cartoons were published for everyone to see, and reprinted many times. In other words, the cartoons offended the social image of Muslims in a very public way—which in an honor culture is both shameful and offensive. In one study, those valuing honor more were more likely to appraise the "illustrations" as harmful to their reputation *as* Muslims, and if they did, they reported both more shame and more anger. So, what was at stake for these Muslims? Presumably, the honor and reputation of their group, and, because honor is a shared commodity, their own honor and reputation. In this cultural context, honor is the very key to being a valuable person.

If honor was at stake, the media focus on "freedom of expression" missed the Muslim "shame" entirely. If honor was at stake, it might not have helped that the Danish government refused to meet with a delegation of Danish Muslim organizations to discuss the cartoons; it certainly did nothing to reassure these organizations that they were in good standing. Unpacking the emotional episode, and seeing what was at stake, would have benefited the dialogue in Denmark and beyond.

In unpacking episodes, it is also important to check *what emotions other people perceive—in themselves or in others—and what these emotions mean* in the situation. People may describe the episode by one or more words or by expressions. The point is to understand how they conceptualize their own emotions, including what the emotion means to them in a particular instance. You cannot stop at a word if you want to unpack the episode: translations of emotion words are rough at best (chapter 6), and may have very different connotations and implications. After all, the associated episodes make up distinct realities. Kaat Van Acker's client Ramla reported "shame." Van Acker's first impulse was to talk it down, and in doing so, raise Ramla's self-esteem. But Ramla's shame was not about harmed self-esteem; to the contrary, it made her more respectable, in her own eyes, but more importantly in the eyes of other people. Van Acker unpacked Ramla's shame by asking her what her shame wanted to do (a question that is common in the kind of therapy she practices). She found that Ramla's shame played a role in restoring the relationship with her mother, and in so doing, being a better daughter. So, it was important that Van Acker checked what the meaning of "shame" was for Ramla.

Unpacking emotional episodes means to understand their projected ending: Is the emotion "right" or "wrong" or neither? This is often a hard one to unpack, but there are concrete questions that people may be able to answer, which would provide you with opportunities to learn about these OURS aspects of emotions. Applied to Ramla's case: Would your mother or your friends approve of your shame? Is it appropriate for you, as a daughter who cannot join her mother in a pilgrimage, to feel shame? Sometimes, posing the opposite question might work better: What would you think of a daughter, who was in your situation, but did not feel shame at all? How would other people perceive this daughter?

Unpacking the meaning of an "emotion" can be done at the level of facial or bodily behavior also. Do not assume that you can infer what another person feels from their behavior: check it. Is the person with the big smile happier than the person with the "calm" smile? American children thought this to be the case, but Taiwanese children did not (chapter 5). Is the doctor with the big smile more confident in what they are doing than the doctor with the "calm" smile? White American healthy adults in the San Francisco area thought so, but their Asian American counterparts assumed the opposite. The consequences were real: in one study, the researchers found that participants adhered to the health recommendations of a doctor who looked "happy" and "confident," but white Americans associated a big smile and an upbeat message with happiness and confidence, while Asian Americans thought the doctor with the "calm" demeanor was more happy and confident.

Was Kaat Van Acker's client Ramla's crying an expression of sadness? By explicitly checking, Kaat found out that for Ramla these were tears of shame. Were my American dinner guests distancing themselves by thanking me (chapter 1)? I could have checked. I now think that thanking me emphasized appreciation over closeness, but did not necessarily do so at its exclusion.

Unpacking emotional episodes also means figuring out *what the next steps in the dance* are supposed to be. It may in fact help the unpacking to think about emotional behaviors as performing certain types of dances: Ramla's shame is a step in the dance of gaining respectability, not in the dance of lost self-esteem. Had I known or understood the dance of mutual enhancement, I might have better understood my friends' thanking me for dinner. I might have complimented Hazel Markus for being such a good host at this successful conference, rather than trying to connect to her by focusing on her fatigued look. Would I have failed to state the truth? Not necessarily: I might have merely focused on a different aspect of the situation.

Importantly, you cannot assume that the way *you* would finish the dance is the most natural one. There is no such thing. Remember that Emiko, Hiroto, and Chiemi reported doing nothing in situations where they were offended. They came to terms with the offense, one way or another, and so did the majority of the other Japanese interviewees in that study (chapter 4). This was not *suppressed* anger: it was simply how their angry episodes evolved. They came to accept the situation, rather than working themselves up to moral indignation, or confronting the offender with the truth. Do not assume that a person who does not behave the way you expect is suppressing their authentic, real emotion. Ask. Don't assume how the episode is ending, and is supposed to end.

In recent studies, Michael Boiger, Alexander Kirchner-Häusler, Anna Schouten, Yukiko Uchida, and I studied emotional interactions in Belgian and Japanese couples who came to the lab to discuss a disagreement. The Belgian and Japanese couples danced to very different types of music: the dance of "meeting each partner's personal needs" and the dance of "relationship harmony," respectively. The Belgian couples reported and showed mutual anger (as rated by independent judges) throughout discussion of conflict—more than any other emotion we measured, and much more so than the Japanese couples. The Japanese couples reported more mutual empathy and showed more validation than any other emotion during the discussions on conflict, and also more than their Belgian counterparts. In focus groups, Belgian men and women told us that anger and conflict were "right" for the relationship, as they helped the couple to figure out and negotiate each partner's needs. Japanese men and women in this study, told us they avoided "bad feelings" in the relationship as much as possible by evading discussion about a disagreement, by adjusting to their partner's wishes, and by empathizing (putting themselves in the shoes of their partners). Of course, it happened that Belgian couples felt empathy and validated each other, and of course, Japanese couples were judged as angry occasionally, but the episode—the dance in which the couple joined—was different. When unpacking the emotional episodes, it is important to try to understand the dance that is being performed: the interpersonal goals.

Expectations for the dance in monocultural couples, and monocultural interaction partners in general, are shared to a certain extent. But what if you are the person to make a next step in an intercultural encounter? Many of us are these days. I do not think there is a shortcut to unpacking the emotional episode. Unpacking becomes easier when you know the many ways in which emotional episodes may develop across cultures, as these cultural differences reveal the junctures at which emotions are OURS. Some cultural competence does make it easier to imagine how emotions are tied to the sociocultural contexts in which they occur—to be aware of "opportunities." Knowing about cultural differences in the ways emotional episodes typically unfold in other cultures also stretches your imagination beyond your habitual way of doing emotions. And yet, understanding the emotions of people from other cultures will never be like botanizing tropical plants. There is no finite number of well delineated entities to be known.

I am very certain that I will never be able to make a go-to reference manual on cultural differences in emotions; nor will anybody else. To grasp the absurdity of the task, ask yourself: How would I deal with the emotions of a Dutch person, any Dutch person? (Substitute, as you wish, "Catholic Irish American," "white American from Boston," "Japanese from Tokyo," . . . for "Dutch.") What emotions do they have? How to understand these emotions? What do these emotions look like in behavior? The answers to those questions would all depend on who the Dutch person is, what their history is, their gender and position in society, their specific predicaments. It depends on what they as an individual specifically care about at that moment, what the relational context is, and what specifically is at stake. It will also depend on whom they are interacting with, and what these people's responses are.

This is true for any person with any ethno-racial or national background. I agree with anthropologist Andrew Beatty that there is no "good reason to expect cultural others to be less complex in their emotional and moral functioning than we take ourselves to be. . . ." and "an emotionally engaged ethnography will fail to deliver if it ignores particulars and assumes that the general frame is determinate or that everyone who fits the categorical profile will think, feel, and relate in the same way. With emotions, the devil is in the details."

Emotional Literacy in Culturally Diverse Schools

Two of the examples at the beginning of this chapter took place in schools: young Ta-Nehisi Coates and Ahmet. This is no coincidence: emotions play a big role in learning environments, and misunderstandings may have large, and sometimes lasting, effects on the futures of students. The young Coates was suspended, and Ahmet accused of something he did not do, in large part because their teachers did not correctly unpack the emotional episodes. Had Coates's teacher understood his behavior as a desperate claim for dignity, and had Ahmet's teacher Ellen understood his shame as conciliatory—a sign of respect—they might have been better teachers for it. Here again, teachers' resonance may precisely lie in a recognition that their students' emotions are *incongruent* with their own—that their students' responses were steps in a different dance than their own. Coates's angry threats were steps in the dance of physical integrity; Ahmet's shameful responses were steps in the dance of respect to elders.

Breakdowns in compassion are particularly likely when teachers perceive infractions of the rules. One teacher intervention encouraged teachers from several U.S. middle schools "to understand and value students' experiences and negative feelings that can cause misbehavior and to sustain positive relationships." Although the intervention did nothing to stop the teachers from disciplining the students for bad behavior, it cut the number of suspensions over the next year in half, with suspensions of Black and Latinx kids being proportional to their numbers. Though the idea behind the intervention was to foster the teacher-student relationship, it arguably encourages teachers to "unpack" their students' emotions, finding common ground with their students, and in the process, humanizing them.

It is the kind of understanding and compassion that may benefit the field of education more broadly. In 2003, UNESCO initiated a worldwide plan to add emotional and social skills to the academically oriented school curriculum, and this initiative was picked up in many countries. No longer are academic subjects, like math, languages, history, and geography, the only focus: how to feel and how to communicate about your own and others' emotions are now an integrative part of what many students learn in school. Some have called it "emotional literacy," a term that underlines how indispensable social and emotion learning are in today's society. The research is clear: it does pay off to include emotional and social skills into the curriculum, at least in North America and in Western Europe. Students whose schools offer social and emotional learning programs show modestly improved emotional and social competence, and fewer emotional and behavioral problems, compared to students whose schools do not have such programs on offer. Some studies even show improved academic performance. The gains made through emotional literacy programs are particularly clear for young children.

What do these programs teach students about emotions? Most important of all, they teach students that it is important to find out what other kids feel, and that this may not be the same as what they themselves feel—an excellent starting point to developing kindness, including kindness across diverse cultural groups. They also teach students that having the "right" feelings is key to making friendships, to resolving conflict, and even to doing their schoolwork. In this particular way, many of the available programs teach children that their emotions are OURS: that emotions position you in life, and are central to building social relationships.

Yet, in another way, many emotional literacy programs treat "emotions" as the letters of the alphabet. The idea seems to be that, just as every child has to learn the same letters of the alphabet if they are to become literate, every child needs to learn the same emotions if they are to be socially equipped. But what about cultural diversity? What about the fact that children grow up in very different households, different neighborhoods, or, in the case of immigrant children, different ethnic or national cultures, and that their respective emotion concepts and understandings are tied to the experiences they had in these different cultural contexts? What about emotions serving different relational goals across sociocultural contexts?

What happens to Reiko, a Japanese American child, who does not find *amae* in the list of important emotions? ("Why? Even puppies have it!") Or what would it do to Ahmet to learn from his Belgian schoolteacher that shame is primarily a *feeling inside us*. I can only imagine that Ahmet would feel at a loss, invalidated, as he himself perceived his shame to be between people—to restore relationships and be respectable. Or what would young Ta-Nehisi Coates have taken away from the message that managing his anger was the "right" thing to do? What is the culture of reference when we say anger management is "right"? Obviously, this message would have invalidated Coates's experience of "right" in that moment. In a world where you need to show you are tough, threats may be right. If "emotional literacy" is unwittingly defined as literacy in the dominant culture, it will hardly reaffirm students who are not part of that culture. Instead, it may serve as one more gatekeeper.

One reason that emotional literacy programs may work could be that they provide a crash course in acculturation. Offering children a shared alphabet or vocabulary, and teaching them to use it in conversation, may create common ground within the school. Emotional literacy programs may be instrumental in socializing students to the school's emotion culture, and this itself may be conducive to the child's relationships with the school and the teachers, and may socialize them to meet the expectations of the school culture. For instance, when we teach students how to "manage their anger," we may simply socialize them to be the kinds of people that we want in our schools. Creating common ground can be a worthwhile project for schools, but only if all students are included.

Parents have an important role in the enterprise of emotional literacy. According to UNESCO, "when home and school collaborate closely to implement social-emotional learning programs, children gain more and program effects are more enduring and pervasive." But is this realistic when there is diversity in doing emotions, and the school and home context may be different? What if the messaging to the child is inconsistent, and leaves the child in the uncomfortable position of bridging the gap with their home culture? Why not give children the tools to understand these differences and cope with them? Rather than teaching students the "right" emotions and their "proper" causes and consequences, why not teach children that different ways of doing emotions may be "right," depending on the goals valued and the kind of person you want to be? In other words, it may be productive if emotional literacy programs teach children that emotions are OURS—tied to our social cultural contexts. This could mean that our school curricula teach children cultural humility and the tools for unpacking emotional episodes.

Teachers could provide their students with the tools to follow their own and other people's emotions to the outside. Teachers and students alike would learn to unpack emotional episodes, in a way similar to what anthropologists and culturally humble clinicians do. Children would learn to pose, as well as answer, the kinds of questions presented in the Toolkit (figure 8.1), above. By learning to unpack emotional episodes, students would be up to the task of bridging the gap between their school and home cultures.

Unpacking emotions, and recognizing their diversity, would fit the growing call for "equity" in emotional literacy programs, not just by generally respecting others, but also by specifically allowing for cultural diversity in emotional and social competence itself. What is more, it will provide an opportunity to value the students (and increasingly, teachers) who have become facile in unpacking different ways of doing emotions, because they belong to more than one culture; we can recognize cultural fluency with a second culture as a desirable relationship skill itself. After *all* ways of doing emotions are made to count, we can be sure that schools and classrooms will find common ground.

Are Emotions the Same Deep Down?

Here I return to the question I asked at the beginning of this book: Is it true that we are all the same when it comes to feelings?

Was the young Ta-Nehisi Coates simply *angry*, but in a situation that would not have prompted anger to those of us who are more privileged? What would be lost if we described Ahmet as simply *ashamed* in response to a situation that might have elicited indignation in his Belgian classmates—the teacher's reprimand? Did Ramla really feel the same as her therapist Kaat Van Acker would have, had she been crying, but did her culture emphasize moral failure rather than a loss of abilities? Did the Simbo women feel *love* like Dureau, but simultaneously feel *sadness*?

These are good, legitimate questions to ask, as their answers allow us to resonate with the feelings of people growing up in different sociocultural contexts. These questions are where the unpacking of emotions should start, because this is where we can resonate. Yet, there is no reason to assume primacy of the ways emotions are done in Western middle-class contexts, and no reason to think that those ways are any more authentic or natural than other ways of doing emotions. There is no reason to assume that the English emotion lexicon cuts nature at its joints any more than other emotion lexicons do. We need to find out what is at stake in emotional episodes, what people perceive to be the emotion(s) during these episodes and what these emotions mean, and how emotional episodes connect people in a directional dance.

We cannot assume that we have "the same emotions" or that our expressions mean the same things. And yet, it is possible to reach across cultural boundaries—across national, positional, and yes, even party lines. For that to happen, we need first and foremost to be humble. Humility vis-à-vis another person's emotions may always be a good idea—we all come from different places, have different experiences, and have unique goals—but it is particularly advisable when you are not part of the OURS of another person's emotions. Yes, emotions differ across cultures in many different ways. At the same time, it is possible to relate to other people's emotions once you meet them on their terms, once you humanize them.

What is important in their lives? What kind of person do they want to be? What do they want from their social relationships? Or how are they constrained by these relationships? These are some of the questions that help you to unpack emotional episodes. My experience is that it is often easy to resonate with emotions, once unpacked, even if you realize they are incongruent with the ones you encounter in your life. It happens by seeing that people in other cultures are as human as the people in our own, having their own goals, and their own compelling concerns, which are sometimes different from the ones we are used to. It happens when you see how their ongoing social interactions and relationships afford different kinds of emotional episodes than the interactions and relationships in your life do. It happens when you realize that their dance is a different one than you are used to doing in your social environment. It happens when you realize their emotions are OURS, just as your emotions are.

Trying to unpack each other's emotions is an indispensable step towards the emotional dance. It does not mean you are dancing yet, but it recognizes that there are a variety of dances to be made. We are partners in it together—emotional episodes are accomplished Between Us.

AFTERWORD

IN THIS BOOK I HAVE ENCOURAGED YOU TO TURN EMOTIONS inside out, to where they actually happen—between us—in our relationships, communities, and cultures. Turning emotions inside out may at first seem to go against the current of an increasingly potent neuroscience whose focus is inside, on the workings of our brains, but it does not. The outward focus of an OURS model of emotions is fully compatible with the inward focus of neuroscience. State-of-the-art neuroscience has clearly demonstrated that our outsides are intrinsically connected to our insides. The brain wires itself through experiences in the social world. Our relationships, communities, and cultural realities make us who we are—emotions not excepted.

Early in life, our caretakers, teachers, and other socializers encourage and hope to instill in us the emotions that are "right" for our culture (and for our position, gender, etc.). They create opportunities, reward, and show the emotions that help you be the kind of person that your cultures value, and grow the relationships that in your cultures are productive and desirable. This first socialization forms the bedrock of the rest of our emotional lives, but later in life emotions continue to be OURS: OUtside the person, Relational and Situated. Time and again, emotional episodes dynamically unfold in the "dance" between people. It is between us that emotions are cultured: other people co-create the emotional episode, sustaining or changing its force or direction, often in alignment with cultural norms, goals and ideals. OURS emotions are relationship acts: they unfold in relationships that they help grow. To the extent that relationship practices and ideals differ across time and place—and yes, they do—so do emotional episodes.

Emotion concepts capture categories of these real-life emotional episodes. This is why emotion lexicons from different languages do not neatly map onto each other—far from it. Emotion concepts do *not* capture innate mental states or fixed patterns of bodily changes, the existence of neither has been demonstrated. For instance, evidence on facial perception, once heralded as the main evidence in support of universal basic emotions, has not held up. People in different cultures do not perceive facial configurations in the same way; in many cultures, they do not perceive these facial configurations as mental states at all. There is also no evidence that concepts such as anger or fear are associated with fixed patterns of bodily or brain responses, even within a given culture. Less so across cultures, as emotion concepts in different cultures do not pair up. So, while emotional episodes are undeniably embodied and enacted, the precise way in which an emotional episodes unfolds—including embodiment and enactment—is dependent on its social and cultural context. Each person's emotion concepts are associated with their own and their culture's experienced realities: the emotion episodes that have happened in their own lives, those encountered by others around them, and the cultural repository of episodes as it is shared.

All of this has profound implications for understanding the emotions of other people, particularly people from other cultures. We cannot assume that we simply understand someone's emotions just by looking at their face, listening to their voice, or translating the emotion word they use to describe themselves. Bridging cultural differences in emotions will require you to do the hard work of unpacking the emotional episodes. Rather than projecting your own emotions onto others, you need to find out what the situation means to them—their context of reference: what they are moved to do, what their feelings and actions mean to the people around them (or what *not* feeling or acting the way they do would have meant to the same people).

There is much to gain from this unpacking, as it can provide you with a valuable window into what is important in another person's life, in their interactions, and in their communities. To take advantage of this window, we need to take seriously how *they* see and act upon the world, make sense *from their point of view,* and understand their actions from their strivings, and from the values and goals of their communities—not replace their perspective with our own. Unpacking emotional episodes means to humanize the people who live through them.

Unpacking emotions in the heat of an emotional interaction is challenging. There is very little research on how to do it successfully, and yet, in our everyday lives, we take part in emotional interactions with partners who may not draw on the same repository, who might make different dance steps to a different musical genre. How to get in step?

There is no easy trick, but the OURS perspective on emotions that I have introduced does shed some new light on how to do it. A first suggestion is to not assume you know or understand others' emotions. Instead, slow down, ask questions, and listen. In the field of mental health care, this is called an attitude of "not knowing" or "cultural humility." Try to stop yourself from drawing fast conclusions based on your own perspective, and check if you understand what it means to your interaction partner, and importantly, sustain a positive relationship while you do. Remember, this is difficult for almost everyone and it takes sustained practice.

The second is to face up to your own feelings and acts. Remember that no emotion is any more "natural" than any other. There are no right and wrong emotions; there are only emotions that are right and wrong in a particular context, by particular standards. So, ask yourself what your own emotion wants to achieve, and how this may be different from the direction that your interaction partner's emotion takes you. Ask yourself how you can act and feel differently. Can you find a dance that accommodates both? Can you end the emotional episode in a way that is right by both perspectives?

Even if your own way of doing emotions is the acceptable, normative one in a given context, ask yourself if other "dances" can be accommodated. Can we stop leading confidently and then question the other's capacity to dance just because they do not follow our own dance?

Let us explore emotions across cultural boundaries (gender, ethnicity, class, and race) by listening and observing, by closely examining, and by not imposing our ways of understanding emotions as the true or "natural" way. Can our schools, business organizations, and courtrooms become flexible enough to accommodate some different understandings of emotion? This is the challenge and the opportunity for researchers and practitioners in the multicultural present and future.

ACKNOWLEDGMENTS

THE RESEARCH AND THINKING ABOUT THE TOPIC OF *BETWEEN US* began with my PhD work under emotion psychologist Nico H. Frijda at the University of Amsterdam. At a time when many in the field believed that emotions were universal, Nico questioned the universality thesis. Our many discussions on the role of culture in emotion have kept me honest and helped articulate my views. I still miss his intellect and his friendship, and I owe him much.

I thank my lucky stars that I met Hazel Markus during my PhD research. She became my postdoctoral advisor at the University of Michigan and was one of the people to create the discipline of cultural psychology that scaffolded my endeavors. She was also my model for being a woman professor; none of my professors the University of Amsterdam were women. I owe much of my emotional acculturation to Hazel: She helped me navigate the culture of American academics. Her friendship and mentorship have meant the world to me.

Throughout my career, I have been fortunate enough to have a peer group of outstanding emotion researchers. My ideas have evolved in dialogue with Lisa Feldman Barrett, Barb Fredrickson, Sheri Johnson, Ann Kring, and Jeanne Tsai. They have been my sounding board, my support group, and the best friends. I thank them for having contributed to the ideas of this book, for having read parts of earlier drafts, and for setting an example by reaching out to a larger audience and writing their own books.

No small part of this book was the product of collaboration. I thank all my collaborators, but special thanks go to Lisa Feldman Barrett, Phoebe Ellsworth, Ashleigh Haire, Mayumi Karasawa, Shinobu Kitayama, Heejung Kim, Bernard Rimé, and Yukiko Uchida for the dialogue and friendship they have offered.

Finally, I thank my colleagues and my students at the Center of Social and Cultural Psychology at the University of Leuven. This book bears the fruits of our everyday research collaboration. I could have never imagined a more collegial, inspiring, and collaborative environment. I particularly thank Michael Boiger, Ellen Delvaux, Jozefien De Leersnyder, Katie Hoemann, Alba Jasini, Alexander Kirchner, Yeasle Lee, Loes Meeussen, Fulya Özcanli, Karen Phalet, Anna Schouten, Kaat Van Acker, and Colette Van Laar. We made this journey together, and I learned so much from you.

This book was conceived during a 2016–2017 residential fellowship at the Center for Advanced Study in the Behavioral Sciences (CASBS) at Stanford University. I thank the director of the center, Margaret Levi, for hosting me, and my cohort of fellows for the many stimulating discussions on this book and related topics. I am particularly grateful to Kate Zaloom and Sapna Cheryan for our morning writing sessions in which I learned that writing a book works like yoga: you go back to the mat every morning and focus; slight improvements happen. I have continued the practice.

The writing of this book was furthermore facilitated by two sabbaticals granted by the University of Leuven (2016–17, 2018–19), by my colleagues' willingness to step up when I was on sabbatical, and by an ERC-Advanced grant (ERC-ADG 834587) from the European Research Council. I want to thank Lisa Feldmann Barrett, Michael Boiger, Katie Hoemann, Jonathan Janssen, Ann Kring, Will Tiemeijer, Jeanne Tsai, Kaat Van Acker, Colette Van Laar, Kate Zaloom, and the members of the Culture Lab 2020–2021 for reading outlines and earlier versions of this book. I thank Yeasle Lee and Michael Boiger for their help with the illustrations of this book.

I thank my agent, Max Brockman, for his confidence in me as an author, for helping me further articulate the purpose of the book, and for allowing me to focus on the writing by taking care of all business in the most efficient way possible. I also thank the unsurpassed Tom Verthé, my project manager, for helping me with all the organizational tasks related to this book, and for doing so in good spirit.

My gratitude also goes to Melanie Tortoroli, my editor at W. W. Norton. It was she who recognized the potential of my ideas, and it was she who helped to develop these ideas to reach their potential. Her enthusiasm, her vision, and her incisive edits have helped the book along. I learned a lot from her in the process.

I am particularly grateful to three scholars, whose close engagement in the writing process made this book possible. Hazel Markus, my mentor and cultural psychologist at Stanford University, sandwiched her critical feedback on every single chapter with love. She encouraged me to reach out to my American audience, and to connect my research with real societal questions and problems. Gert Storms, linguistic psychologist at my own university, read every chapter, offering reassurance in his understated European way, and pointing out my inconsistencies and errors (as Europeans do when they feel close enough to care). Finally, Owen Flanagan, philosopher of mind at Duke University, generously shared his astute mind, his incredible command of the literature, and his wisdom about the process of writing books. Our continued dialogue and friendship sustained me during the writing of this book and gave me confidence.

I thank my parents for teaching me the vital importance of accommodating a diversity of perspectives. Their personal histories showed me that intolerance can kill, and they carried the value of tolerance close at heart, practicing what they preached. I thank them for encouraging me to be an independent, critical thinker. I would have liked to show my dad, Albert Gomes de Mesquita, "that book of yours"; he did not live to see it. I thank my mom, Lien de Jong, for her sustained support, her unconditional love, her interest and involvement in the book, and for showing vicarious pride.

I thank my family and close friends for having been not only supportive and curious, but also patient during the writing of this book. I specifically thank Mat Aguilar, Ton Broeders, Sytse Carlé, Waldo Carlé, Ulli D'Oliveira, Debbie Goldstein, Daniël Gomes de Mesquita,

Diane Griffioen, Mieke Hulens, Roos Kroon, Renée Lemieux, Arjeh Mesquita, Ada Odijk, Jacqueline Peeters, Reshmaa Selvakumar, Paul Van Hal, Ewald Verfaillie, Michael Zajonc, Daisy Zajonc, Donna Zajonc, Jonathan Zajonc, Krysia Zajonc, Lucy Zajonc, Peter Zajonc, and Joe Zajonc.

All my love and gratitude goes to Benny Carlé, who has been on my side during the ups and downs of the writing process. He is not the fictive husband I describe in Chapter 4, who was late for dinner without notifying me. Instead, Benny spiced up my days with delicious dinners and conversations about the world beyond the book.

I dedicate this book to my children, Oliver and Zoë Zajonc. I love you so much. The future is yours, and I hope this book can help, if even just a little, to help build a better future—one that accommodates diversity.

NOTES

Preface

vii **my parents survived the Holocaust in hiding:** My mom's biography is *The Cut Out Girl* (Bart van Es, *The Cut Out Girl: A Story of War and Family, Lost and Found* [New York: Random House, 2018]). My dad was a classmate of Anne Frank's and is mentioned in her diary; some of his memories have been recorded in *We All Wore Stars* (Theo Coster, *We All Wore Stars*, trans. Marjolijn de Jager [New York: St. Martin's Press, 2011]).

viii **cultural focus on feelings:** Ralph H. Turner, "The Real Self: From Institution to Impulse," *American Journal of Sociology* 81, no. 5 (1976): 989–1016.

viii **WEIRD:** The term was introduced in Joseph Henrich, Steven J. Heine, and Ara Norenzayan, "The Weirdest People in the World?," *Behavioral and Brain Sciences* 33, no. 2–3 (June 2010): 61–83.

viii **study of culture and emotion in psychology:** Other major contributions around the same time included: Shinobu Kitayama and Hazel R. Markus, *Emotion and Culture: Empirical Studies of Mutual Influence* (Washington, DC: American Pscyhological Association, 1994); Russell, James A, "Culture and the Categorization of Emotion," *Psychological Bulletin* 110, no. 3 (1991): 426–50.

viii **"make each other up":** Richard A. Shweder, "Cultural Psychology: What Is It?" in *Thinking through Cultures. Expeditions in Cultural Psychology*, ed. Richard A. Shweder (Cambridge, MA: Harvard University Press, 1991), 73–110. Quote on p. 73.

Chapter 1 Lost in Translation

4 **collector's item of culture-specific emotion words:** A recent collection can be found in Tiffany W. Smith, *The Book of Human Emotions* (New York: Little, Brown and Company, 2016).

4 **contribute to each other's sense of value or self-esteem:** See for a similar description: Shinobu Kitayama and Hazel R. Markus, "The Pursuit of Happiness and the Realization of Sympathy: Cultural Patterns of Self, Social Relations, and Well-Being," in *Culture and Subjective Well-Being*, ed. Ed Diener and Eunkook M. Suh (Cambridge, MA: Bradford Books, 2000), 113–61.

5 **no one should feel or act any better:** Also described by Han van der Horst, *The Low Sky: Understanding the Dutch* (The Hague: Scriptum Books, 1996), 34–35.

5 **Differences also show in unpleasant emotions:** The Dutch confrontational style that does not shy away from unpleasant emotions is in stark contrast to the "American cool" that historian Peter N. Stearns describes in *American Cool: Constructing a Twentieth-Century Emotional Style* (New York: New York University Press, 1994).

5 **You confront each other:** The examples in the preceding sentence are from Eva Hoffman, *Lost in Translation: A Life in a New Language* (London: William Heinemann, 1989), 146, who draws a similar contrast between Polish and North American styles of connection.

5 **paint you or the relationship in the most favorable light:** See Stearns, *American Cool*, for the contrast with American emotion culture; this book came out just around the time that I first arrived in the United States.

6 **"into painful reminders":** Catherine A Lutz, *Unnatural Emotions: Everyday Sentiments on a Micronesian Atoll and Their Challenge to Western Theory* (Chicago: University of Chicago Press, 1988), 44.

6 *Never in Anger:* J. L. Briggs, "Emotion Concepts," in *Never in Anger: Portrait of an Eskimo Family* (Cambridge, MA: Harvard University Press, 1970), 257–58, 284, 286. Copyright © 1970 by the President and Fellows of Harvard College.

8 **"painful process of self-discovery":** Quoted from Lutz, *Unnatural Emotions*, 11.

8 **a small set of emotions that were "hard-wired":** E.g., Paul Ekman, "Are There Basic Emotions?," *Psychological Review* 99, no. 3 (1992): 550–53; Carroll E. Izard, *Human Emotions* (New York: Springer Science + Business Media, LLC, 1977); Keith Oatley and Philip N. Johnson-Laird, "Towards a Cognitive Theory of Emotions," *Cognition and Emotion* 1, no. 1 (1987): 29–50.

8 **They proposed that six emotions:** It is not my intention to summarize the basic emotions here. Suffice to say that the theory has evolved over the years. In no way do I suggest that state-of-the-art insights have not surpassed the one presented by Paul Ekman and Wallace V. Friesen, *Unmasking the Face: A Guide to Recognizing Emotions from Facial Clues* (Englewood Cliffs, NJ: Prentice Hall, 1975). Ekman himself suggested that there may be at least nine basic emotions (Ekman, *Are There Basic Emotions?*). In addition to the six introduced in 1975, he proposed that embarrassment, awe, and excitement would qualify as (i.e., meet the criteria for) basic emotions. The meaning of these findings has been heavily debated, and this book is not the place to resuscitate the full critique of basic emotion approaches.

8   **"When people look at someone's face and . . . wrong or right?":** This quote
and the ones on the next page are taken from Ekman and Friesen, *Unmasking
the Face*, on pp. 22, 23, and 24, respectively.

10   **universal emotions being in the soul . . . the brain:** e.g., Paul Ekman, "An
Argument for Basic Emotions," *Cognition & Emotion* 6, no. 3–4 (1992): 169–
200; Jaak Panksepp, "Basic Affects and the Instinctual Emotional Systems of
the Brain: The Primordial Sources of Sadness, Joy, and Seeking," in *Feelings
and Emotions: The Amsterdam Symposium*, ed. Antony S. R. Manstead, Nico
Frijda, and Agneta Fischer (New York: Cambridge University Press, 2004),
174–93.

10   ***shame, embarrassment,* and *pride*:** Research claiming to provide evidence for
embarrassment and shame (Dacher Keltner, "Signs of Appeasement: Evidence
for the Distinct Displays of Embarrassment, Amusement, and Shame,"
Journal of Personality and Social Psychology 68, no. 3 [1995]: 441–45); pride
(Jessica L. Tracy and Richard W. Robins, "Show Your Pride: Evidence for a
Discrete Emotion Expression," *Psychological Science* 15, no. 3 [2004]: 194–97];
and awe, amusement, and pride (Michelle N. Shiota, Belinda Campos, and
Dacher Keltner, "The Faces of Positive Emotion: Prototype Displays of Awe,
Amusement, and Pride," *Annals of the New York Academy of Sciences* 1000, no.
1 [2003]: 296–99).

10   **universal "emotion recognition":** Would imply that emotions can
be recognized from the face. More recent evidence suggests that facial
information makes sense only in connection to other information being used
(Brian Parkinson, *Heart to Heart* [Cambridge, UK: Cambridge University
Press, 2019]); Lisa F. Barrett, Batja Mesquita, and Maria Gendron, "Context
in Emotion Perception," *Current Directions in Psychological Science* 20, no.
5 (2011): 286–90; Maria Gendron, Batja Mesquita, and Lisa F. Barrett,
"Emotion Perception: Putting the Face in Context," in *The Oxford Handbook
of Cognitive Psychology*, ed. Daniel Reisenberg (New York: Oxford University
Press, 2013), 539–56.

10   **artefact of the methods:** Russell (*Universal Reg of Emotion from Facial
Expression*) reviews all facial judgment studies after 1969, and finds several
aspects of the method contribute to the rate of "recognition" of the particular
emotion intended.

10   **never examined "emotions":** In the '80s and '90s, componential theories
broke the meaning of emotion concepts down into constituents, such as
the appraisals of a situation (e.g., Craig A. Smith and Phoebe C. Ellsworth,
"Patterns of Cognitive Appraisal in Emotion," *Journal of Personality and Social
Psychology* 48, no. 4 [1985]: 813–38); the action readiness (e.g., Nico H. Frijda,
Peter Kuipers, and Elisabeth ter Schure, "Relations among Emotion, Appraisal,
and Emotional Action Readiness," *Journal of Personality and Social Psychology*
57, no. 2 [1989]: 212–28); and physiological and behavioral responses (Nico H.
Frijda, *The Emotions* [Cambridge, UK: Cambridge University Press / Éditions
de la Maison des Sciences de l'Homme, 1986]).

10 **examining the words for emotion:** Phillip R. Shaver et al., "Emotion Knowledge: Further Exploration of a Prototype Approach," *Journal of Personality and Social Psychology* 52, no. 6 (1987): 1061–86; Aneta Wierzbicka, "Talking about Emotions: Semantics, Culture, and Cognition," *Cognition & Emotion* 6, no. 3–4 (1992): 285–319.

10 **"cuts nature at its joints":** Plato compares philosophers' taxonomy to the way a butcher carves things, at their natural junctures (Plato, "Phaedrus," n.d.); implying that the world comes pre-divided.

10 **in U.S. research:** Shaver, Schwartz, Kirson, and O'Connor, "Emotion Knowledge . . . . "

11 **Chinese participants were asked to do the same task:** Phillip R. Shaver, Shelley Wu, and Judith C. Schwartz, "Cross-Cultural Similarities and Differences in Emotion and Its Representation: A Prototype Approach," in *Review of Personality and Social Psychology, No. 13. Emotion*, ed. Margaret S. Clark (Newbury Park, CA: Sage Publications, Inc., 1992), 175–212.

12 **method that had been introduced by others:** see, e.g., Beverley Fehr and James A. Russell, "Concept of Emotion Viewed from a Prototype Perspective," *Journal of Experimental Psychology: General* 113, no. 3 (1984): 464–86.

12 **"on the inside" of the person:** This definition of emotions as phenomena on the inside of the person is also used by anthropologist Catherine Lutz, who proceeds to describe emotions among the Ifaluk as taking place in the social realm (Lutz, *Unnatural Emotions*, 41).

13 **in Western (mostly U.S.) science:** Henrich, Heine, and Norenzayan note that most psychological studies have been produced in Western (particularly U.S.) contexts, and more particularly with college students ("The Weirdest People in the World?" *Behavioral and Brain Sciences* 33, no. 2–3 [June 2020]: 6183).

13 **my subsequent research:** Batja Mesquita, "Cultural Variations in Emotions: A Comparative Study of Dutch, Surinamese, and Turkish People in the Netherlands" (PhD diss.,University of Amsterdam, 1993). Some parts of this thesis research have been published (Batja Mesquita, "Emotions in Collectivist and Individualist Contexts," *Journal of Personality and Social Psychology* 80, no. 1 [2001]: 68–74; Mesquita and Frijda, "Cultural Variations in Emotions: A Review", 1992).

14 **talked about emotions:** Referred to as "emotion talk" (Paul Heelas, "Emotion Talk across Cultures," in *The Social Construction of Emotions*, ed. Rom Harré [New York: SAGE Publications, 1986], 234–65), or "emotion discourse" (Catherine A. Lutz and Lila Abu-Lughod, *Language and the Politics of Emotion: Studies in Emotion and Social Interaction*, ed. C. Lutz and L. Abu-Lughod [Cambridge, UK: Cambridge University Press, Éditions de la Maison des Sciences de l'Homme, 1990]).

14 **"unquestioned use of American-English emotion concepts":** Quote from Lutz, *Unnatural Emotions*, 42.

14 **"public, social, and relational":** Lutz, *Unnatural Emotions*, 82.

15 **"vulnerability to humiliation":** Lila Abu-Lughod, *Veiled Sentiments: Honor and Poetry in a Bedouin Society* (Berkeley: University of California Press, 1986), 112.

15 **a review article on culture and emotion:** Mesquita and Frijda, "Cultural Variations in Emotions: A Review."

16 **discover the power of culture:** E.g., Harry C. Triandis, "The Self and Social Behavior in Differing Cultural Contexts," *Psychological Review* 96, no. 3 (1989): 506–20; Hazel R. Markus and Shinobu Kitayama, "Culture and the Self: Implications for Cognition, Emotion, and Motivation," *Psychological Review* 98, no. 2 (1991): 224–53; see for a good introductory textbook on Cultural Psychology: Steven J. Heine, *Cultural Psychology* (New York: W. W. Norton & Company, 2020).

18 **pre-wired for certain emotions:** Erika H. Siegel, Molly K. Sands, Wim Van den Noortgate, Paul Condon, Yale Chang, Jennifer Dy, Karen S. Quigley, and Lisa Feldman Barrett, "Emotion Fingerprints or Emotion Populations? A Meta-Analytic Investigation of Autonomic Features of Emotion Categories," *Psychological Bulletin* 144, no. 4 (2018): 343; Kristen A. Lindquist, Tor D. Wager, Hedy Kober, Eliza Bliss-Moreau, and Lisa Feldman Barrett, "The Brain Basis of Emotion: A Meta-Analytic Review," *Behavioral and Brain Sciences* 35, no. 3 (2012): 121.

18 **adjusted to our communities and cultures:** Maria Gendron, Batja Mesquita, and Lisa Feldman Barrett, "The Brain as a Cultural Artifact: Concepts, Actions, and Experiences within the Human Affective Niche," in *Culture, Mind, and Brain: Emerging Concepts, Models, and Applications*, ed. Laurence J. Kirmayer et al. (Cambridge, UK: Cambridge University Press, 2020), 188–222.

19 **happens through experience:** L. J. Kirmayer, C. M. Worthman, and S. Kitayama, "Introduction: Co-Constructing Culture, Mind, and Brain," in *Culture, Mind, and Brain*, ed. L. J. Kirmayer et al. (Cambridge, UK: Cambridge University Press, 2020), 1–49; Shinobu Kitayama and Cristina E. Salvador, "Culture Embrained: Going Beyond the Nature-Nurture Dichotomy," *Perspectives on Psychological Science* 12, no. 5 (2017): 841–54; Samuel P. L. Veissière, Axel Constant, Maxwell J. D. Ramstead, Karl J. Friston, and Laurence J. Kirmayer, "Thinking through Other Minds: A Variational Approach to Cognition and Culture," *Behavioral and Brain Sciences* 43 (2020).

19 **the out-of-the-ordinary:** In "The Laws of Emotion," Frijda captures these regularities as "The Law of Change, Habituation, and Comparative Feeling": "Emotions are elicited not so much by the presence of favorable or unfavorable conditions but by actual or expected changes in favorable or unfavorable conditions." (Frijda, Nico H. 2007. *The Laws of Emotion*. Mahwah: Lawrence Erlbaum Associates, Inc.).

19 **recruit many body processes:** Lisa Feldman Barrett Barrett, *How Emotions Are Made: The Secret Life of the Brain* (New York: Houghton Mifflin Harcourt, 2017); Gendron, Mesquita, and Barrett, "The Brain as a Cultural Artifact.

Concepts, Actions, and Experiences within the Human Affective Niche," 2020; Karen S. Quigley and Lisa Feldman Barrett, "Is There Consistency and Specificity of Autonomic Changes during Emotional Episodes? Guidance from the Conceptual Act Theory and Psychophysiology," *Biological Psychology* 98, no. 1 (2014): 82–94. Among these bodily processes are cardiovascular, skeletomuscular, neuroendocrine, and autonomic nervous system processes.

19 **these bodily changes**: In a series of studies, computer scientist Lauri Nummenmaa and colleagues suggest that "bodily maps" of emotions are culturally universal. (Lauri Nummenmaa et al., "Bodily Maps of Emotions," *Proceedings of the National Academy of Sciences of the United States of America* 111, no. 2 [2014]).

20 **meaningful in our relationships**: E.g., Michael Boiger and Batja Mesquita, "The Construction of Emotion in Interactions, Relationships, and Cultures," *Emotion Review* 4, no. 3 (2012): 221–29; Parkinson, *Heart to Heart*.

20 **love**: Examples taken from the prototype study by Shaver et al. ("Emotion Knowledge: Further Exploration of a Prototype Approach," 1075).

Chapter 2 EMOTIONS: MINE OR OURS?

23 **portrayal of emotions themselves**: Lisa F. Barrett has used the example in talks for very similar purposes (Lisa F. Barrett and Daniel J. Barrett, "Brain Scientist: How Pixar's 'Inside Out' Gets One Thing Deeply Wrong," WBUR, July 5, 2015).

23 **set of fixed properties**: For similar characterizations of this model of emotions, see Barrett, *How Emotions Are Made*, 157; Lutz, *Unnatural Emotions*, 53–54.

25 **associated emotional episodes**: The people in my interview study told us why the event was meaningful to them, how they had acted during and after, who else had been involved and what they did or said, and what the current or lasting consequences of the event were. We compared the emotional experiences associated with a single theme (e.g., being successful because of an achievement) across different cultural groups. I did not interview the respondents myself, but had female interviewers matched on the ethnicity of the respondents, who conducted the interviews in the language(s) of the respondents. Interviews were fully transcribed (and translated in the Turkish sample).

26 **shifts in relative status, honor, or power**: Mesquita, "Emotions in Collectivist and Individualist Contexts."

27 **MINE and OURS features**: MINE and OURS are acronyms that combine the initials of different dimensions. Emotions can be described as INside or OUtside the person, as Mental or Relational, and as Essences or Situated. Granted, the initials have to be scrambled a bit to get these meaningful acronyms.

27 **A MINE cultural model . . . OURS cultural model**: MINE and OURS define the core attributes of the "category" or the slots of the "narrative" of emotions differently (e.g., Lawrence W. Barsalou, *Cognitive Psychology: An*

Overview for Cognitive Scientists [Hillsdale, NJ: Erlbaum, 1992]; Jerome Bruner, *Acts of Meaning* [Cambridge, MA: Harvard University Press, 1990]). For example, internal sensations could be a core attribute of the category of MINE, but not OURS emotions.

28 **sabotaged their status or opportunities:** In a separate large-scale questionnaire study comparing the same cultural groups in the Netherlands, Surinamese respondents who reported having been offended by someone they knew well were more convinced than respondents from the majority Dutch and minority Turkish group that the harm-doer him- or herself had gained or benefited from their negative actions; they also perceived the harm-doer to be more intentionally harmful and the harmful act as more premeditated (Mesquita, "Emotions in Collectivist and Individualist Contexts," 2001). These findings are consistent with the idea that competition for status was foregrounded in the Surinamese group.

28 **"about enemies in intimate spaces":** Glenn Adams, "The Cultural Grounding of Personal Relationship: Enemyship in North American and West African Worlds," *Journal of Personality and Social Psychology* 88, no. 6 (2005): 948.

28 **"There is no man without an enemy":** A poem by Kojo G. Kyei and Hannah Schreckenbach (*No Time to Die* [London: Walden Books, 1975], 72), as cited by Adams, "The Cultural Grounding of Personal Relationship."

29 **the contrast with "other cultures":** Anthropologist Tanya Luhrmann notes that "Anthropologists tend to be cranky when it comes to making comparative claims about cultural difference because they want to believe that cultures are remarkably complex and relatively unbounded" ("Subjectivity," *Anthropological Theory* 6, no. 3 [2006]: 345). I understand the concern about stereotyping and essentializing, and yet I think there is much to learn from contrasting cultures and communities, however heterogeneous they are internally.

29 **A now classic study:** Robert W. Levenson et al., "Emotion and Autonomic Nervous System: Activity in the Minangkabu of West Sumatra," *Journal of Personality and Social Psychology* 62, no. 6 (1992): 972–88.

30 **modalities . . . strongly connected:** Levenson et al., "Emotion and Autonomic Nervous System," 972: Emotions are "evolved phenomena, having been established through natural selection so the organism can respond most efficiently to certain prototypical environmental demands."

30 **the Minangkabau:** Levenson et al., "Emotion and Autonomic Nervous System"; Birgitt Röttger-Rössler et al., "Socializing Emotions in Childhood: A Cross-Cultural Comparison between the Bara in Madagascar and the Minangkabau in Indonesia," *Mind, Culture, and Activity* 20, no. 3 (2013): 260–87.

30 **For disgust, the instruction was:** Levenson et al., "Emotion and Autonomic Nervous System," 975. Copyright © 1992, American Psychological Association.

30 **associated autonomic arousal:** Robert W. Levenson, Paul Ekman, and Wallace V. Friesen, "Voluntary Facial Action Generates Emotion-Specific Autonomic Nervous System Activity," *Psychophysiology* 27, no. 4 (July 1, 1990): 363–84. The meaning of the physiological data for this particular

task has been contested: Boiten provides evidence that the autonomic activity associated with voluntarily adopted facial expression may be merely explained by effort-related changes in respiration (Frans A. Boiten, "Autonomic Response Patterns during Voluntary Facial Action," *Psychophysiology* 33 [1996]: 123–31). See also Quigley and Barrett, "Is There Consistency and Specificity of Autonomic Changes during Emotional Episodes?," 2014; Robert B. Zajonc and Daniel N. McIntosh, "Emotions Research: Some Promising Questions and Some Questionable Promises," *Psychological Science* 3, no. 1 (1992): 70–74, for empirical reviews that challenge the existence of specific ANS patterns that, across studies, consistently distinguish between emotions.

31 **"focusing on . . . interpersonal interactions and relationships":** Levenson et al., "Emotion and Autonomic Nervous System," 974. Copyright © 1992, American Psychological Association.

31 **failed to cue emotional experience in the Minangkabau:** This is my conclusion. The Levenson team provides different explanations for this finding, rather suggesting that the Minangkabau had been less successful in making the various expressions, and that this could have been a reason that they did not feel the associated emotional state. (Levenson et al., "Emotion and Autonomic Nervous System," 1992).

31 **only if socially contextualized or shared:** Cultural psychologists Hazel Markus and Shinobu Kitayama were the first to suggest "Americans and Minangkabau define emotions differently, and that they have different expectations about when and why an emotion will be experienced . . . one could argue that the subjectivity of the Minangkabau was keyed or tuned to the presence of others . . . the activity of the autonomic nervous system stemming from the configuration of the facial musculature did not [for them] constitute an emotion" (Hazel R. Markus and Shinobu Kitayama, "The Cultural Construction of Self and Emotion: Implications for Social Behavior," in *Emotion and Culture: Empirical Studies of Mutual Influence* [Washington, DC: American Psychological Association, 1994, 89–130]). To my knowledge, this hypothesis has never been directly tested.

31 **Uchida decided to study the phenomenon more systematically:** Yukiko Uchida et al., "Emotions as within or between People? Cultural Variation in Lay Theories of Emotion Expression and Inference," *Personality and Social Psychology Bulletin* 35, no. 11 (November 10, 2009): 1427–39; the quote of the Japanese athlete further down comes on p. 1432.

32 **For Japanese, emotions were OURS; for Americans, they were MINE:** Japanese and American research participants were randomly assigned to one of four conditions: (1) a Japanese athlete by themselves, (2) a Japanese athlete with three others, (3) an American athlete by themselves, and (4) an American athlete with three others. The described differences were found in the within-culture conditions, where American participants projected the emotions for American athletes, and Japanese participants projected emotions onto the

Japanese athletes. Differences were not found for the conditions in which participants reported emotions for athletes from the other culture (Uchida et al., "Emotions as within or between People? Cultural Variation in Lay Theories of Emotion Expression and Inference").

34 **our study examined *which* emotions:** Takahiko Masuda et al., "Placing the Face in Context: Cultural Differences in the Perception of Facial Emotion," *Journal of Personality and Social Psychology* 94, no. 3 (2008): 365–81. Copyright © 2008, American Psychological Association.

34 **looked at the expressions of the other figures:** Note that the traditional paradigm for "face recognition" would have been just fine for our North American participants: they did not use the information from the surrounding people's faces. Yet, this paradigm failed to capture an important aspect of "emotion" perception in the Japanese. This is one example where Western researchers, by modeling their very paradigm according to a MINE model of emotions, would never have picked up on important cultural differences in the way emotional episodes evolve (Batja Mesquita et al., "A Cultural Lens on Facial Expression in Emotions," *Observer* 17, no. 4 [2004]: 50–51).

34 **using pictures of real faces:** Takahiko Masuda et al., "Do Surrounding Figures' Emotions Affect Judgment of the Target Figure's Emotion? Comparing the Eye-Movement Patterns of European Canadians, Asian Canadians, Asian International Students, and Japanese," *Frontiers in Integrative Neuroscience* 6, no. 72 (2012): 1–9.

35 **Historically, this seems to be the common way:** Many of the examples in this and the next paragraph are taken from Paul Heelas, "Emotion Talk across Cultures," 1986. In ordinary language, the English "emotion" (introduced from French) is said to have become associated with the mind no earlier than the eighteenth century; before that it was located in the body (as in physical disturbance or bodily movement) (Thomas Dixon, "Emotion: One Word, Many Concepts," *Emotion Review* 4, no. 4 [2012]: 387–88).

35 **the Homeric Greeks:** Bennett Simon and Herbert Weiner, "Models of Mind and Mental Illness in Ancient Greece: I. The Homeric Model of Mind," *Journal of the History of the Behavioral Sciences* 2, no. 4 (October 1, 1966): 306.

35 **early modern people in the United States:** John R. Gillis, "From Ritual to Romance," in *Emotion and Social Change: Toward a New Psychohistory*, ed. Carol Z. Stearns and Peter N. Stearns (New York: Holmes & Meier, 1988), 90–91.

35 **the Kaluli, living in Papua New Guinea:** Edward L. Schieffelin, "Anger and Shame in the Tropical Forest: On Affect as a Cultural System in Papua New Guinea," *Ethos* 11, no. 3 (1983): 183–84.

36 **going beyond observations to infer feelings:** This is part of a more general reluctance to present interpretations of other people's state of purpose (Schieffelin, "Anger and Shame in the Tropical Forest," 174).

36 **no reference made to the subjective feeling:** Elinor Ochs, *Culture and Language Development: Language Acquisition and Language Socialization in a Samoan Village* (Cambridge, UK: Cambridge University Press, 1988).

36   **"feelings are not . . . worthy of being understood":** Sulamith H. Potter, "The Cultural Construction of Emotion in Rural Chinese Social Life," *Ethos* 16, no. 2 (1988): 187.

36   **Maria Gendron . . . studied how Himba individuals perceived emotions in others:** The study was part of Gendron's dissertation research under the guidance of psychologist Lisa F. Barrett, and with help of anthropologist Debi Robertson (Maria Gendron, Debi Roberson, Jacoba Marietta van der Vyver, and Lisa F. Barrett, "Perceptions of Emotion from Facial Expressions Are Not Culturally Universal: Evidence from a Remote Culture," *Emotion* 14, no. 2 [2014]: 251).

36   **"each person in the pile experienced the same emotion" . . . "What is in the pile?":** Literal instructions from Maria Gendron et al., "Perceptions of Emotion from Facial Expressions Are Not Culturally Universal: Evidence from a Remote Culture," *Emotion* 14, no. 2 (April 2014): 253–54.

37   **Americans have learned to infer "mental states":** Gendron et al., "Perceptions of Emotion from Facial Expressions Are Not Culturally Universal," 260.

37   *can* **read acts from faces:** Nico H. Frijda and Anna Tcherkassof, "Facial Expression as Modes of Action Readiness," in *The Psychology of Facial Expression. Studies in Emotion and Social Interaction*, ed. James A. Russell and José Miguel Fernández-Dols (Cambridge, UK: Cambridge University Press, 1997), 78–102.

37   *can* **infer mental states from acts:** Jinkyung Na and Shinobu Kitayama, "Spontaneous Trait Inference Is Culture-Specific: Behavioral and Neural Evidence," *Psychological Science* 22, no. 8 (2011): 1025–32.

38   **Psychologist Qi Wang:** Examples are from Qi Wang, "'Did You Have Fun?': American and Chinese Mother-Child Conversations about Shared Emotional Experiences," *Cognitive Development* 16, no. 2 (2001): 711–13. Reprinted with permission from Elsevier.

39   **on Java, Indonesia:** Andrew Beatty, *Emotional Worlds: Beyond an Anthropology of Emotion* (Cambridge, UK: Cambridge University Press, 2019), 258. Reprinted with permission by Cambridge University Press.

39   **share most of their emotional episodes with others:** Bernard Rimé et al., "Beyond the Emotional Event: Six Studies on the Social Sharing of Emotion," *Cognition & Emotion* 5, no. 5–6 (1991): 435–65.

40   **people who *feel* happy tend to be healthier:** E.g., Julia K. Boehm and Laura D. Kubzansky, "The Heart's Content: The Association between Positive Psychological Well-Being and Cardiovascular Health," *Psychological Bulletin* 138, no. 4 (2012): 655–91; Sheldon Cohen and Sarah D. Pressman, "Positive Affect and Health," *Current Directions in Psychological Science* 15, no. 3 (2006): 122–25; Kostadin Kushlev et al., "Does Happiness Improve Health? Evidence from a Randomized Controlled Trial," *Psychological Science* 31, no. 7 (2020): 807–21, https://doi.org/10.1177/0956797620919673.

40   **representative samples of Americans and Japanese in their midlife:** Magali Clobert et al., "Feeling Excited or Taking a Bath: Do Distinct Pathways Underlie the Positive Affect–Health Link in the U.S. and Japan?," *Emotion* 20, no. 2 (2019): 164–78.

40 **difference in emotions . . . well established in cultural psychology:** The evidence comes from the lab of Stanford psychologist Jeanne Tsai; e.g., Jeanne L. Tsai, Brian Knutson, and Helene H. Fung, "Cultural Variation in Affect Valuation," *Journal of Personality and Social Psychology* 90, no. 2 (2006): 288–307; Jeanne L. Tsai, "Ideal Affect: Cultural Causes and Behavioral Consequences," *Perspectives on Psychological Science* 2, no. 3 (2007): 242–59; Jeanne Tsai and Magali Clobert, "Cultural Influences on Emotion: Empirical Patterns and Emerging Trends," in *Handbook of Cultural Psychology*, ed. Shinobu Kitayama and Dov Cohen, 2nd ed. (New York: Guildford Press, 2019), 292–318. I will describe the research in more detail in chapter 5 of this book.

40 **In the U.S., the healthiest individuals:** Healthy U.S. participants also reported more activities of excitement, but activities were not as good a predictor of mental and physical health as were feelings (Clobert et al., "Feeling Excited or Taking a Bath").

41 **contribute to longevity:** A few caveats are in order. The study was cross-sectional, so it teaches us very little about the processes involved. Even if emotions contribute to health outcomes directly, they are far from the only health determinants. Finally, having high activation positive emotions (in the U.S.) or calm activities (in Japan) does not need to come at the exclusion of other emotional experiences: a variety of emotions is the norm. It is the relative occurrence of high activation positive emotions and calm activities, respectively, that was associated with different health indicators.

41 **language is full of reminders:** Zoltán Kövecses, *Emotion Concepts* (New York: Springer-Verlag, 1990).

41 **"grief work":** Sigmund Freud, "Trauer Und Melancholic [Mourning and Melancholia]," *Internationale Zeiischrift Fur Arztliche Psychoanalyse* 4 (1917): 288–301; John Bowlby, "Loss, Sadness and Depression," *Attachment and Loss* 3 (1981); Camille Wortman and Roxane Silver, "The Myths of Coping with Loss," *Journal of Consulting and Clinical Psychology* 57 (1989): 349–57. More recent work has suggested that grief work may not always be essential to a healthy adjustment after loss, is oversimplified (Margaret Stroebe and Wolfgang Stroebe, "Does 'Grief Work' Work?," *Journal of Consulting and Clinical Psychology* 59, no. 3 [1991]: 479–82; George A. Bonanno, Camille Wortman, and Randolph M. Nesse, "Prospective Patterns of Resilience and Maladjustment During Widowhood," *Psychology and Aging* 19, no. 2 [2004]: 260).

41 **A 2004 study:** Oliver P. John and James J. Gross, "Healthy and Unhealthy Emotion Regulation: Personality Processes, Individual Differences, and Life-Span Development," *Journal of Personality* 72, no. 6 (2004): 1301–33. To measure suppression, they asked the respondents such questions as "I control my emotions by not expressing them," or "I keep my emotions to myself."

42 ***The Managed Heart*:** Arlie R. Hochschild, *The Managed Heart: Com-mercialization of Human Feeling* (Berkeley: University of California Press, 1983).

42 **"Our flight attendants' smiles will be more human":** Cited from Hochschild, *The Managed Heart*, 5.

42 **"[o]pen aggression was the official policy":** Cited from Hochschild, *The Managed Heart*, 146.

42 **"understanding as one would be with a good friend":** Cited from Hochschild, *The Managed Heart*, 109.

42 **"seemed too much like a cabin full of 300 demanding strangers":** Cited from Hochschild, *The Managed Heart*, 134.

42 **"a sense of being phony or insincere":** Cited from Hochschild, *The Managed Heart*, 21.

43 **"faces that did not show emotion at all":** Quotes from Julia L. Cassaniti, "Moralizing Emotion: A Breakdown in Thailand," *Anthropological Theory* 14, no. 3 (August 6, 2014): 284. Copyright © 2014 by Sage Journals. Reprinted by Permission of SAGE Publications.

45 **match up to others' needs and expectations:** Eunkook Suh et al., "The Shifting Basis of Life Satisfaction Judgments across Cultures: Emotion vs Norms," *Journal of Personality and Social Psychology* 74, no. 2 (1998): 483.

45 **a large-scale international questionnaire study:** David Matsumoto, Seung H. Yoo, and Sanae Nakagawa, "Culture, Emotion Regulation, and Adjustment," *Journal of Personality and Social Psychology* 94, no. 6 (2008): 925–37. Suppression was measured with the four-item suppression scale developed by Gross and John, which Matsumoto and colleagues established to be equivalent across different cultures (James J. Gross and Oliver P. John, "Individual Differences in Two Emotion Regulation Processes: Implications for Affect, Relationships, and Well-Being," *Journal of Personality and Social Psychology* 85, no. 2 [August 2003]: 348–62).

46 **emotions to be "negotiated" with the social environment:** The point was originally made by Lutz (*Unnatural Emotions*).

46 **sign of personal immaturity:** Hazel R. Markus and Shinobu Kitayama, "Models of Agency: Sociocultural Diversity in the Construction of Action," in *Cross-Cultural Differences in Perspectives on the Self*, ed. Virginia Murphy-Berman and John J. Berman, vol. 49 (Lincoln: University of Nebraska Press, 2003), 1–58.

46 **cultivate the emotions . . . with greater ease:** Joseph A. Allen, James M. Diefendorff, and Yufeng Ma, "Differences in Emotional Labor across Cultures: A Comparison of Chinese and U.S. Service Workers," *Journal of Business and Psychology* 29 (2014): 21–35; Batja Mesquita and Ellen Delvaux, "A Cultural Perspective on Emotion Labor," in *Emotional Labor in the 21st Century: Diverse Perspectives on Emotion Regulation at Work*, ed. Alicia Grandey, James Diefendorff, and Deborah E. Rupp (New York: Routledge, 2013), 251–72.

46 **Chinese service workers did not see it as faking at all:** "Surface acting" items (i.e., items on changing emotional expression) loaded on the same factor as items on "faking" in the U.S., but not in China. Suppression is simply not the same as faking it in China: the faking items had a zero loading on the

surface acting factor (Allen, Diefendorff, and Ma, "Differences in Emotional Labor across Cultures").

47 **have the emotions to match their display:** Display rules (e.g., "Part of my job is to make the customer feel good") predicted as much surface acting ("Put on an act in order to deal with customers in an appropriate way") as deep acting ("Try to actually experience the emotions I must feel towards a customer") in the U.S. sample, but it only predicted deep acting in China. Similarly, Matsumoto, Yoo, and Nakagawa find that in cultures that emphasize the maintenance of social order (outward perspective), suppression and reappraisal (which may be part of deep acting) were positively related, whereas in cultures that emphasized individualism, affective autonomy and egalitarianism (arguably an inward perspective), suppression was negatively related with reappraisal ("Culture, Emotion Regulation, and Adjustment," 2008, 931). Both findings suggest that managing the display of emotions has a very different meaning in cultures with OURS models than in cultures with MINE models.

47 **burnout:** Measured by the Burnout Inventory (MBI; Christina Maslach and Susan E. Jackson, "The Measurement of Experienced Burnout," *Journal of Organizational Behavior* 2, no. 2 [April 1, 1981]: 99–113). The scales are emotional exhaustion (e.g., "I feel emotionally drained from this work"); depersonalization (e.g., "I have become more callous toward people since I took the job"); and personal accomplishment (e.g., "I feel I am positively influencing people's lives through my work").

47 **made . . . undergraduate students angry:** Iris B. Mauss and Emily A. Butler, "Cultural Context Moderates the Relationship between Emotion Control Values and Cardiovascular Challenge versus Threat Responses," *Biological Psychology* 84, no. 3 (2010): 521–30.

47 **higher value on emotional control:** The following six items were used to assess emotion control values (ECV): (1) "People should not express their emotions openly"; (2) "It is wrong for people to always display how they feel" (3) "It is better for people to let out pent up emotions" (reversed); (4) "People should show their emotions when overcome with strong feelings" (reversed); (5) "People in general should control their emotions more"; and (6) "I think it is appropriate to express emotions, no matter whether negative or positive" (reversed).

47 **(as perceived by judges):** Two judges coded the behavior; no specifics for the cultural background of the judges were given (Mauss and Butler, "Cultural Context Moderates the Relationship between Emotion Control Values and Cardiovascular Challenge versus Threat Responses").

48 **The sisters "hurried to his house":** Lutz, *Unnatural Emotions*, 33.

48 **Alba Jasini tells me:** Personal communication, December 9, 2020.

48 **rituals have a similar function:** Batja Mesquita and Nico H. Frijda, "Cultural Variations in Emotions: A Review," *Psychological Bulletin* 112, no. 2 (1992): 197; see also Marcel Mauss, "L'Expression Obligatiore Des Sentiments: Rituels

Oraux Funeraires Australiens," *Journal de Psychologie* 18, no. 1 (1921): 425–33; Michelle Z. Rosaldo, *Knowledge and Passion: Ilongot Notions of Self and Social Life, An Interdisciplinary Journal for Cultural Studies* (Cambridge, UK: Cambridge University Press, 1980).

49 **force the display by highlighting the norm:** Birgitt Röttger-Rössler et al., "Socializing Emotions in Childhood: A Cross-Cultural Comparison between the Bara in Madagascar and the Minangkabau in Indonesia," *Mind, Culture, and Activity* 20, no. 3 (2013): 260–87.

49 **In Andi's own words:** Röttger-Rössler et al., "Socializing Emotions in Childhood." Quote on p. 271. Reprinted by permission of the publisher (Taylor & Francis Ltd, http://www.tandfonline.com).

49 **reflection on the terms *emotional expression* and *emotional suppression*:** A similar point was made by Robert B. Zajonc in a beautiful essay entitled "The Preemptive Power of Words" (*Dialogue* 18, no. 1 [2003]: 10–13). He calls *emotional expression* "a preemptive term," a term that "impose[s] on a given reality." He argues this term "did more harm than good." "If we accept Darwin's preemptive concept of emotional expression we must also accept all the implicit meanings and associations that go with it," he writes. "For instance, emotional expression implies that for each emotion there exists a distinct internal state. That there are these distinct and identifiable states is clearly implied by the fact that Darwin's title reads THE expression of THE emotions in man and animals . . . The concept of emotional expression also implies that this distinctive state, the emotion, seeks externalization. It follows therefore, that if external manifestation does not occur for some emotional instigations, then there must exist a process capable of suppressing it."

50 **When American individuals speak about emotions:** Examples are taken from Shaver et al., "Emotion Knowledge."

50 **smiling is instrumental in making a connection with their customers:** E.g., Jared Martin et al., "Smiles as Multipurpose Social Signals," *Trends in Cognitive Sciences* 21, no. 11 (2017): 864–77.

52 **anger gets you the better business deal:** Gerben A. Van Kleef, Carsten K. W. De Dreu, and Antony S. R. Manstead, "The Interpersonal Effects of Emotions in Negotiations: A Motivated Information Processing Approach," *Journal of Personality and Social Psychology* 87, no. 4 (October 2004): 510–28.

53 **How do our emotions act to change our relationship with the world?:** Question taken from introduction to Nico H. Frijda, "The Evolutionary Emergence of What We Call Emotions," *Cognition & Emotion* 30, no. 4 (2016), 609–20.

53 **What does this emotion want in the social world?:** Taken from Kaat Van Acker et al., "Hoe Emoties Verschillen Tussen Culturen," in *Handboek Culturele Psychiatrie En Psychotherapie*, 2nd ed. (Amsterdam: De Tijdstroom, 2020), 163–78.

53 **Arlie Hochschild suggests:** Hochschild, *The Managed Heart*, 1983.

53 **parents give in to their desires:** Carol Tavris, *Anger: The Misunderstood*

Emotion (New York: Simon & Schuster, 1989), 144; Keith Oatley, Dacher Keltner, and Jennifer M. Jenkins, *Understanding Emotions*, 2nd ed. (Malden, MA: Wiley, 2006), 305.

53 **parents only respond to their negative emotions:** Susan Goldberg, Sherri MacKay-Soroka, and Margot Rochester, "Affect, Attachment, and Maternal Responsiveness," *Infant Behavior and Development* 17, no. 3 (1994): 335–39.

54 **more rewarding for men:** For differences in anger expression see Leslie R. Brody, Judith A. Hall, and Lynissa R. Stokes, "Gender and Emotion: Theory, Findings, and Context," in *Handbook of Emotions*, ed. Lisa F. Barret, Michael Lewis, and Jeannette M. Haviland-Jones, 4th ed. (New York: Guilford Press, 2016), 369–92; see chapter 4 of this book for more examples.

54 **women started to be more angry:** Tavris, *Anger*, 133–34. The original experiment is by Jack E. Hokanson, K. R. Willers, and Elizabeth Koropsak, "The Modification of Autonomic Responses during Aggressive Interchange," *Journal of Personality* 36, no. 3 (1968): 386–404.

54 **some feeling, some embodiment:** See Beatty, *Emotional Worlds: Beyond an Anthropology of Emotion*, who, following Bedford, suggests that emotion words are not used to name a feeling but to describe behavioral contexts, in which feelings often occur. Even if the use of a word doesn't hinge on embodiment, there may still be physical sensations.

Chapter 3 TO RAISE YOUR CHILD

55 **(miss many of the adult features):** Children are thought to need objective self-awareness: they need to pay attention to the self. This cognitive milestone is thought to happen no sooner than the second half of the second year (Michael Lewis and Dennis P. Carmody, "Self-Representation and Brain Development," *Developmental Psychology* 44, no. 5 [2008]: 1329–34).

55 **Taiwanese mothers cultivated shame:** Heidi Fung, "Becoming a Moral Child: The Socialization of Shame among Young Chinese Children," *Ethos* 27, no. 2 (1999): 180–209; Heidi Fung and Eva C.-H. Chen, "Affect, Culture, and Moral Socialization: Shame as an Example," in *Emotion, Affect, and Culture*, ed. T. L. Hu, M. T. Hsu, and K. H. Yeh (Taipei, Taiwan: Institute of Ethnology, Academie Sinica, 2002), 17–48. The quotes that follow in this paragraph are taken from Fung, "Becoming a Moral Child," 202–203. Copyright © 1999 by the American Anthropological Association. Reprinted by permission of John Wiley and Sons Journals.

56 **Anthropologist Naomi Quinn observes:** Naomi Quinn, "Universals of Child Rearing," *Anthropological Theory* 5, no. 4 (December 1, 2005): 505.

56 **American moms and kids . . . with Taiwanese:** Peggy J. Miller et al., "Self-Esteem as Folk Theory: A Comparison of European American and Taiwanese Mothers' Beliefs," *Parenting: Science and Practice* 2, no. 3 (August 2002): 209–39.

56 **feeling good about yourself:** Chicago moms' lay ideas about self-esteem are largely consistent with psychological findings: Baumeister, Campbell, Krueger, and Vos, summarizing the literature (based on U.S. samples mostly), found that self-esteem was closely linked with happiness and enhanced initiative; self-esteem seems to be a result rather then a precursor of school success (Roy F. Baumeister et al., "Does High Self-Esteem Cause Better Performance, Interpersonal Success, Happiness, or Healthier Lifestyles?," *Psychological Science in the Public Interest* 4, no. 1 [2003]: 1–44).

57 **"build, cultivate or protect their children's self-esteem":** Miller et al., "Self-Esteem as Folk Theory." Reprinted by permission of the publisher (Taylor & Francis Ltd, http://www.tandfonline.com).

57 **one Chicago mom relates to the researcher:** P. J. Miller, H. Fung, and J. Mintz, "Self-Construction through Narrative Practices: A Chinese and American Comparison of Early Socialization," *Ethos* 24, no. 2 (1996): 258.

58 **face-to-face interactions:** E.g., Heidi Keller et al., "Cultural Models, Socialization Goals, and Parenting Ethnotheories: A Multicultural Analysis," *Journal of Cross-Cultural Psychology* 37, no. 2 (March 2006): 155–72.

59 **"a generalized self-reliance":** Naomi Quinn and Holly F. Mathews, "Emotional Arousal in the Making of Cultural Selves," *Anthropological Theory* 16, no. 4 (December 1, 2016): 359–89, 376.

59 **predisposes children to feel happy, proud, or full of self-esteem:** Miller et al., "Self-Esteem as Folk Theory"; Quinn, "Universals of Child Rearing"; Quinn and Mathews, "Emotional Arousal in the Making of Cultural Selves."

59 **As one website puts it:** Pamela Li, "Top 10 Good Parenting Tips—Best Advice," *Parenting for Brain*, February 3, 2021, https://www.parentingforbrain .com/how-to-be-a-good-parent-10-parenting-tips/.

59 **"shaming children . . . damage self-esteem . . . ":** Miller et al., "Self-Esteem as Folk Theory." Reprinted by permission of the publisher (Taylor & Francis Ltd, http://www.tandfonline.com).

59 **low self-esteem and proneness to depression . . . aggressive and antisocial tendencies:** E.g., Tamara J. Ferguson et al., "Guilt, Shame, and Symptoms in Children," *Developmental Psychology* 35, no. 2 (1999): 347–57; So Young Choe, Jungeun Olivia Lee, and Stephen J. Read, "Self-concept as a Mechanism through Which Parental Psychological Control Impairs Empathy Development from Adolescence to Emerging Adulthood," *Social Development* 29, no. 3 (2020): 713–31.

60 **"Do not spank, no matter what":** Arash Emamzadeh, "Do Not Spank Your Children," *Psychology Today*, 2018, https://www.psychologytoday.com/sg/ blog/finding-new-home/201809/do-not-spank-your-children.

60 **right from wrong:** Mark R. Lepper, "Social Control Processes and the Internalization of Social Values: An Attributional Perspective," *Social Cognition and Social Development*, 1983; Judith G. Smetana, "Parenting and the Development of Social Knowledge Reconceptualized: A Social Domain

Analysis," in *Parenting and the Internalization of Values*, ed. J. E. Grusec and L. Kuczynski (New York: John Wiley & Sons, Inc., 1997), 162–92.

60 **puts children's psychological health at risk:** E.g., Diana Baumrind, "Current Patterns of Parental Authority," *Developmental Psychology* 4, no. 1, Pt. 2 (1971): 1–103; Judith G. Smetana, "Parenting Styles and Conceptions of Parental Authority during Adolescence," *Child Development*, 1995, 299–316.

60 **the central role of *malu*:** Röttger-Rössler et al., "Socializing Emotions in Childhood."

61 **teach her little boy propriety:** Fung, "Becoming a Moral Child: The Socialization of Shame among Young Chinese Children."

62 **no good translation for self-esteem in Chinese:** Miller et al., "Self-Esteem as Folk Theory," 2002. It is not uncommon to have no word for self-esteem (for Japanese, see Steven J. Heine et al., "Is There a Universal Need for Positive Self-Regard?," *Psychological Review* 106, no. 4 [1999]: 766–94), and self-esteem has a negative connotation in some cultures. As Quinn notes: one Inuit woman tells Briggs that it is dangerous to think you are perfectly good (Quinn, "Universals of Child Rearing," 496).

62 **vicarious shame:** Heidi Fung and Eva C.-H. Chen, "Across Time and beyond Skin: Self and Transgression in the Everyday Socialization of Shame among Taiwanese Preschool Children," *Social Development* 10, no. 3 (2001): 419–37; Jin Li, Lianqin Wang, and Kurt W. Fisher, "The Organisation of Chinese Shame Concepts," *Cognition and Emotion* 18, no. 6 (2004): 767–97; Batja Mesquita and Mayumi Karasawa, "Self-Conscious Emotions as Dynamic Cultural Processes," *Psychological Inquiry* 15 (2004): 161–66; Röttger-Rössler et al., "Socializing Emotions in Childhood."

62 **seven middle-class Taiwanese families:** Fung and Chen, "Across Time and beyond Skin," 2001; quote from Axin's mom appears on p. 43. Copyright © 2001 by Wiley. Reprinted by permission of John Wiley and Sons Journals.

64 **"*Malu* makes us behave carefully":** Röttger-Rössler et al., "Socializing Emotions in Childhood," 273. Reprinted by permission of the publisher (Taylor & Francis Ltd, http://www.tandfonline.com).

64 **they should "know *tahotsy*":** Röttger-Rössler et al., "Socializing Emotions in Childhood," 274; other quotes on the Bara appear on pp. 275 and 277. Reprinted by permission of the publisher (Taylor & Francis Ltd, http://www.tandfonline.com).

66 **respect the social norms:** It is not my intention to give a full review of socializing emotions, but there are other examples of communities where fear is a central socializing emotion. Fear (*metagu*) among the Ifaluk (Lutz, *Unnatural Emotions*, 1988) follows as well as anticipates *song* (justifiable anger) of others, especially elders, and is also provoked by threats of a certain kind of ghost which is said to kidnap and eat children. It is used as a way to keep children in place. Among the Mfantse, a fishing community in West Ghana, fear (*suro adze*) is a socializing emotion as well (Quinn, "Universals of Child Rearing"). Beating is a prominent way of provoking this emotion, and "in some

households, the cane was left on prominent display"; to "warn misbehaving children to desist and, sometimes, to head off anticipated misbehavior before it happened" (p. 493).

66 **parental aggression:** "Based on field studies and the Human Relations Area Files (HRAF), parental punishment appears to increase aggressiveness in children, whereas parental warmth and permissiveness appear to reduce it. . . . In addition, harsh and aggressive initiation rites are assumed to instigate a retaliation motive . . . in cultures in which one believes in 'malevolent' gods, children are attacked and hurt in their early socialization and they become more aggressive" (Gisela Trommsdorff and Hans-Joachim Kornadt, "Parent-Child Relations in Cross-Cultural Perspective," in *Handbook of Dynamics in Parent-Child Relations*, ed. Leon Kuczynski [London: Sage, 2003], 295).

67 **"in defense of hierarchy and religious orthodoxy":** Quote from P. N. Stearns, *American Cool*, 62.

67 **"[T]he whippings the child constantly received":** David Hunt, 1970, quoted in Carol Z. Stearns, " 'Lord Help Me Walk Humbly': Anger and Sadness in England and America, 1570–1750," in *Emotion and Social Change: Toward a New Psychohistory*, ed. Carol Z. Stearns and Peter N. Stearns (Teaneck, NJ: Holmes & Meier, 1988), 49.

67 **"As the God-fearing qualities":** Stearns, *American Cool*, 22.

67 **"loving" in the first place:** Several historical developments may have laid at the root of this changed emphasis on mother love. Historians attribute this change in family relations to a starkly decreased child mortality, to a reduction in family size, and to industrialization (the latter having the effect of refocusing the nuclear family on itself).

68 **a reverend wrote in an 1839 issue of *The Mother's Magazine*:** Quote from Stearns, *American Cool*, 20; next quote, "Children of a loving mother cannot but desire to conform themselves to such models," from Stearns, *American Cool*, 35.

68 **Love . . . has arguably not ceded its place since:** Love, as we will see in chapter 4, grants a child some autonomy, but it can also be seen as the social glue in a society with declining cohesion and embedding, where families are separated during their daily activities. These speculations, while inspired by Stearns, *American Cool*, were not articulated by him.

68 **Japanese and German mothers responding to their disobedient five-year-olds:** Hans-Joachim Kornadt and Yoshiharu Tachibana, "Early Child-Rearing and Social Motives after Nine Years: A Cross-Cultural Longitudinal Study," in *Merging Past, Present, and Future in Cross-Cultural Psychology*, ed. Walter J. Lonner et al. (London: Swets & Zeitlinger, 1999), 429–41; Trommsdorff and Kornadt, "Parent-Child Relations in Cross-Cultural Perspective," 2003; quote in this paragraph appears on Trommsdorff and Kornadt, p. 296.

68 **Japanese children were more empathetic:** This conclusion is based on Hans-Joachim Kornadt and Yoshiharu Tachibana, "Early Child-Rearing and Social Motives after Nine Years," 1999 (reprinted as "Early Child-Rearing and Social

Motives after Nine Years: A Cross-Cultural Longitudinal Study," *Merging Past, Present, and Future in Cross-Cultural Psychology*, 2020, 429–41), who used helping scenarios to elicit different components of "behavior motivation." The details of this method are only sparsely documented in the article.

68 ***amae*:** T. Doi, "Amae: A Key Concept for Understanding Japanese Personality Structure," in *Japanese Culture: Its Development and Characteristics*, ed. R. J. Smith and R. K. Beardsley (Psychology Press, 1962), 132–52; Michael Boiger, Yukiko Uchida, and Igor de Almeida, "Amae, Saudade, Schadenfreude," in *The Routledge Handbook of Emotion Theory*, ed. Andrea Scarantino (New York: Taylor & Francis, n.d.).

69 ***Omoiyari* " . . . satisfy their wishes":** Takie S. Lebra, *Japanese Patterns of Behaviour* (Honolulu: University of Hawaii Press, 1976), 38.

69 **harmonious relatedness that is culturally valued in Japan:** Fred Rothbaum et al., "The Development of Close Relationships in Japan and the United States: Paths of Symbiotic Harmony and Generative Tension," *Child Development* 71, no. 5 (September 2000): 1121–42; Takie S. Lebra, "Mother and Child in Japanese Socialization: A Japan-U.S. Comparison," in *Cross-Cultural Roots of Minority Child Development*, ed. Patricia M. Greenfield and Rodney R. Cocking (Hillsdale, NJ: Lawrence Erlbaum Associates, 1994), 259–74; Hiroshi Azuma, "Two Modes of Cognitive Socialization in Japan and the United States," in *Cross-Cultural Roots of Minority Child Development*, ed. Patricia M. Greenfield and Rodney R. Cocking (Hillsdale, NJ: Psychology Press, 1994), 275–84.

69 **Perspective taking:** Lebra, "Mother and Child in Japanese Socialization"; Azuma, "Two Modes of Cognitive Socialization in Japan and the United States"; Heine et al., "Is There a Universal Need for Positive Self-Regard?"

69 **Japanese preschool practices:** Akiko Hayashi, Mayumi Karasawa, and Joseph Tobin, "The Japanese Preschool's Pedagogy of Feeling: Cultural Strategies for Supporting Young Children's Emotional Development," *Ethos* 37, no. 1 (March 2009): 32–49, quotes appear on pp. 37, 38, and 46.

70 **U.S. teachers:** Joseph Tobin, Yeh Hsueh, and Mayumi Karasawa, *Preschool in Three Cultures Revisited: China, Japan, and the United States* (Chicago: University of Chicago Press, 2009), e.g., p. 110.

71 **sensitive enough to take perspective:** A similar conjecture is made by Lebra, "Mother and Child in Japanese Socialization"; Azuma, "Two Modes of Cognitive Socialization in Japan and the United States"; Rothbaum et al., "The Development of Close Relationships in Japan and the United States."

71 **"a good child is one who is always calm":** Heidi Keller and Hiltrud Otto, "The Cultural Socialization of Emotion Regulation during Infancy," *Journal of Cross-Cultural Psychology* 40, no. 6 (November 2009): 1002; "If the child is crying at times . . ." appears on p. 1003.

71 **a kid that "stays put":** Keller and her colleagues created a culturally adapted strange situation, an experimental paradigm used to measure "attachment." In this paradigm mothers leave the baby and a stranger comes in. The majority of

Western infants start crying or whimpering at that point, but the majority of Nso infants did not show any emotion. Keller points out that "This behavior is definitely not the same as the secure behavior shown by the majority of Western middle class infants. The latter are stressed in the presence of a stranger, and only at ease in the presence of the mother." Keller and Otto, "The Cultural Socialization of Emotion Regulation during Infancy," 1007.

71 **Nso babies . . . adjust to circumstances:** In research in the '60s and '70s, notably William Caudill and Lois Frost, "A Comparison of Maternal Care and Infant Behavior in Japanese-American, American, and Japanese Families," in W. P. Lebra (ed.), *Youth, Socialization, and Mental Health* (University Press of Hawaii, 1972); William Caudill and Helen Weinstein, "Maternal Care and Infant Behavior in Japan and America," *Psychiatry* 32, no. 1 (1969): 12–43, Japanese mothers have been similarly described to soothe their babies, certainly compared to U.S, American (likely white) mothers in the same studies who aimed at stimulating their babies. For a good review with more recent examples, see also Jeanne L Tsai, "Ideal Affect: Cultural Causes and Behavioral Consequences," *Perspectives on Psychological Science* 2, no. 3 (2007): 245.

72 **"You have to smile":** Keller and Otto, "The Cultural Socialization of Emotion Regulation during Infancy," p. 1004; "Don't you want to lie down anymore? Do you need your pacifier?" appears on the same page.

72 **face-to-face contact:** Heidi Keller, *Cultures of Infancy* (New York: Psychology Press, 2009).

72 **a "big smile," or . . . a "small smile":** Jeanne L Tsai et al., "Learning What Feelings to Desire: Socialization of Ideal Affect through Children's Storybooks," *Personality and Social Psychology Bulletin* 33, no. 1 (2007): 17–30.

73 **"I am not gonna care for you if you keep crying":** Fung and Chen, "Across Time and beyond Skin," 432. Copyright © 2001 by Wiley. Reprinted by permission of John Wiley and Sons Journals.

73 **Jeanne Tsai's theory:** Jeanne L. Tsai et al., "Influence and Adjustment Goals: Sources of Cultural Differences in Ideal Affect," *Journal of Personality and Social Psychology* 92, no. 6 (2007): 1102–17; Tsai, "Ideal Affect: Cultural Causes and Behavioral Consequences."

74 **influencers . . . more excited, and adjusters more calm:** Tsai et al., "Influence and Adjustment Goals," 2007.

74 **"German mothers . . . Nso mothers":** Keller, *Cultures of Infancy*; Keller and Otto, "The Cultural Socialization of Emotion Regulation during Infancy."

75 **"terrible twos":** Bright Horizons Education Team, "Toddlers and Twos: Parenting during the 'No' Stage," *Bright Horizons,* accessed February 10, 2021, https://www.brighthorizons.com/family-resources/toddlers-and-twos-the-no-stage.

75 **An article on adolescence in *Psychology Today*:** Carl E. Pickhardt, "Adolescence and Anger," *Psychology Today,* July 26, 2010, https://www.psychologytoday.com/us/blog/surviving-your-childs-adolescence/201007/adolescence-and-anger.

75 **Psychologist Pamela Cole and her colleagues:** Pamela M. Cole, Carole J. Bruschi, and Babu L. Tamang, "Cultural Differences in Children's Emotional Reactions to Difficult Situations," *Child Development*, 2002. The eraser vignette appears on p. 993. Copyright © 2002 by the Society for Research in Child Development. Reprinted by permission of John Wiley and Sons Journals.

76 **"I snatched the eraser":** Cole, Bruschi, and Tamang, "Cultural Differences in Children's Emotional Reactions to Difficult Situations," 992. Copyright © 2002 by the Society for Research in Child Development. Reprinted by permission of John Wiley and Sons Journals.

76 **The observational study of German and Japanese:** Kornadt and Tachibana, "Early Child-Rearing and Social Motives after Nine Years: A Cross-Cultural Longitudinal Study"; Trommsdorff and Kornadt, "Parent-Child Relations in Cross-Cultural Perspective"; "he wants to make me angry" appears on p. 296 of Trommsdorff and Kornadt, "Parent-Child Relations in Cross-Cultural Perspective."

77 **three working-class mothers:** Peggy Miller and Linda L. Sperry, "The Socialization of Anger and Aggression," *Merril-Palmer Quarterly* 33, no. 1 (1987): 1–31. Reprinted by permission of the publisher (Taylor & Francis Ltd, http://www.tandfonline.com). Interactions between mothers and daughters were followed and video-taped over a period of eight months (once every three weeks); "be strong, to suppress hurt feelings, and to defend themselves when wronged" appears on p. 18; narrative starting with "He started that shit . . ." on p. 12; exchange starting with "You want to fight about it? . . ." is described on p. 21; the exchange describing Wendy's temper tantrum about her "ninny" is described on pp. 21–22.

78 **the ideal child:** The sociologist Adrie Kusserow distinguishes between soft individualism and hard defensive individualism. She describes child-rearing in a upper-middle-class neighborhood and a working-class one, both in the New York area. In the middle-class neighborhood, parents focus on their children's emotions and desires, as a way to develop their unique personalities; in contrast, in the working-class neighborhood, parents teach their children to rely on themselves, and create tough boundaries as a way to deal with hardship ("De-Homogenizing American Individualism: Socializing Hard and Soft Individualism in Manhattan and Queens," *Ethos* 27, no. 2 [1999]: 210–34). The South Baltimore moms in Miller and Sperry's study seem to foster hard defensive individualism, and in doing so, are less interested in what the child feels than what the child does.

79 **"no *ihuma*":** Jean L. Briggs, *Never in Anger: Portrait of an Eskimo Family* (Cambridge, MA: Harvard University Press, 1970): 111; her "hostility took the form not of attack but of sullenness: a passive, but total resistance to social overtures" appears on p. 137. Copyright © 1970 by the President and Fellows of Harvard College.

80 **good adults in our communities:** Of course, not all caretaking is deliberately directed toward the goal of raising a culturally valued adult: a lot of what

parents do is just making sure their children are safe and fed, although cultural values even seep into those everyday routines (e.g., Richard A. Shweder, Lene A. Jensen, and William M. Goldstein, "Who Sleeps by Whom Revisited: A Method for Extracting the Moral Goods Implicit in Practice," in *Cultural Practices as Contexts for Development*, vol. 67, 1995, 21–39; Keller, *Cultures of Infancy*; Patricia M. Greenfield et al., "Cultural Pathways Through Universal Development," *Annual Review of Psychology* 54, no. 1 [2003]: 461–90).

80 **emotions that support the cultural social norms and values:** Birgitt Röttger-Rössler et al., "Learning (by) Feeling: A Cross-Cultural Comparison of the Socialization and Development of Emotions," *Ethos* 43, no. 2 (2015): 188.

80 **methods . . . are strongly moralized:** There are many other examples. In Bara community, but also in many African American families, beating is what caring parents do (leading to the instilment of proper fear); in other cultures beating is condemned as disrespect for the integrity of the child. In middle-class European American households, caring parents talk to their infants; Guisii mothers (Western Kenya) told anthropologists that it would be silly to talk to a baby (Robert A. LeVine et al., *Communication and Social Learning during Infancy* [Cambridge, UK: Cambridge University Press, 1994]); N. Quinn and H. F. Mathews. 2016. "Emotional Arousal in the Making of Cultural Selves." *Anthropological Theory* 16 (4): 359–89.

81 **met disapproval or were being ignored:** Similar ideas can be found in Quinn and Otto, "Emotional Arousal in the Making of Cultural Selves."

Chapter 4 "RIGHT" AND "WRONG" EMOTIONS

83 **cultural differences (and similarities) in every aspect of emotions:** Batja Mesquita and Nico Frijda, "Cultural Variations in Emotions: A Review," *Psychological Bulletin* 112, no. 2 (1992): 179–204.

83 **I now understand a logic to it:** Batja Mesquita, "Emotions as Dynamic Cultural Phenomena," in *Handbook of Affective Sciences*, ed. Richard J. Davidson, Klaus R. Scherer, and H. Hill Goldsmith (Oxford, UK: Oxford University Press, 2003), 871–90; Batja Mesquita, Michael Boiger, and Jozefien De Leersnyder, "The Cultural Construction of Emotions," *Current Opinion in Psychology* 8 (2016): 31–36; Batja Mesquita and Janxin Leu, "The Cultural Psychology of Emotion," in *Handbook of Cultural Psychology*, ed. Shinobu Kitayama and Dov Cohen (New York: Guilford Press, 2007), 734–59; Tsai and Clobert, "Cultural Influences on Emotion: Empirical Patterns and Emerging Trends."

84 **culture of close interdependence . . . culture . . . not depend on anybody:** Fred Rothbaum et al., "The Development of Close Relationships in Japan and the United States: Paths of Symbiotic Harmony and Generative Tension," *Child Development* 71, no. 5 (September 2000): 1121–42.

84 **"right" in some cultures . . . , but "wrong" in others:** Michael Boiger et al.,

"Condoned or Condemned: The Situational Affordance of Anger and Shame in the United States and Japan," *Personality and Social Psychology Bulletin* 39, no. 4 (2013): 540–53; Michael Boiger et al., "Defending Honour, Keeping Face: Interpersonal Affordances of Anger and Shame in Turkey and Japan," *Cognition and Emotion* 28, no. 7 (January 3, 2014): 1255–69; Owen Flanagan, *How to Do Things with Emotions: The Morality of Anger and Shame across Cultures* (Princeton, NJ: Princeton University Press, 2021).

85 **Anger *itself* takes a stance:** Robert C. Solomon, *Not Passion's Slave: Emotions and Choice* (Oxford, UK: Oxford University Press, 2003), 88. In an astute analysis of anger, he calls it a "judgmental emotion, a perception of offense. . . . Getting angry is making an indictment (whether overtly or not)."

85 **dependent on its reception:** See also Michael Boiger and Batja Mesquita, "The Construction of Emotion in Interactions, Relationships, and Cultures," *Emotion Review* 4, no. 3 (2012): 221–29; Emily A. Butler and Ashley K. Randall, "Emotional Coregulation in Close Relationships," *Emotion Review* 5, no. 2 (2013): 202–10; Parkinson, *Heart to Heart.*

86 **a representative study of middle-aged U.S. Americans:** The particular finding is reported by Jiyoung Park et al., "Social Status and Anger Expression: The Cultural Moderation Hypothesis," *Emotion* 13, no. 6 (2013): 1122–31.

86 **selfless love was the cornerstone of marriage:** Stearns, *American Cool.*

86 **difficulty describing themselves as angry:** Carol Z. Stearns, "'Lord Help Me Walk Humbly': Anger and Sadness in England and America, 1570–1750." Interestingly, Stearns also notes that most diarists lacked interest in their mental lives at all. The ones who did focus on their feelings, failed to label themselves as angry. Quotes are from Roger Lowe's diary, as reported by Stearns, Lord, 41.

87 **an extremely destructive emotion:** Richard A. Shweder et al., "The Cultural Psychology of the Emotions: Ancient and Renewed," in *Handbook of Emotions*, ed. Michael Lewis, Jeannette M. Haviland-Jones, and Lisa F. Barrett, 3rd ed. (New York: Guilford Press, 2008), 409–27.

87 **condemned anger in their everyday lives:** Lutz, *Unnatural Emotions.*

87 **the complete condemnation of anger:** Owen Flanagan, "Introduction: The Moral Psychology of Anger," in *The Moral Psychology of Anger*, ed. Myisha Cherry and Owen Flanagan (London: Rowman & Littlefield International Ltd., 2018), vii–xxxi; Flanagan, *How to Do Things with Emotions*; see also B. H. Rosenwein, *Anger. The Conflicted History of an Emotion* (New Haven, CT: Yale University Press, 2020).

88 **U.S. American college students have more anger:** Boiger et al., "Condoned or Condemned: The Situational Affordance of Anger and Shame in the United States and Japan"; Shinobu Kitayama, Batja Mesquita, and Mayumi Karasawa, "Cultural Affordances and Emotional Experience," *Journal of Personality and Social Psychology* 91, no. 5 (2006): 890–903.

88 **so do middle-aged American:** Park et al., "Social Status and Anger Expression"; no evidence was reported that the cultural differences only held for one of the gender.

88 **more readily angered . . . in similar situations:** Kitayama, Mesquita, and Karasawa, "Cultural Affordances and Emotional Experience," Study 2.

88 **Anger as nonacceptance is woven into a general view on life:** The argument was also (and first) made by Robert C. Solomon in "Getting Angry: The Jamesian Theory of Emotion in Anthropology," 1984, 249. In his view, legitimacy, blame, and responsibility, and therefore "anger," are culture-bound concepts.

88 **sales team whose mission failed:** L. Z. Tiedens, P. C. Ellsworth, and B. Mesquita, "Sentimental Stereotypes: Emotional Expectations for High- and Low-Status Group Members," *Personality & Social Psychology Bulletin* 26, no. 5 (2000): 560–74.

88 *song* **("justifiable anger"):** Lutz, *Unnatural Emotions.*

88 **report angry behaviors:** Park et al., "Social Status and Anger Expression."

89 **anger . . . in Japan is . . . healthy:** Shinobu Kitayama et al., "Expression of Anger and Ill Health in Two Cultures: An Examination of Inflammation and Cardiovascular Risk," *Psychological Science* 26, no. 2 (2015): 211–20. Expressing anger was associated with less biological health risk in Japan, whereas it was associated with more biological health risk in the U.S. Participants were subsamples of representative studies of middle-aged Japanese and U.S. Americans. Biological health risk was measured by two inflammatory measures and two measures of cardiovascular malfunction. The authors suggest that the different meanings of anger, as an index of power or dominance in Japan and as an index of frustration in the U.S., may be responsible for the culturally different association. It is a good hypothesis (which I have adopted in the main text) that deserves follow-up study.

89 **anger as a power move may pay off:** Larissa Z. Tiedens, "Anger and Advancement versus Sadness and Subjugation: The Effect of Negative Emotion Expression on Social Status Conferral," *Journal of Personality and Social Psychology* 80, no. 1 (2001): 86–94.

90 **"showed bad character, pure and simple":** Quoted come from Stearns, *American Cool*, 25. Anger was condemned in men too, but "an angry woman was worse than an angry man" (also on p. 25).

90 **struck by the fate of another Clinton:** Victoria L. Brescoll and Eric Luis Uhlmann, "Can an Angry Woman Get Ahead?," *Psychological Science* 19, no. 3 (2008): 268–75. The quote is from Maureen Dowd, "Who's Hormonal? Hillary or Dick?," *New York Times*, February 8, 2006, as cited on Brescoll and Uhlmann, "Can an Angry Woman Get Ahead?," 2008, p. 268.

90 **there is an emotional glass ceiling:** Among female job applicants, those who did not express any emotion, rather than being either sad or angry, were perceived to be most effective leaders. Angry men were perceived effective, as were neutral-looking men (Brescoll and Uhlmann, "Can an Angry Woman Get Ahead?").

90 **Davin Phoenix makes this point precisely:** Davin Phoenix, "Anger Benefits Some Americans Much More than Others," *New York Times*, June 6, 2020,

https://www.nytimes.com/2020/06/06/opinion/george-floyd-protests-anger
.html?referringSource=articleShare.

91 **anger among the Kaluli . . . is a power move:** Edward L. Schieffelin, "Anger and Shame in the Tropical Forest: On Affect as a Cultural System in Papua New Guinea," *Ethos* 11, no. 3 (1983): 181–91. The quote appears on p. 183. It is not clear if the anger dynamics of Kaluli women are the same as those of men.

91 **in so-called honor cultures:** There are honor cultures around the world, and anger has been described as playing the role of claiming or reclaiming honor in the ones I know. There is quite a bit of anthropological work on honor cultures in Mediterranean regions (most notably Lila Abu-Lughod, *Veiled Sentiments: Honor and Poetry in a Bedouin Society* [Berkeley: University of California Press, 1986]; J. G. Peristiany, *Honour and Shame: The Values of Mediterranean Society* [Chicago: University of Chicago Press, 1974]).

91 **claim to precedence:** Ayse K. Uskul et al., "Honor Bound: The Cultural Construction of Honor in Turkey and the Northern United States," *Journal of Cross Cultural Psychology* 43, no. 7 (2012): 1131–51; Angela K.-Y. Leung and Dov Cohen, "Within- and between-Culture Variation: Individual Differences and the Cultural Logics of Honor, Face, and Dignity Cultures," *Journal of Personality and Social Psychology* 100, no. 3 (2011): 507–26.

91 **honor in the southern United States:** Richard E. Nisbett and Dov Cohen, *Culture of Honor: The Psychology of Violence in the South* (Boulder, CO: Westview Press, 1996); quote appears on p. 5; The original "asshole" experiment was reported also in D. Cohen et al., "Insult, Aggression, and the Southern Culture of Honor: An 'Experimental Ethnography,'" *Journal of Personality and Social Psychology* 70, no. 5 (1996): 945–60.

92 **separating children . . . at the Mexican border:** The family separation policy was introduced under U.S. President Donald Trump's tough immigration policy and adopted across the U.S.-Mexico border from April 2018 until June 2018. Under the policy, more than four thousand children were separated from their parents, some of whom never saw each other again ("Immigration Policy of Donald Trump," Wikipedia, 2021, https://en.wikipedia.org/wiki/Immigration_policy_of_Donald_Trump).

92 **a core theme of anger:** The reason to start from those prompts rather than from the equivalents of anger was precisely that we were not sure if the meaning of anger and its translation in Japanese (*ikari*) would be equivalent. In comparing the emotional stories, we did not want to bias our results by differences implicated by the words; more on this in chapter 6.

96 **What if anger . . . stance in the relationship?:** See Solomon, "Getting Angry"; Solomon, *Not Passion's Slave,* for a similar idea.

96 **shame is "wrong":** E.g., Helen B. Lewis, "Shame and Guilt in Neurosis," *Psychoanalytic Review* 58, no. 3 (1971): 419–38; June P. Tangney et al., "Are Shame, Guilt, and Embarrassment Distinct Emotions?," *Journal of Personality and Social Psychology* 70, no. 6 (1996): 1256–69.

96 **being evaluated by others and found to be deficient:** Boiger et al., "Condoned or Condemned." In a U.S. sample of college students, vignettes in which others pointed out your personal flaws were in fact rated as most shameful.

97 **this type of event had never happened to them:** A study with American college students, predominantly white, suggested that the more shame situations are judged to elicit, the lower their frequency was. The situations at hand were vignettes based on previously self-reported shame situations, and respondents who read them both rated the intensity of shame they would feel in such a situation, and their perceived frequency (Boiger et al., "Condoned or Condemned").

98 **salespeople in the financial sector:** Richard P. Bagozzi, Willem Verbeke, and Jacinto C. Gavino, "Culture Moderates the Self-Regulation of Shame and Its Effects on Performance: The Case of Salespersons in the Netherlands and the Philippines," *Journal of Applied Psychology* 88, no. 2 (2003): 219–33.

98 **shame stories that involved customers:** Shame stories were collected in focus groups with financial salespeople from a firm that did not participate in the final study. Bagozzi, Verbeke, and Gavino, "Culture Moderates the Self-Regulation of Shame and Its Effects on Performance." The article does not provide much detail on the process by which those stories were selected.

99 **feel like "crawling in a hole," "suddenly shrinking," and "physically weak" and "tongue-tied":** Items used to measure the phenomenology of shame. Bagozzi, Verbeke, and Gavino, "Culture Moderates the Self-Regulation of Shame and Its Effects on Performance," 232.

99 **Dutch salespeople . . . would "strive to be unique . . .":** Bagozzi, Verbeke, and Gavino, "Culture Moderates the Self-Regulation of Shame and Its Effects on Performance," 220.

99 **no longer able to deliver appropriate service:** I use slightly different labels than Bagozzi et al. do, but my labels are equally based on the actual scale items that were used. All findings are self-reported.

99 **situations that had elicited shame:** Boiger et al., "Condoned or Condemned"; the examples are real experiences reported in previous studies—names are fictitious—that were used as vignettes in the study. The precise wording of the vignettes can be found in the supplemental materials to the article.

100 **strong defenses:** Sana Sheikh, "Cultural Variations in Shame's Responses," *Personality and Social Psychology Review* 18, no. 4 (2014): 387–403; Alexander Kirchner et al., "Humiliated Fury Is Not Universal: The Co-Occurrence of Anger and Shame in the United States and Japan," *Cognition and Emotion* 32, no. 6 (2018): 1317–28.

100 **"humiliated fury":** Term was coined by Lewis, "Shame and Guilt in Neurosis."

100 **transforms it into aggression towards others:** E.g., June P. Tangney et al., "Shamed into Anger? The Relation of Shame and Guilt to Anger and Self-Reported Aggression," *Journal of Personality and Social Psychology* 62, no. 4 (1992): 669–75.

100 **the bleak future of recidivism:** When inmates did not externalize blame, their shame predicted less crime after they were released from prison (June P. Tangney, Jeffrey Stuewig, and Andres G. Martinez, "Two Faces of Shame: The Roles of Shame and Guilt in Predicting Recidivism," *Psychological Science* 25, no. 3 [2014]: 799–805).

100 **mostly psychoanalysts:** E.g., Karen Horney, *The Neurotic Personality of Our Time* (New York: W. W. Norton & Company, 1937), as cited in Sheikh, "Cultural Variations in Shame's Responses," 2014; Gershen Kaufman, *The Psychology of Shame: Theory and Treatment of Shame-Based Syndromes* (New York: Springer Publishing Co., 2004).

100 **vulnerable to depression, anxiety, and somatic symptoms:** Jeffrey Stuewig et al., "Children's Proneness to Shame and Guilt Predict Risky and Illegal Behaviors in Young Adulthood," *Child Psychiatry and Human Development* 46, no. 2 (2015): 217–27. The attention of clinical psychologists has been devoted to the "shame-prone" individual, rather than to isolated instances of shame.

100 **"a short step . . . disapproving":** June P. Tangney and Ronda L. Dearing, *Shame and Guilt* (New York: Guilford Press, 2002), 93.

101 **care about your bond with others:** The common thread across shame instances may be that it is a bid for acceptance, or at the very least, an acknowledgment that acceptance by others may be problematic. Some have proposed that shame has grown out of an act of subordinance: the less powerful yielding to the more powerful (Daniel M. T. Fessler, "Shame in Two Cultures: Implications for Evolutionary Approaches," *Journal of Cognition and Culture* 4, no. 2 [2004]: 207–62. See also, Dacher Keltner and LeeAnne Harker, "The Forms and Functions of the Nonverbal Signal of Shame," in *Shame: Interpersonal Behavior, Psychopathology, and Culture*, ed. P. Gilbert and B. Andrews [Oxford University Press, 1998], 78–98). Shame is not universally limited to situations in which the self is poorly evaluated (Fessler, 2004).

101 **"An Admirable Culture of Shame":** Nassrine Azimi, "An Admirable Culture of Shame," *New York Times*, 2010, https://www.nytimes.com/2010/06/08/opinion/08iht-edazimi.html.

101 **Shame fits this focus on self-criticism:** Steven J. Heine et al., "Is There a Universal Need for Positive Self-Regard?," *Psychological Review* 106, no. 4 (1999): 770.

101 **Shame is . . . less unpleasant in Japanese:** Kimball A. Romney, Carmella C. Moore, and Craig D. Rusch, "Cultural Universals: Measuring the Semantic Structure of Emotion Terms in English and Japanese," *Proceedings of the National Academy of Sciences* 94, no. 10 (1997): 5489–94.

102 **keen motivation not to burden others:** E.g., Hiroshi Azuma, "Two Modes of Cognitive Socialization in Japan and the United States," in *Cross-Cultural Roots of Minority Child Development*, ed. Patricia M. Greenfield and Rodney R. Cocking (Hillsdale, NJ: Psychology Press, 1994), 275–84; Akiko Hayashi, Mayumi Karasawa, and Joseph Tobin, "The Japanese Preschool's Pedagogy

of Feeling: Cultural Strategies for Supporting Young Children's Emotional Development," *Ethos* 37, no. 1 (March 2009): 32–49.

102 **risks jeopardizing the relationship:** Psychologists Yukiko Uchida and Shinobu Kitayama make a similar observation ("Happiness and Unhappiness in East and West: Themes and Variations," *Emotion* 9, no. 4 [2009]: 442): "Unhappiness in East and West: Themes and Variations," *Emotion* 9, no. 4 [2009]: 442): "Accomplishing one's goals might be perceived as good insofar as others also feel happy about it. If it should invite envy of others, the sense of accomplishment might be compromised."

102 **remedying your shortcomings:** E.g., Heine et al., "Is There a Universal Need for Positive Self-Regard?"; Shinobu Kitayama et al., "Individual and Collective Processes in the Construction of the Self: Self-Enhancement in the United States and Self-Criticism in Japan," *Journal of Personality and Social Psychology* 72, no. 6 (1997): 1245–67; Lewis, C. C. 1995. *Educating Hearts and Minds*. New York: Cambridge Press.

102 **Japanese respondents reported higher frequencies of shame:** Kitayama, Mesquita, and Karasawa, "Cultural Affordances and Emotional Experience"; Boiger et al., "Condoned or Condemned." Similarly, respondents in Benkulu (on the Sumatran island of Indonesia) reported shame to be one of the most frequent emotions, while middle-class Southern Californians reported it to be one of the rarest (D. M. T. Fessler, "Shame in Two Cultures: Implications for Evolutionary Approaches," *Journal of Cognition and Culture* 4, no. 2 [2004]: 207–62).

102 **their Filipino counterparts:** Bagozzi, Verbeke, and Gavino, "Culture Moderates the Self-Regulation of Shame and Its Effects on Performance."

103 **can count on their friend's or spouse's acceptance and support:** Kitayama and Markus, "The Pursuit of Happiness and the Realization of Sympathy: Cultural Patterns of Self, Social Relations, and Well-Being."

103 **Japanese . . . encountered many situations eliciting strong shame:** Boiger et al., "Condoned or Condemned."

103 **his friend Mehmet falsely accused him:** "False accusations" were the most frequently reported honor-attacking situations in a study with a large sample of Turkish undergraduates (Uskul et al., "Honor Bound," study 1).

104 **almost all Turkish respondents told us they ended the relationship:** In fact, in this small study almost all (out of seven) Turkish and only one (out of six) Dutch participants reported that they ended the relationship with the close other who had offended them; and more than half of the (nine) Turkish participants reported they had ended the relationship with a more distant other who had offended them versus two (out of nine) Dutch participants (Batja Mesquita, "Cultural Variations in Emotions: A Comparative Study of Dutch, Surinamese, and Turkish People in the Netherlands" [University of Amsterdam, 1993]): 144).

104 **concerned with the impact of the event on the respect they, their family, or their ingroup received:** Mesquita, "Cultural Variations in Emotions." In a

survey study, I confirmed that Turkish participants perceived a greater impact of these situations on their own, their family, and their ingroup respect (Batja Mesquita, "Emotions in Collectivist and Individualist Contexts," *Journal of Personality and Social Psychology* 80, no. 1 (2001): 68–74). Turkish respondents in Uskul et al.'s research also reported that honor-attacking situations would have greater impact on the feelings relatives and friends would have about themselves than did the U.S. respondents in this research (Uskul et al., "Honor Bound").

104 **which in other honor cultures are highly connected with shame:** Patricia M. Rodriguez Mosquera, Antony S. R. Manstead, and Agneta H. Fischer, "The Role of Honour Concerns in Emotional Reactions to Offences," *Cognition & Emotion* 16, no. 1 (2002): 143–63. This study compared insults in Spain, another honor culture, and the Netherlands. Spanish but not the Dutch students reported that they would feel as much shame as they would feel anger in response to imaginary insults; Spanish students reporting the most shame perceived a threat to their family honor.

105 **ripple effect of shame:** Uskul et al., "Honor Bound."

105 **specifically studied family honor:** Patricia M. Rodriguez Mosquera, Leslie X. Tan, and Faisal Saleem, "Shared Burdens, Personal Costs on the Emotional and Social Consequences of Family Honor," *Journal of Cross Cultural Psychology* 45, no. 3 (2013): 400–16.

105 **the highest threat to the family honor:** Rodriguez Mosquera, Tan, and Saleem, "Shared Burdens, Personal Costs on the Emotional and Social Consequences of Family Honor."

106 **Shame is everywhere in honor cultures:** In one of our studies, we did in fact find that events that were seen to be shameful in Turkey were perceived to be frequent (Boiger et al., "Defending Honour, Keeping Face"; see also Batja Mesquita and Nico H. Frijda, "Cultural Variations in Emotions: A Review," *Psychological Bulletin* 112, no. 2 [1992]: 179–204).

106 **not even the most important one:** Rodriguez Mosquera, "Cultural Concerns," 2018; Patricia M. Rodriguez Mosquera, "On the Importance of Family, Morality, Masculine, and Feminine Honor for Theory and Research," *Social and Personality Psychology Compass* 10, no. 8 (2016): 431–42.

106 **you must act:** E.g., Leung and Cohen, "Within- and between-Culture Variation" (variation on what they write on p. 3).

107 **the (sexual) modesty of the female relatives:** Abu-Lughod, *Veiled Sentiments*, 1986; Peristiany, "Honour and Shame in a Cypriot Highland"; Rodriguez Mosquera, "On the Importance of Family, Morality, Masculine, and Feminine Honor for Theory and Research."

107 **a dignified way for women . . . to achieve respect and honor:** Abu-Lughod, *Veiled Sentiments*.

108 **"wanting to dissolve into nothing":** Nico H. Frijda, *The Emotions* (Cambridge, UK: Cambridge University Press / Éditions de la Maison des Sciences de l'Homme, 1986).

108 **being judged by others . . . falling short of the standard:** Michael Boiger

et al., "Protecting Autonomy, Protecting Relatedness: Appraisal Patterns of Daily Anger and Shame in the United States and Japan," *Japanese Psychological Research* 58, no. 1 (2016): 28–41.

108 **"public evaluations" . . . "self-failure":** Rodriguez Mosquera, Manstead, and Fischer, "The Role of Honor-Related Values in the Elicitation, Experience, and Communication of Pride, Shame, and Anger."

Chapter 5 BEING CONNECTED AND FEELING GOOD

111 **the enterprise has been WEIRD:** E.g., Charles R. Snyder and Shane J. Lopez, *Handbook of Positive Psychology* (New York: Oxford University Press, 2001). Shane J. Lopez and Charles R. Snyder, *The Oxford Handbook of Positive Psychology*, 2nd ed. (New York: Oxford University Press, 2012).

111 **"broadening and building":** E.g., Barbara L. Fredrickson, "The Role of Positive Emotions in Positive Psychology: The Broaden-and-Build Theory of Positive Emotions," *American Psychologist* 56, no. 3 (2001): 218–26.

111 **building . . . the social connection with others:** Barbara L. Fredrickson, "The Role of Positive Emotions in Positive Psychology: The Broaden-and-Build Theory of Positive Emotions," *American Psychologist*, 56, no. 3 (2001), 218–26; Sara B. Algoe, Jonathan Haidt, and Shelly L. Gable, "Beyond Reciprocity: Gratitude and Relationships in Everyday Life," *Emotion* 8, no. 3 (2008): 425–29; Sara B. Algoe, Shelly L. Gable, and Natalya C. Maisel, "It's the Little Things: Everyday Gratitude as a Booster Shot for Romantic Relationships," *Personal Relationships* 17, no. 2 (2010): 217–33.

112 **loves and happinesses are tailored:** The point was made for love by A. E. Beall and R. J. Sternberg, "The Social Construction of Love," *Journal of Social and Personal Relationships* 12, no. 3 (August 30, 1995): 417–38.

112 **Love is a staple:** Lutz, *Unnatural Emotions,* 145.

112 **love as "the best example":** Shaver et al., "Emotion Knowledge: Further Exploration of a Prototype Approach." Fessler similarly finds that a group of English-speaking Southern Californians reports the emotion of love to be the most frequent emotion of all in daily life ("Shame in Two Cultures: Implications for Evolutionary Approaches," 213–14). Many traditional emotion theories fail to list *love* as an emotion (see Phillip R. Shaver, Hillary J. Morgan, and Shelley Wu, "Is Love a 'Basic' Emotion?," *Personal Relationships* 3, no. 1 [1996]: Table 1, for an overview).

112 **"is one of the most important human emotions":** Beverley Fehr and James A. Russell, "The Concept of Love Viewed from a Prototype Perspective," *Journal of Personality and Social Psychology* 60, no. 3 (1991): Study 4. They distinguished at least 123 different types of love, but found maternal, paternal, friendship, sibling, and romantic love the best examples of love (Fehr and Russell, Study 1). Of course, not all instances of *love* are exactly the same, and features that occur in one instance (and for one concept) of love may not occur in another.

112 **A person who loves someone else:** Descriptions are taken from Study 2 of Shaver et al., "Emotion Knowledge: Further Exploration of a Prototype Approach," 1987, but many of the description also overlap with attributes that were seen to be shared by many types of love by Canadian college students in the eighties (Fehr and Russell, "The Concept of Love Viewed from a Prototype Perspective," Study 6). The idea of the latter study is that love concepts share a "family resemblance": "Although no single attribute may be shared by all, [different types of love] are linked through a complex pattern of criss-crossing and overlapping attributes" (p. 433). In both studies, respondents freely reported attributes of different types of love.

112 **"[Love] is a lot of sacrifice . . .":** Quote from Lutz (*Unnatural Emotions*, 146), who was the interviewer.

113 **Love . . . elevates one particular individual:** Lutz, *Unnatural Emotions*.

113 **to be united in mutual admiration:** A very similar analysis of North American close relationships is provided by Kitayama and Markus, "The Pursuit of Happiness and the Realization of Sympathy: Cultural Patterns of Self, Social Relations, and Well-Being."

113 **prioritize relationship and group goals:** E.g., C. Harry Hui and Harry C. Triandis, "Individualism-Collectivism: A Study of Cross-Cultural Researchers," *Journal of Cross-Cultural Psychology* 17, no. 2 (1986): 225–48; Harry C. Triandis, *Individualism and Collectivism* (Boulder, CO: Westview Press, 1995).

113 **an Indian woman giggled:** The clip comes from *Today Tonight*, an Australian TV show, and was recorded around 2011.

114 **understood love as "sad":** Shaver, Wu, and Schwartz, "Cross-Cultural Similarities and Differences in Emotion and Its Representation: A Prototype Approach"; Michael F. Mascolo, Kurt W. Fischer, and Jin Li, "Dynamic Development of Component Systems in Emotions: Pride, Shame and Guilt in China and the United States," in *Handbook of Affective Sciences*, ed. Richard J. Davidson, Klaus R. Scherer, and H. Hill Goldsmith (New York: Oxford University Press, 2003), 295–408.

114 **deference that children owed their parents:** Mascolo, Fischer, and Li, "Dynamic Development of Component Systems in Emotions"; Potter, "The Cultural Construction of Emotion in Rural Chinese Social Life"; James A. Russell and Michelle S. M. Yik, "Emotion among the Chinese," in *The Handbook of Chinese Psychology*, ed. Michael H. Bond (New York: Oxford University Press, 1996), 166–88.

114 **more negative features:** Chinese describing love spontaneously listed more negative features such as pain, sadness, sacrifice, and loneliness than American respondents; when both groups were explicitly asked about negative features, the differences were less pronounced (Shaver, Morgan, and Wu, "Is Love a 'Basic' Emotion?").

115 **very different from *love*:** Takeo Doi, *The Anatomy of Dependence* (Tokyo: Kodansha International, 1973); Susumu Yamaguchi, "Further Clarifications

of the Concept of Amae in Relation to Dependence and Attachment," *Human Development* 47, no. 1 (2004): 28–33; see also Boiger, Uchida, and de Almeida, "Amae, Saudade, Schadenfreude."

115 **The prototype of an *amae* relationship:** Lebra, "Mother and Child in Japanese Socialization: A Japan-U.S. Comparison," 261.

115 **created an interdependent relationship:** Hazel R. Markus and Shinobu Kitayama, "Culture and the Self: Implications for Cognition, Emotion, and Motivation," *Psychological Review* 98, no. 2 (1991): 224–53. *Amae* may be rejected, in which case the relationship is in jeopardy. The response of the rejected requester would be loneliness or sadness, but these emotions themselves reach for the valued type of relationship: interdependence.

115 ***fago*:** Lutz, *Unnatural Emotions*. The quote about *fago* for the visitor appears on pp. 137–38.

116 **The bad always comes with the good:** Li-Jun Ji, Richard E. Nisbett, and Yanjie Su, "Culture, Change, and Prediction," *Psychological Science* 12, no. 6 (2001): 450–56; J. Leu et al., "Situational Differences in Dialectical Emotions: Boundary Conditions in a Cultural Comparison of North Americans and East Asians," *Cognition and Emotion* 24, no. 3 (2010): 419–35.

117 ***more intimacy* in relationships:** Shelley E. Taylor et al., "Culture and Social Support: Who Seeks It and Why?," *Journal of Personality and Social Psychology* 87, no. 3 (2004): 354–62; Heejung S. Kim et al., "Pursuit of Comfort and Pursuit of Harmony: Culture, Relationships, and Social Support Seeking," *Personality and Social Psychology Bulletin* 32, no. 12 (2006): 1595–1607; Heejung S. Kim, David K. Sherman, and Shelley E. Taylor, "Culture and Social Support," *American Psychologist* 63, no. 6 (2008): 518–26.

117 **caution about friends:** All examples come from G. Adams, "The Cultural Grounding of Personal Relationship: Enemyship in North American and West African Worlds," *Journal of Personality and Social Psychology* 88, no. 6 (2005): 948–68; Glenn Adams and Victoria C. Plaut, "The Cultural Grounding of Personal Relationships: Friendship in North American and West African Worlds," *Personal Relationships* 10, no. 1 (2003): 333–47.

117 **A Ghanaian poem sounded:** Kyei and Schreckenbach, *No Time to Die*, 59, as cited in Adams and Plaut, "The Cultural Grounding of Personal Relationships."

118 **"loved and cared for":** Kim et al., "Pursuit of Comfort and Pursuit of Harmony: Culture, Relationships, and Social Support Seeking," 1596.

119 **seeking less . . . social support:** Shelley E. Taylor et al., "Culture and Social Support: Who Seeks It and Why?," *Journal of Personality and Social Psychology* 87, no. 3 (2004): Study 1.

119 **easy rather than a hard puzzle:** Kim et al., "Pursuit of Comfort and Pursuit of Harmony: Culture, Relationships, and Social Support Seeking." By default, Asian Americans were concerned with their partners' needs, but if they were asked to focus on their own needs, they sought social support more like white Americans did. In one study (Kim et al., Study 2), Asian American students who were asked to list five self-goals first (and thus focused on their own

needs), were found to seek more social support than Asian Americans who were not asked to do this task first. The point is, under normal circumstances, relationship goals rather than narrow self-goals are prioritized in Korean settings.

119 **did not reduce stress in Asian American individuals:** Stress was measured both as self-reported and in terms of cortisol levels; Shelley E Taylor et al., "Cultural Differences in the Impact of Social Support on Psychological and Biological Stress Responses," *Psychological Science* 18, no. 9 (2007): 831–37. Conclusions about reduced stress levels are based on the comparison with a control condition in which participants wrote on an the irrelevant topic.

120 **"right" emotion in the relationship between parents and children:** E.g., Stearns, *American Cool: Constructing a Twentieth-Century Emotional Style.*

120 **"I love you" is a fairly modern invention:** By some historical estimates, "romantic love" as a feeling was only starting to be recognized by the upper-class English in the late eighteenth century (Gillis, "From Ritual to Romance," 103). Only in the late Victorian era did love become an important goal for couples (Stearns, *American Cool*). Similarly, sexual desire, while it always has existed, did not become central in the relationship between spouses until the early twentieth century, when the individual rewards of sexual satisfaction became highlighted (Stearns, 173).

120 **you probably value happiness:** For an excellent discussion of American happiness as a virtue—or vice, as it may be—see Barbara Ehrenreich, *Bright-Sided: How Positive Thinking Is Undermining America* (London: Picador, 2009).

121 **". . . perceived as friendly and *cheerful*":** Anna Wierzbicka, "Emotion, Language, and Cultural Scripts," in *Emotion and Culture: Empirical Studies of Mutual Influence*, ed. Shinobu Kitayama and Hazel R. Markus (Washington, DC: American Psychological Association, 1994), 182. (Italics are mine.)

121 **list "features" of happiness:** Uchida and Kitayama, "Happiness and Unhappiness in East and West: Themes and Variations," Study 1.

121 **"proud," . . . "on top of the world," . . . "superior," . . . "self-esteem":** Kitayama, Mesquita, and Karasawa, "Cultural Affordances and Emotional Experience: Socially Engaging and Disengaging Emotions in Japan and the United States."

121 **both good and successful:** Phillip R. Shaver et al., "Emotion Knowledge: Further Exploration of a Prototype Approach," *Journal of Personality and Social Psychology* 52, no. 6 (1987): 1078.

121 **your own achievements:** Other research confirms the high value placed on achievement in the U.S. (S. H. Schwartz, "Cultural Value Orientations: Nature and Implications of National Differences" [Moscow State University—Higher School of Economics Press, 2008]; S. H. Schwartz and A. Bardi, "Value Hierarchies across Cultures: Taking a Similarities Perspective," *Journal of Cross-Cultural Psychology* 32, no. 3 [May 1, 2001]: 268–90; Jennifer L. Hochschild, *Facing up to the American Dream: Race, Class, and the Soul of the Nation* [Princeton, NJ: Princeton University Press, 1995]).

121 **outgoing, energetic, and approach-oriented:** Descriptions in this paragraph rendered by Shaver et al., "Emotion Knowledge: Further Exploration of a Prototype Approach," 1078.

121 **"enthusiastic," "interested," "determined," "excited," and "inspired":** These are the highest loading "positive" items on the PANAS, one of the most commonly used scales (David Watson, Lee Anna Clark, and Auke Tellegen, "Development and Validation of Brief Measures of Positive and Negative Affect: The PANAS Scale," *Journal of Personality and Social Psychology* 54, no. 6 [1988]: 1063–70).

121 **make things go your way:** Tsai et al., "Influence and Adjustment Goals: Sources of Cultural Differences in Ideal Affect." See also mastery values, S. H. Schwartz and M. Ros, "Values in the West: A Theoretical and Empirical Challenge to the Individualism-Collectivism Cultural Dimension," *World Psychology* 1, no. 2 (1995): 91–122.

122 **"influencers" from very different cultures:** Tsai et al., "Influence and Adjustment Goals: Sources of Cultural Differences in Ideal Affect," 2007. After having been assigned to the role of influencer (or adjuster), participants asked to select either a calm or excited CD to help them with the task. Participants assigned to the role of influencer tended to chose the excited CD. Participants were white and Asian American college students and college students from Hong Kong; students from all groups were more likely to select the excited CD when in the role of influencer.

122 **American mothers stimulate their babies:** Tsai, "Ideal Affect: Cultural Causes and Behavioral Consequences," 245. Characterization of children's life in the U.S. is taken from Tsai, "Ideal Affect: Cultural Causes and Behavioral Consequences," as well.

122 **"explore and do exciting things":** All examples come from Tsai, "Ideal Affect: Cultural Causes and Behavioral Consequences." Tsai's research shows main cultural tendencies and their emotional correlates, but does not dictate that these tendencies are stable or all encompassing (e.g., calming herbal teas are widely available now).

122 **Happiness . . . informs choice:** Hazel Rose Markus and Barry Schwartz, "Does Choice Mean Freedom and Well-Being?," *Journal of Consumer Research* 37, no. 2 (2010): 344–55.

122 **happiness to describe an individual:** Shigehiro Oishi et al., "Concepts of Happiness across Time and Cultures," *Personality and Social Psychology Bulletin* 39, no. 5 (2013): 559–77.

123 **more likely to choose to play basketball:** Shigehiro Oishi and Ed Diener, "Culture and Well-Being: The Cycle of Action, Evaluation, and Decision," *Personality and Social Psychology Bulletin* 29, no. 8 (2003): 939–49. For a similar finding with different tasks, see S. J. Heine et al., "Divergent Consequences of Success and Failure in Japan and North America: An Investigation of Self-Improving Motivations and Malleable Selves," *Journal of Personality and Social Psychology* 81, no. 4 (2001): 599–615.

124 **"For misery, happiness is leaning against it; for happiness, misery is hiding in it"**: B. Wei, "Gu Wen Can Tong Qi Ji Jie (Y. Jiang, ed.). Changsha, China: Shang Wu Yin Shu Guan," 1939, chap. 58., as cited in Ji, Nisbett, and Su, "Culture, Change, and Prediction."

124 **"perfect happiness . . . is not attainable in this life"**: Oishi et al., "Concepts of Happiness across Time and Cultures," 569.

124 **U.S. with Japanese conceptions of happiness**: Uchida and Kitayama found the same results, using three different words for happiness in Japan (*shiawaze, ureshii, manzoku*). The same negative connotations were associated with all three words.

125 **The predecessor of America's present culture**: Ehrenreich, *Bright-Sided*, 74–75.

126 **Japanese . . . college students consistently report less happiness**: B. Mesquita and M. Karasawa, "Different Emotional Lives," *Cognition and Emotion* 16, no. 1 (2002): 127–41; Christie N. Scollon et al., "Emotions across Cultures and Methods," *Journal of Cross Cultural Psychology* 35, no. 3 (2004): 304–26.

126 **people act according to their societal roles**: E.g., Markus and Kitayama, "Models of Agency: Sociocultural Diversity in the Construction of Action."

126 **The East Asian participants did not *like* to persist**: Oishi and Diener, "Culture and Well-Being: The Cycle of Action, Evaluation, and Decision"; Heine et al., "Divergent Consequences of Success and Failure in Japan and North America: An Investigation of Self-Improving Motivations and Malleable Selves."

127 **White American college students savored the happiness**: Xiaoming Ma, Maya Tamir, and Yuri Miyamoto, "Socio-Cultural Instrumental Approach to Emotion Regulation: Culture and the Regulation of Positive Emotions," *Emotion* 18, no. 1 (2018): 138–52.

127 **preferred feelings were related to their actual feelings**: Tsai, Knutson, and Fung, "Cultural Variation in Affect Valuation," Study 2.

128 **"to think about the Leader's frame of mind"**: Jeanne L. Tsai et al., "Influence and Adjustment Goals: Sources of Cultural Differences in Ideal Affect," *Journal of Personality and Social Psychology* 92, no. 6 (2007): 1102–17.

128 **Japanese and Chinese mothers soothe and quiet their babies**: Tsai, "Ideal Affect: Cultural Causes and Behavioral Consequences." See also Caudill and Frost, "A Comparison of Maternal Care and Infant Behavior in Japanese-American, American, and Japanese Families"; Caudill and Weinstein, "Maternal Care and Infant Behavior in Japan and America"; Keller, *Cultures of Infancy*.

128 **Taiwanese children's books also describe fewer arousing activities**: Tsai, "Ideal Affect: Cultural Causes and Behavioral Consequences." In fact, Tsai et al. ("Learning What Feelings to Desire: Socialization of Ideal Affect through Children's Storybooks") find evidence that exposure to calmer models

strengthens children's preference for LAP feelings. What is called "calm smiles" are closed-mouth smiles, often with closed eyes; what is called "excited smiles" are in fact smiles with jaw dropped, teeth showing, and, often, wide-open eyes.

128 **"Calm happiness" remains favorite among adults too:** Tsai, "Ideal Affect: Cultural Causes and Behavioral Consequences." In the same review of practices cited above for white Americans, psychologist Jeanne Tsai and her colleagues find that East Asians prefer leisure activities, drugs, and music that are geared towards calm happiness. Hong Kong Chinese dream of vacations where they can "totally relax" rather than doing exciting things. And it is possible that a preference for calm happiness also explains the widespread intake of tea (instead of coffee) and, among recreational illicit drug users, the preference for opiates (over stimulants) in East Asian contexts.

128 **the most commonly used psychological scales of emotions:** Notably, David Watson, Lee Anna Clark, and Auke Tellegen, "Development and Validation of Brief Measures of Positive and Negative Affect: The PANAS Scales," *Journal of Personality and Social Psychology* 54, no. 6 (1988): 1063–70.

128 **contrasted this desire with the Belgian acceptance of emotions:** This was in a recent study where we conducted focus groups in Japan about couple interactions on disagreements (Schouten et al., in preparation).

129 **associated with culturally valued feelings:** E.g., Jozefien De Leersnyder et al., "Emotional Fit with Culture: A Predictor of Individual Differences in Relational Well-Being," *Emotion* 14, no. 2 (2014): 241–45; Nathan S. Consedine, Yulia E. Chentsova-Dutton, and Yulia S. Krivoshekova, "Emotional Acculturation Predicts Better Somatic Health: Experiential and Expressive Acculturation among Immigrant Women from Four Ethnic Groups," *Journal of Social and Clinical Psychology* 33, no. 10 (2014): 867–89.

129 **not being calm enough . . . lack of excitement:** Tsai, Knutson, and Fung, "Cultural Variation in Affect Valuation."

130 **the smiles of leaders:** Jeanne L. Tsai et al., "Leaders' Smiles Reflect Cultural Differences in Ideal Affect," *Emotion* 16, no. 2 (2016): 183–95.

130 **not be explained by . . . development:** Tsai et al., "Leaders' Smiles Reflect Cultural Differences in Ideal Affect," Study 3. This study compared smiles of legislators in ten different countries. More democratic and more developed nations were more likely to have legislators who smiled, but excited smiles specifically where predicted by ideal HAP, even after controlling for these country-level variables of democracy and development, and similarly calm smiles specifically where predicted by ideal LAP after controlling for these variables (p. 192).

130 **Korean students who played a computer game:** Bo Kyung Park et al., "Neurocultural Evidence That Ideal Affect Match Promotes Giving," *Social Cognitive and Affective Neuroscience* 12, no. 7 (2017): 1083–96.

130 **the happiest people in my studies:** For similar published results, see Scollon et al., "Emotions across Cultures and Methods"; Belinda Campos and

Heejung S. Kim, "Incorporating the Cultural Diversity of Family and Close Relationships into the Study of Health," *American Psychologist* 72, no. 6 (2017): 543–54, suggest that the role of East Asian and Latino cultures in attaining interdependence is starkly different, as is the type of interdependence sought. In order to obtain harmony collectivism, East Asians moderate emotions and place emphasis on fulfilling duties over personal preferences and wishes. Latinos' fulfillment of family duties is expected to be emotionally positive and rewarding; positive emotional interactions are thought to attain convivial collectivism.

131   **pleasant relationships, or *simpatía*:** Triandis, Marín, Lisansky, and Betancourt, "Simpatía as a Cultural Script of Hispanics." 1984; Amanda M Acevedo et al., "Cultural Diversity and Ethnic Minority Psychology Measurement of a Latino Cultural Value: The Simpatía Scale Measurement of a Latino Cultural Value: The Simpatía Scale," *Cultural Diversity and Ethnic Minority Psychology*, 2020.

131   **a situation in which they felt happy:** Interestingly, we had used the same description as for Turkish, Dutch, Surinamese, and also white American and Japanese interviews, which was "a situation in which they felt extremely valued or important." Mexican descriptions of happiness were connectedness-oriented, despite the overtones of achievement that many individuals in other cultural groups had perceived in the happiness prompt.

133   **Krishna Savani and colleagues:** K. Savani et al., "Feeling Close and Doing Well: The Prevalence and Motivational Effects of Interpersonally Engaging Emotions in Mexican and European American Cultural Contexts," *International Journal of Psychology* 48, no. 4 (2012): 682–94.

134   **It is important to do well for your family:** In contrast, the kind of happiness they had written about did not affect how well white American college students did. Happiness in the context of family was not particularly motivating for white American students, as it was for Latinx and Mexican students (Savani et al.).

134   **calm, and no longer worried:** A similar point is made by Angela Y. Lee, Jennifer L. Aaker, and Wendi L. Gardner ("The Pleasures and Pains of Distinct Self-Construals: The Role of Interdependence in Regulatory Focus," *Journal of Personality and Social Psychology* 78, no. 6 [2000]: 1122–34), who found that prevention-focused Hong Kong Chinese students projected more calm (or worry) when imagining themselves in an important tennis match that they won (versus lost), whereas the promotion-focused white American students projected more happiness (or dejection), respectively (Lee, Aaker, and Gardner, 1122).

135   **love as we know it is natural:** This argument can be found in Fisher, *Anatomy of Love: The Natural History of Monogamy*; Jankowiak and Fischer, "A Cross-Cultural Perspective on Romantic Love."

135   **the child who is excitedly happy but gets reprimanded:** Lutz, *Unnatural Emotions.*

Chapter 6 WHAT'S IN A WORD?

136 **a caregiver does not have access:** Ludwig Wittgenstein, *Philosophical Investigations* (New York: MacMillan, 1953), as cited in Parkinson, *Heart to Heart*.

136 **towards the second year:** Patricia M. Clancy, "The Socialization of Affect in Japanese Mother-Child Conversation," *Journal of Pragmatics* 31, no. 11 (November 1, 1999): 1397–1421; Judy Dunn, Inge Bretherton, and Penny Munn, "Conversations about Feeling States between Mothers and Their Young Children," *Developmental Psychology* 23, no. 1 (1987): 132–39.

136 **between once and twice per *minute*:** Clancy, "The Socialization of Affect in Japanese Mother-Child Conversation."

137 **The more emotion words caregivers use:** Dunn, Bretherton, and Munn, "Conversations about Feeling States between Mothers and Their Young Children."

137 **the container of the many episodes:** Peter Kuppens et al., "Individual Differences in Patterns of Appraisal and Anger Experience," *Cognition & Emotion* 21, no. 4 (2007): 689–713; Michael Boiger et al., "Beyond Essentialism: Cultural Differences in Emotions Revisited," *Emotion* 18, no. 8 (2018): 1142–62.

137 **this process of concept learning:** Barrett, *How Emotions Are Made*, chap. 5.

137 **emotion concepts make connections:** The point is eloquently made by Barrett, *How Emotions Are Made*, 99–100.

137 **situations that urge deferent behavior:** While at an abstract level the functional goal of the emotion may be defined as "being deferent" or "knowing one's position," what this means concretely may be very different. Concrete functional goals are situated, even if they can be described to be similar at some very abstract level. See also Mesquita and Frijda, "Cultural Variations in Emotions: A Review."

138 **collective knowledge that scaffolds your own experiences:** In no way do I want to suggest that infants are born with emotion concepts; rather, they are born into a culture with a language and webs of meaning.

138 **the tools that your parents use:** E. T. Higgins, "Shared-Reality Development in Childhood," *Perspectives on Psychological Science* 11, no. 4 (2016): 466–95.

138 **historically new, and geographically unique:** In fact, many languages do not have a term equivalent to *emotion*. Even in the English language the word *emotion* has only been in use since the nineteenth century. E.g., Thomas Dixon, *From Passions to Emotions: The Creation of a Secular Psychological Category* (Cambridge, UK: Cambridge University Press, 2003); John Leavitt, "Meaning and Feeling in the Anthropology of Emotions," *American Ethnologist* 23, no. 3 (1996): 514–39; James A. Russell, "Culture and the Categorization of Emotions," *Psychological Bulletin* 110, no. 3 (1991): 426–50.

139 **boundaries around the domain of emotions:** Linguist Aneta Pavlenko astutely notes that researchers are often not aware that the term "emotion" is

a cultural construct (Pavlenko, *The Bilingual Mind and What It Tells Us about Language and Thought* [New York: Cambridge University Press, 2014], 296): "Whorfian effects in emotion research are found in learned scholars who reify the term *emotion* as 'natural,' treat emotions as inner states consistent with the morphosyntactic encoding in English, and use a distinction between *emotions, feelings,* and *affect,* peculiar to English, and an idiosyncratic set of everyday English emotion words as technical terms."

139 **Emotion vocabularies:** Russell, "Culture and the Categorization of Emotions," 428.

139 **different numbers of distinctions:** Anna Wierzbicka, "Introduction: Feelings, Languages, and Cultures," in *Emotions Across Languages and Cultures: Diversity and Universals,* 1st ed. (New York: Cambridge University Press, 1999), 1–48. Anna Wierzbicka, *Emprisoned in English: The Hazards of English as a Default Language* (New York: Oxford University Press, 2014).

139 *okusunguwala,* **for "anger" and "sadness":** John H. Orley, "Culture and Mental Illness: A Study from Uganda," in *East African Studies* (Nairobi: East African Publishing House, 1970), 3 (as cited in Russell, "Culture and the Categorization of Emotions," 430).

139 *kızmak*: This literally means "to be angry." It is a verb. Note that "hurt feelings" may be a good translation; cf. Mark R. Leary and Sadie Leder, "The Nature of Hurt Feelings: Emotional Experience and Cognitive Appraisals," in *Feeling Hurt in Close Relationships,* ed. Anita L. Vangelisti (New York: Cambridge University Press, 2009), 15–33.

140 *afökho dödö* **(literally "pain-hearted"):** Andrew Beatty, *Emotional Worlds: Beyond an Anthropology of Emotion* (Cambridge, UK: Cambridge Univeristy Press, 2019), 63. Reprinted with permission by Cambridge University Press.

140 **Ifaluk emotion *fago*:** Lutz, *Unnatural Emotions.*

140 *alofa*: Eleanor Ruth Gerber, "Rage and Obligation: Samoan Emotion in Conflict," in *Person, Self and Experience: Exploring Pacific Ethnopsychologies,* ed. Geoffrey M. White and John Kirkpatrick (Berkeley: University of California Press, 1985), 121–67.

140 *hasham*: Abu-Lughod, *Veiled Sentiments.*

140 *betang*: Michelle Z. Rosaldo, *Knowledge and Passion: Ilongot Notions of Self and Social Life* (Cambridge, UK: Cambridge University Press, 1980).

140 **emotion lexicons in almost 2,500 languages:** Joshua Conrad Jackson et al., "Emotion Semantics Show Both Cultural Variation and Universal Structure," *Science* 366, no. 6472 (2019): 1517–22.

141 **the absence of a word for *disgust* in Polish:** A. Wierzbicka, "Human Emotions: Universal or Culture-Specific?," *American Anthropologist* 88, no. 3 (September 1986): 590.

141 **Tahitians suffering a loss:** Robert I. Levy, *Tahitians: Mind and Experience in the Society Islands* (Chicago: University of Chicago Press, 1973), 305.

141 **more trouble understanding the new emotion terms:** Jackson et al., "Emotion Semantics Show Both Cultural Variation and Universal Structure."

142 **"a mental state that could be felt":** See p. 3 of supplementary materials for Jackson et al., "Emotion Semantics Show Both Cultural Variation and Universal Structure."

142 **Crying . . . has not been treated as "an emotion":** Limited work on crying does exist in the psychological literature; see, e.g., A. J. J. M. Vingerhoets et al., "Adult Crying: A Model and Review of Literature," *Review of General Psychology* 4, no. 4 (2000): 354–77; A. J. J. M. Vingerhoets and Lauren M. Bylsma, "The Riddle of Human Emotional Crying: A Challenge for Emotion Researchers," *Emotion Review* 8, no. 3 (2016): 207–17.

143 **"inclination to depend on or accept another's nurturant indulgence":** Lebra, "Mother and Child in Japanese Socialization: A Japan-U.S. Comparison," 291, as cited in Trommsdorff and Kornadt, "Parent-Child Relations in Cross-Cultural Perspective," 286.

143 **"Why, even puppies do it!":** Doi, *The Anatomy of Dependence*, 15, as cited in H. Morsbach and W. J. Tyler, "A Japanese Emotion: Amae," in *The Social Construction of Emotions*, ed. Rom Harré (New York: Blackwell, 1986), 290.

144 **pride and shame concepts:** Mascolo, Fischer, and Li, "Dynamic Development of Component Systems in Emotions: Pride, Shame and Guilt in China and the United States." The different elements of pride episodes in the U.S. and China have been distinguished by Mascolo and his colleagues. They call this pride, and propose a timeline for its development; the timeline may be questioned (Katie Hoemann, Fei Xu, and Lisa Feldman Barrett, "Emotion Words, Emotion Concepts, and Emotional Development in Children: A Constructionist Hypothesis," *Developmental Psychology* 55, no. 9 [2019]: 1830–49; Maria Gendron et al., "Emotion Perception in Hadza Hunter-Gatherers," *Scientific Reports* 10, no. 1 [2020]: 1–17), yet the description of the different episodes that together constitute the respective cultural concepts of pride is useful.

145 **it is *they* who are responsible:** Some psychologists think that this is the first sign of pride (e.g., Michael Lewis, "The Emergence of Human Emotions," in *Handbook of Emotions*, ed. Michael Lewis, Jeannette M. Haviland-Jones, and Lisa F. Barrett, 3d ed. (New York: Guildford Press, 2008), but there is no principled reason to exclude previous "stories" (or stages) of pride.

146 **social roles and obligations:** M. F. Mascolo and K. W. Fischer, "Developmental Transformations in Appraisals for Pride, Shame, and Guilt," in *Self-Conscious Emotions. The Psychology of Shame, Guilt, Embarrassment, and Pride*, ed. J. P. Tangney and K. W. Fischer (New York: Guilford Press, 1995), 64–113; Mascolo, Fischer, and Li, "Dynamic Development of Component Systems in Emotions: Pride, Shame and Guilt in China and the United States."

148 **anger instances across different kinds of situations:** Boiger et al., "Beyond Essentialism: Cultural Differences in Emotions Revisited." The example described in this paragraph was adapted from this article. Copyright © 2018, American Psychological Association.

148 **students of either gender:** In this study we did in fact consider gender dichotomous; call it one of the limitations of the study.

149 **After they read a vignette:** The appraisal and action readiness questions included in this study were derived from a broad range of previous studies, including studies that were designed to capture non-Western appraisals and modes of action readiness. Simultaneous component analyses for shame yielded three appraisal components and four components of action readiness that held across cultures. For details, see Boiger et al., "Beyond Essentialism: Cultural Differences in Emotions Revisited."

149 **the same sets did occur in all cultures:** It is possible that the similarities were overestimated, given we started from a limited set of similar situation descriptions. In reality, situation ecologies may vary substantially across cultures.

150 **protecting their close relationships . . . protecting their autonomy:** Boiger et al., "Beyond Essentialism: Cultural Differences in Emotions Revisited," 1152.

150 **store collections of episodes:** Boiger et al., "Beyond Essentialism: Cultural Differences in Emotions Revisited"; Hoemann, Xu, and Barrett, "Emotion Words, Emotion Concepts, and Emotional Development in Children: A Constructionist Hypothesis."

150 **stepping into the encounters of another world:** Pavlenko (*The Bilingual Mind and What It Tells Us about Language and Thought*) makes a similar observation. In a recent review article, anthropologist Alan Fiske similarly observes that the "vernacular words" of different languages far from neatly map onto each other (Alan Page Fiske, "The Lexical Fallacy in Emotion Research: Mistaking Vernacular Words for Psychological Entities," *Psychological Review* 127, no. 1 [2020]: 95–113). Fiske rightly warns against reifying the emotion words of any context, he also rightly observes that instances of emotions are more than merely words. I agree with Fiske that there is a lexical fallacy: Just because we have a translation for a word, does not mean we understand the emotion in the other culture. Where Fiske and I start to differ is not on the claims he makes based on evidence (his evidence largely converges with the examples I use in this book), but on his assumptions about "natural kinds" of emotions which unfortunately remain just that—assumptions. His plea to search for these natural kinds, independently from vernacular words is interesting, but starkly underestimates the role of concepts (not necessarily words) in experience (e.g., Barrett, *How Emotions Are Made: The Secret Life of the Brain*).

151 **many languages have words for happy:** It is also clear that vocabularies in different languages are not the same. Russell, "Culture and the Categorization of Emotions"; Jackson et al., "Emotion Semantics Show Both Cultural Variation and Universal Structure." (especially the supplementary materials).

151 **"Because . . . cradle to grave":** Beatty, *Emotional Worlds*, 111. Reprinted with permission by Cambridge University Press.

151 **You can move towards or away from another human being or a group:**
Frijda, "The Evolutionary Emergence of What We Call 'Emotions.'" In this
paper that appeared after his death, Frijda suggested that moving towards and
moving away are precursors of valuation: "Elementary animal movements on
occasion show direction, and this prefigures affective processes. For instance,
bacteria move towards higher concentrations of glucose, and away from toxic
substances such as phenol" (p. 609).

151 **Western scholars have proposed taxonomies:** E.g., Frijda, *The Emotions*;
Klaus R. Scherer and Harald G. Wallbott, "Evidence for Universality and
Cultural Variation of Differential Emotion Response Patterning," *Journal of
Personality and Social Psychology* 66, no. 2 (1994): 310–28; Joseph de Rivera, *A
Structural Theory of the Emotions, Psychological Issues* (New York: International
University Press, 1977).

151 **"guilt," and "disgust" with *moving away*:** Scherer and Wallbott ("Evidence
for Universality and Cultural Variation of Differential Emotion Response
Patterning") found that "shame" and "guilt" were associated with moving
away, but in this research the only two options were moving towards and
moving away. I think these emotions are better qualified as moving down
(which sometimes is best achieved by taking distance).

152 **"Love" . . . moving towards another person:** De Rivera, *A Structural Theory
of the Emotions.*

152 **"Anger" . . . moving someone else away . . . and "fear" . . . moving away:**
De Rivera. Some of these characterizations are more intuitive than others.
In an empirical study, most were recognized by a sample of Canadian
college students (Joseph de Rivera and Carmen Grinkis, "Emotions as Social
Relationships," *Motivation and Emotion* 10 [1986]: 351–69).

152 **dominant (*move up*) or submissive (*move down*):** Described as "potency"
(Charles E. Osgood, William H. May, and Murray S. Miron, *Cross-Cultural
Universals of Affective Meaning* [Urbana: University of Illinois Press, 1975]; as
"power" (Johnny R. J. Fontaine and Klaus R. Scherer, "The Global Meaning
Structure of the Emotion Domain: Investigating the Complementarity of
Multiple Perspectives on Meaning," in *Components of Emotional Meaning: A
Sourcebook*, ed. Johnny R. J. Fontaine, Klaus R. Scherer, and Cristina Soriano
[Oxford, UK: Oxford University Press, 2013], 106–28; as "strong" versus
"weak" position (C. Lutz, "The Domain of Emotion Words on Ifaluk," ed.
M. Harré, *American Ethnologist* 9, no. 1 [1982]: 113–28).

152 **Western adults (including some psychologists) turn this around:** Even
congenitally blind athletes who won postured as big, with "the expanded
posture and outstretched arms" (Jessica L. Tracy and David Matsumoto, "The
Spontaneous Expression of Pride and Shame: Evidence for Biologically Innate
Nonverbal Displays," *Proceedings of the National Academy of Sciences* 105, no.
16 (2008): 11655–60). While this has been interpreted as evidence that the
expression of pride is not learned, there is no evidence that these athletes felt
proud. They may have just posed as dominant. As Tracy and Matsumoto

themselves suggest, this posture "may have originated as a way of appearing larger, allowing for the assertion of dominance and attracting attention" (11655–60).

152 **infer pride from strong and dominant posturing:** Jessica L. Tracy and Richard W. Robins, "Emerging Insights into the Nature and Function of Pride," *Current Directions in Psychological Science* 16, no. 3 (2007): 147–50; Batja Mesquita and Susan Polanco, "Pride," in *Oxford Companion to the Affective Sciences*, ed. David Sander and Klaus R. Scherer (Oxford, UK: Oxford University Press, 2009), 313–14.

152 **down in the relationship:** Fontaine and Scherer ("The Global Meaning Structure of the Emotion Domain: Investigating the Complementarity of Multiple Perspectives on Meaning," 115) found that these emotions were the lowest loading items on the power dimension in their study. It is interesting to notice that the highest positive loading items on this dimension were "increased the volume of voice," "assertive voice," and "felt dominant."

152 **concepts come with submission:** The term "submission" is used by Nico H. Frijda and W. Gerrod Parrott, "Basic Emotions or Ur-Emotions?," *Emotion Review* 3, no. 4 (2011): 406–15.

152 **Awe . . . awareness of how small you are compared:** Yang Bai et al., "Awe, the Diminished Self, and Collective Engagement: Universals and Cultural Variations in the Small Self," *Journal of Personality and Social Psychology* 113, no. 2 (2017): 185–209.

152 **acceptance and calmness . . . depression:** Frijda and Parrott, "Basic Emotions or Ur-Emotions?"

152 **or not know where to move . . . (depressed, hopeless):** Frijda, *The Emotions*, 97.

152 **will occur in all human societies:** Some of these moves described by Frijda, "The Evolutionary Emergence of What We Call 'Emotions.'"

153 *amaeru . . . amayakasu:* Lebra, *Japanese Patterns of Behaviour.*

153 **depends on the emotion concepts that are available in your culture:** Barrett, *How Emotions Are Made*; Beatty, *Emotional Worlds.*

153 **Marie, a U.S. American student:** Shaver et al., "Emotion Knowledge: Further Exploration of a Prototype Approach." The name is fictitious, the original vignette was written in first person voice (p. 1073).

154 **bring online . . . cultural knowledge:** Beatty, *Emotional Worlds*, but also Barrett, *How Emotions Are Made.*

154 **without a concept, there is no emotion as we know it:** I do not mean to say that there needs to be one word for an emotion; the emotion can get conceptualized in many ways, including expressions consisting of several words, drawings, gestures. I also want to point out that my friend and colleague Lisa Feldman Barrett has often been misunderstood as to say that we need a *word* to have a feeling (e.g., Fiske, "The Lexical Fallacy in Emotion Research: Mistaking Vernacular Words for Psychological Entities"). That is not what she writes (e.g., 2017). Rather, her argument is that we need a *concept* to have an emotion (and it is true that many important concepts are lexicalized).

154   **sparking movements for justice:** Myisha Cherry and Owen Flanagan, *The Moral Psychology of Anger* (London: Rowman & Littlefield, 2017).

154   **This is not true everywhere:** Owen Flannagan, *How to Do Things with Emotions. The Morality of Anger and Shame across Cultures* (New York; Oxford University Press, 2021). See also chapter 4 of this book.

155   **"a fundamentally destructive sentiment":** Shweder et al., "The Cultural Psychology of the Emotions: Ancient and Renewed," 416.

155   **"expresses a person's reluctance to do what is required":** Gerber, "Rage and Obligation: Samoan Emotion in Conflict," 128–29.

155   **shame . . . is taboo:** Scheff, "Shame and Conformity: The Deference-Emotion System."

155   **And, if acknowledged as shame:** June Price Tangney et al., "Are Shame, Guilt, and Embarrassment Distinct Emotions?," *Journal of Personality and Social Psychology* 70, no. 6 (1996): 1256–69, measured these as: "felt inferior to others," "felt physically smaller," "was overcome in inward experience of feeling."

156   **not having a word for sadness in Tahitian:** Levy, *Tahitians: Mind and Experience in the Society Islands*, 305.

156   **anything else than "fatigued" or "gentle":** As referenced above: Orley, "Culture and Mental Illness: A Study from Uganda," 3, as cited in Russell, "Culture and the Categorization of Emotions," 430.

156   **harder to perceive emotions in the face:** Maria Gendron et al., "Emotion Words Shape Emotion Percepts," *Emotion* 12, no. 2 (April 2012): 314–25; K. A. Lindquist et al., "Language and the Perception of Emotion," *Emotion* 6, no. 1 (February 2006): 125–38; Nicole Betz, Katie Hoemann, and Lisa Feldman Barrett, "Words Are a Context for Mental Inference," *Emotion* 19, no. 8 (December 1, 2019): 1463–77.

156   **constitute your emotional experience differently:** This is no different from the role any concept has on experience (e.g., L. W. Barsalou et al., "Social Embodiment," in *The Psychology of Learning and Motivation*, ed. B. H. Ross, vol. 43 [New York: Elsevier Science, 2003], 43–92; G. Lupyan and B. Bergen, "How Language Programs the Mind," *Topics in Cognitive Science* 8, no. 2 [April 2016]: 408–24).

156   **My American friends:** Barrett, *How Emotions Are Made*, 105.

156   **American college students recognized *amae* situations:** Y. Niiya, P. C. Ellsworth, and S. Yamaguchi, "Amae in Japan and the United States: An Exploration of a 'Culturally Unique' Emotion," *Emotion* 6, no. 2 (2006): 279–95.

157   **"were not sure about its range of reference . . .":** Pavlenko, *The Bilingual Mind and What It Tells Us about Language and Thought*, 260.

158   **different cultural episodes are associated with these concepts:** Pavlenko (*Emotions and Multilingualism*) distinguishes between semantic and conceptual representations, and argues that "Research on second language acquisition and bilingualism convincingly demonstrates that to recognize and understand the basic meaning of a particular word [i.e. have a semantic representation] is not

the same as having an authentic conceptual representation of the linguistic item and acting on it. Only through a prolonged process of L2 socialization can L2 users form L2-based conceptual representations that, among other things, force them to pay attention to distinctions not encoded in their L1 and allow them to determine the prototypicality of particular events or displays of emotion" (pp. 85–86).

158 **The stories or scripts are the emotions:** E.g., Russell, "Culture and the Categorization of Emotions"; Flanagan, *How to Do Things with Emotions. The Morality of Anger and Shame across Cultures*; Gendron et al., "Emotion Perception in Hadza Hunter-Gatherers."

159 **I am taking a stance in the relationship:** The term "stance" was coined by R. Solomon, "Beyond Ontology: Ideation, Phenomenology and the Cross Cultural Study of Emotion," *Journal for the Theory of Social Behaviour* 27, no. 2–3 (1997): 289–303; R. C. Solomon, "Emotions, Thoughts, and Feelings: Emotions as Engagements with the World," in *Thinking about Feeling: Contemporary Philosophers on Emotions*, ed. R. C. Solomon (New York: Oxford Univeristy Press, 2004), 76–88. The examples in this paragraph of the content of such stance come from N. H. Frijda, P. Kuipers, and E. ter Schure, "Relations among Emotion, Appraisal, and Emotional Action Readiness," *Journal of Personality and Social Psychology* 57, no. 2 (1989): 212–28; P. C. Ellsworth and K. R. Scherer, "Appraisal Processes in Emotion," in *Handbook of Affective Sciences*, ed. R. J. Davidson, K. R. Scherer, and H. H. Goldsmith (New York: Oxford University Press, 2003), 572–95.

159 **"my angry warning of aggression may constitute a compelling threat":** Parkinson, *Heart to Heart*, 56.

159 **to give them attention, and to seek closeness:** This description is taken from Study 2 of Shaver et al., "Emotion Knowledge: Further Exploration of a Prototype Approach."

160 **without necessarily feeling the emotion:** This is, I think, the point of focusing on OURS aspects of emotions when using an emotion word. Specific examples can be found in Abu-Lughod, *Veiled Sentiments: Honor and Poetry in a Bedouin Society*; Beatty, *Emotional Worlds*; Rosaldo, *Knowledge and Passion*.

160 **Inauthentic? Not necessarily:** Beatty makes a similar point on p. 54 of *Emotional Worlds*: "Emotions are often performative—intended to influence, persuade, or repel. We learn how to feel emotions by observing its behavioral contexts, how it is manifested and pragmatically used. . . . Feeling angry is just a way of saying 'feeling as people do when they are *being* angry.'" Reprinted with permission by Cambridge University Press.

160 **The people living on Nias:** Beatty, *Emotional Worlds*, 47–48. Reprinted with permission by Cambridge University Press.

160 **" . . . by referring to their hearts . . .":** Beatty, *Emotional Worlds*, 53. The earlier quote in this paragraph appears on the same page. Reprinted with permission by Cambridge University Press.

161 **"you'll make your pants wet . . .":** Briggs, *Never in Anger*, 172. Copyright © 1970 by the President and Fellows of Harvard College.

161 **"as a way of promoting gentle . . . behavior":** Lutz, *Unnatural Emotions*, 136.

161 **should *fago* a young man:** Lutz, *Unnatural Emotions*, 137–38.

163 **that something may not be an invariant emotion:** E.g., Maria Gendron, Carlos Crivelli, and Lisa Feldman Barrett, "Universality Reconsidered: Diversity in Making Meaning of Facial Expressions," *Current Directions in Psychological Science* 27, no. 4 (2018): 211–19; see also Nico H. Frijda and Anna Tcherkassof, "Facial Expression as Modes of Action Readiness," in *The Psychology of Facial Expression. Studies in Emotion and Social Interaction*, ed. James A. Russell and José Miguel Fernández-Dols (Cambridge, UK: Cambridge University Press, 1997), 78–102.

Chapter 7 LEARNING THE WALTZ

164 **Like partners in a dance:** See also Emily A. Butler, "Temporal Interpersonal Emotion Systems: The 'TIES' That Form Relationships," *Personality and Social Psychology Review* 15, no. 4 (2011): 367–93; Parkinson, *Heart to Heart*.

165 **difficulty understanding the emotions of Utku Inuit:** Briggs, *Never in Anger*.

165 **linguist Aneta Pavlenko:** Pavlenko, *The Bilingual Mind*, 275.

165 **her autobiography *Lost in Translation*:** Hoffmann, *Lost in Translation and What It Tells Us about Language and Thought*, 220.

165 **At the time we had this conversation:** The examples of psychological changes provided in this paragraph are examples of psychological acculturation catalogued by previous research. See, for an overview of psychological acculturation research, Batja Mesquita, Jozefien De Leersnyder, and Alba Jasini, "The Cultural Psychology of Acculturation," in *Handbook of Cultural Psychology*, ed. Shinobu Kitayama and Dov Cohen, 2nd ed. (New York: Guilford Press, 2019), 502–35.

166 **one of the hardest things to learn:** Some evidence for this is provided by David K. Sherman and Heejung S. Kim, "Affective Perseverance: The Resistance of Affect to Cognitive Invalidation," *Personality and Social Psychology Bulletin* 28, no. 2 (2002): 224–37; Yasuka Minoura, "A Sensitive Period for the Incorporation of a Cultural Meaning System: A Study of Japanese Children Growing up in the United States," *Ethos* 20, no. 3 (September 1992): 304–39.

166 **"more colors in the world than [you] ever knew":** Hoffmann, *Lost in Translation*, 220.

166 **the proper names of emotions in the new language:** See Pavlenko, *The Bilingual Mind and What It Tells Us about Language and Thought*, for a very similar analysis.

166 **flew in the face of these assumptions:** Mesquita, De Leersnyder, and Jasini, "The Cultural Psychology of Acculturation."

166 **tasks awaiting a second-language (L2) learner:** Pavlenko, *The Bilingual Mind and What It Tells Us about Language and Thought*, 247.

167 **the lyrics of a famous Dutch song:** Original title "Mens durf the leven"; translation van der Horst, *The Low Sky: Understanding the Dutch*, 231.

167 **"intellectual autonomy":** This is a value domain specified by Schwartz, "Cultural Value Orientations: Nature and Implications of National Differences." Curiosity, freedom, and broadmindedness are values in this domain. Northern Europeans in fact did prioritize this value more than U.S. samples.

168 **avoid becoming a laughingstock:** Nisbett and Cohen, *Culture of Honor*; D. Cohen et al., " 'When You Call Me That, Smile!' How Norms for Politeness, Interaction Styles, and Aggression Work Together in Southern Culture," *Social Psychology Quarterly* 62, no. 3 (1999): 257–75.

169 **reprimanded by her teacher:** This is an example of an interaction at school that "as a result of which you felt bad about yourself." Students were being asked about three other types of interactions that varied according to valence (bad, good) and the dimension of protective of personal goals (about yourself) vs. relational outcomes (about your relationship with other people). After reporting a situation that happened "not so long ago," our respondents rated the emotions they felt in the situation on a long list: anger, shame, guilt, pride, respect (e.g., Alba Jasini et al., "Tuning in Emotionally: Associations of Cultural Exposure with Distal and Proximal Emotional Fit in Acculturating Youth," *European Journal of Social Psychology* 49, no. 2 [2019]: 352–65).

170 **Ayse's feelings did not "fit" the Belgian average:** Note that our research allowed us to measure emotional acculturation without ever *asking* immigrants how acculturated they were; we simply compared immigrant emotions to the majority emotional norm (Jozefien De Leersnyder, Batja Mesquita, and Heejung S. Kim, "Where Do My Emotions Belong? A Study of Immigrants' Emotional Acculturation," *Personality and Social Psychology Bulletin* 37, no. 4 [2011]: 451–63; Jasini et al., "Tuning in Emotionally: Associations of Cultural Exposure with Distal and Proximal Emotional Fit in Acculturating Youth"; Mesquita, De Leersnyder, and Jasini, "The Cultural Psychology of Acculturation").

170 **"emotions" shifted:** In each of the studies reported, we used simultaneous component analyses to check structural equivalence of the emotion items (Kim De Roover, Eva Ceulemans, and Marieke E. Timmerman, "How to Perform Multiblock Component Analysis in Practice," *Behavior Research Methods* 44, no. 1 [March 2012]). For the Korean and European American samples, we found three structurally equivalent factors: positive emotions (e.g., close, proud), negative engaged emotions (e.g., ashamed), and negative disengaged emotion (e.g., irritable); three items loaded differently across the cultural groups (jealous, relying, surprised) (De Leersnyder, Mesquita, and

Kim, "Where Do My Emotions Belong? A Study of Immigrants' Emotional Acculturation," Study 1). For the Turkish Belgian and Turkish groups, we found four structurally equivalent factors: positive engaged (e.g., close), positive disengaged (e.g., proud), negative engaged (e.g., ashamed), and negative disengaged (e.g., irritable); again three items loaded differently (feeling resigned, jealous, embarrassed) (De Leersnyder, Mesquita, and Kim, Study 2). In the large-scale Belgian school study, we found four structurally equivalent factors: positive engaged (e.g., connected), positive disengaged (e.g., proud), negative engaged (e.g., ashamed), and negative disengaged (e.g., angry); three items loaded differently (felt good, sad, surprised) (Jasini et al., "Tuning in Emotionally: Associations of Cultural Exposure with Distal and Proximal Emotional Fit in Acculturating Youth"). We made sure to exclude emotion words that failed to group in similar ways across different groups. This way, group differences in ratings remained comparable. Of course, the changes in Ayse's emotions may have gone well beyond the shifts on these two dimensions, but we would not have documented these other changes.

170 **closest to the majority emotion norm:** The emotions of the majority were closest to the majority norm, even though we always recalculated the majority average to exclude the ratings of the particular majority individual; we avoided conflation of cultural fit.

171 **if "they" want to stay here:** Kaat Van Acker et al., "Flanders' Real and Present Threat: How Representations of Intergroup Relations Shape Attitudes towards Muslim Minorities" (KU Leuven, 2012).

171 **emotional fit with the white American norm:** De Leersnyder, Mesquita, and Kim, "Where Do My Emotions Belong? A Study of Immigrants' Emotional Acculturation," Study 1.

171 **when the facial displays come from their own . . . culture:** H. A. Elfenbein and N. Ambady, "When Familiarity Breeds Accuracy: Cultural Exposure and Facial Emotion Recognition," *Journal of Personality and Social Psychology* 85, no. 2 (2003): 276–90. Elfenbein and Ambady suppose that "universal affect programs can largely determine emotional expression, whereas stylistic differences across cultures create small adjustments to these core programs." Their research does not allow to draw conclusions in this hypothesis.

171 **pictures of Chinese faces:** Chinese posers, who had never lived outside of mainland China, were asked to imagine a situation of "happiness," "surprise," "sadness," "fear," "anger," or "disgust," and to make the "appropriate expression for that emotional state." (L. Wang and R. Markham, "Facial Expression Megamix: Tests of Dimensional and Category Accounts of Emotion Recognition," *Journal of Cross Cultural Psychology* 30 [1999]: 397–410, as cited by Elfenbein and Ambady, "When Familiarity Breeds Accuracy: Cultural Exposure and Facial Emotion Recognition," 279). Pictures of the actual faces could not be traced back in the literature.

172 **Jon or Taro:** The study was described in chapter 2; Masuda, Takahiko, Phoebe C. Ellsworth, Batja Mesquita, Janxin Leu, Shigehito Tanida, and Ellen Van

de Veerdonk, "Placing the Face in Context: Cultural Differences in the Perception of Facial Emotion." Journal of Personality and Social Psychology 94 (3) (2008): 365–81.

172 **Tweaking our original research:** Masuda et al., "Do Surrounding Figures' Emotions Affect Judgment of the Target Figure's Emotion? Comparing the Eye-Movement Patterns of European Canadians, Asian Canadians, Asian International Students, and Japanese." What I call "tweaks" here are important improvements on the earlier design from another point of view: (a) stimulus materials consisted of actual photographs, (b) female central figures were added to the male central figures, (c) the context figures were made of equal size to the central figures (in contrast to the cartoon study where they were drawn to be in the background), (d) the observation time was set at ten seconds. Other changes included a reduction in the number of emotions under study: The current study focuses on sad, happy, and neutral (which comes down to studying valence, and is a reduction in specificity compared to the early study).

173 **Asian Canadian and Asian international students:** We have little information about the Asian Canadian sample, but even without it, it is safe to assume that Japanese students in Japan have the least exposure to North American culture, followed by Asian international students who had arrived not so long ago, followed by Asian Canadians who as a group could span several generations.

173 **The eye-tracking data:** Masuda and his colleagues used an eye-tracking machine to see where the participants gazed. They separately counted how often the participants gazed at the central person versus the surrounding people, and how much time they spent on each. Samples differed in expected ways in how much attention they gave the central (versus the surrounding) figure(s). European Canadians who judged the central person's feelings largely kept their gaze on this person; Japanese students in Japan and Asian international students did not differ from each other on most measures. Both groups fixated less often as well as less long on the central person than European Canadian students. The pattern of gaze attention of Asian Canadians held the middle between that of European Canadians and Japanese.

173 **my Sephardic Jewish ancestors:** I am borrowing from the history of another Sephardic Jewish family that was creditably described in Jaap Cohen, *De Onontkoombare Afkomst van Eli d'Oliveira* (Amsterdam: Querido, 2015).

173 **followed . . . seventy Japanese-born school-aged children:** Minoura, "A Sensitive Period for the Incorporation of a Cultural Meaning System: A Study of Japanese Children Growing up in the United States."

174 **continued to align to their new . . . environments:** Minoura herself concludes that there may be a critical age for emotion socialization, because children who had entered the United States before the age of nine were more emotionally acculturated. I do not think Minoura's data provide evidence for a critical age. Her informants were all fifth and sixth grade students at the Japanese weekend school. This means that the kids who entered the United States at an

earlier age were also the ones who had spent most time in the United States. In Minoura's sample, age of entry and length of stay were confounded. Other research converges with the conclusion that there is no critical age of emotion socialization. Pavlenko (*Emotions and Multilingualism*, 10), summarizing the research on second language learning, similarly concludes that "there is no conclusive support for the existence of a critical period for second language learning."

174 **proportion of life:** De Leersnyder, Mesquita, and Kim, "Where Do My Emotions Belong? A Study of Immigrants' Emotional Acculturation"; Jasini et al., "Tuning in Emotionally: Associations of Cultural Exposure with Distal and Proximal Emotional Fit in Acculturating Youth."

174 **having close majority friends:** To decide which minority students were friends with majority peers, we asked both the minority and the majority students in each class to list their best friends. Only when majority and minority students had listed each other as "friends" did we consider it a real friendship, and we found the highest emotional fit for minority students who had mutual feelings of friendship with a majority student (Alba Jasini et al., "Show Me Your Friends, I'll Tell You Your Emotions," *under review*).

175 **more time with majority friends:** Jasini et al., "Tuning in Emotionally: Associations of Cultural Exposure with Distal and Proximal Emotional Fit in Acculturating Youth"; Jasini et al., "Show Me Your Friends, I'll Tell You Your Emotions."

175 **others may also *categorize* emotional episodes:** Barrett, *How Emotions Are Made*.

176 **emotions are any less real:** See, for a similar point, Lisa Feldman Barrett, "Emotions Are Real," *Emotion* 12, no. 3 (2012): 413–29.

176 **incorporating the concept of "feeling good about myself":** The process is described in Batja Mesquita and Hazel R. Markus, "Culture and Emotion: Models of Agency as Sources of Cultural Variation in Emotion," in *Feelings and Emotions: The Amsterdam Symposium*, ed. Antony S. R. Manstead, Nico H. Frijda, and Agneta Fischer (Cambridge, UK: Cambridge University Press, 2004), 341–58.

177 **Sofia knew approximately *when stenahoria* was used:** The example is described by Pavlenko, *Emotions and Multilingualism* (chap. 4).

177 **the concepts from their native culture:** Pavlenko, *Emotions and Multilingualism*, 8–9; Jean-Marc Dewaele, "Reflections on the Emotional and Psychological Aspects of Foreign Language Learning and Use," *Anglistik: International Journal of English Studies* 22, no. 1 (2011): 23–42.

177 **a study on Spanish second-language learning:** Howard Grabois, "The Convergence of Sociocultural Theory and Cognitive Linguistics: Lexical Semantics and the L2 Acquisition of Love, Fear, and Happiness," in *Languages of Sentiment: Cultural Constructions of Emotional Substrates*, ed. Gary B. Palmer and Debra J. Occhi (Amsterdam: John Benjamins Publishing Co., 1999), 201–36.

178 **never lived in a Spanish-speaking environment:** Of course, individuals who have lived in a country for a long time would not only have the native's associations with the words, but also be more proficient in the language, than other learners of L2. However, the word associations of groups with different levels of proficiency, who had not lived in a Spanish-speaking environment, were no different from each other. This makes it less likely that shifts in word associations for those who had lived in Spain for at least three years could be attributed to language proficiency only (Grabois).

178 *anger* **was different from the Dutch** *boos***:** Michael Boiger, Simon De Deyne, and Batja Mesquita, "Emotions in 'the World': Cultural Practices, Products, and Meanings of Anger and Shame in Two Individualist Cultures," *Frontiers in Psychology* 4, no. 867 (2013): Study 3. The links between *anger* words and the behavioral tendencies reported in this paragraph were derived from huge semantic association networks produced by tens of thousands of respondents in each language. Each respondent provided associations for a number of cue words; in total, respondents in each language produced associations for thousands of cue words. The associations reported in this particular study were just a few from the large body of associations that was produced this way.

179 **clouds our understanding:** Pavlenko (*Emotions and Multilingualism*, 173) calls this "the fallacy of understanding."

179 **reluctance of many scientists:** Pavlenko (*Emotions and Multilingualism*, 18–19) is particularly critical of the field of psychology when she astutely observes that it "is perhaps most noteworthy for its detailed reporting of research design and methodology and the use of verification procedures, yet [it is remarkable] how much 'glossing over' of the process of translation takes place." I agree with her.

179 **"I had to make a Japanese out of myself":** Minoura, "A Sensitive Period for the Incorporation of a Cultural Meaning System: A Study of Japanese Children Growing up in the United States," 320.

180 **the fate of many immigrants:** Jozefien De Leersnyder, Heejung S. Kim, and Batja Mesquita, "My Emotions Belong Here and There: Extending the Phenomenon of Emotional Acculturation to Heritage Culture Fit," *Cognition & Emotion* 34, no. 8 (2020): 1–18.

180 **lost some of their original emotional culture:** Fit of the first-generation Turkish immigrants was neither significantly different from the Belgian sample's nor from the Turkish sample's fit with the Turkish pattern; fit of the second-generation Turkish immigrants was no different from the Belgian sample's fit, but different from the Turkish sample's fit with the Turkish emotional pattern (De Leersnyder, Kim, and Mesquita, "My Emotions Belong Here and There: Extending the Phenomenon of Emotional Acculturation to Heritage Culture Fit").

180 **he can relate to them both:** Minoura, "A Sensitive Period for the Incorporation of a Cultural Meaning System: A Study of Japanese Children Growing up in the United States," 320.

181 **an indelible influence:** Stephens, Hamedani, and Townsend, "Difference

Matters: Teaching Students a Contextual Theory of Difference Can Help Them Succeed," 2019, introduce a contextual theory of difference that similarly proposes that (all) people's different backgrounds and social group memberships shape their life experiences (and outcomes).

182 **lose a culture's ways of doing:** De Leersnyder, Kim, and Mesquita, "My Emotions Belong Here and There: Extending the Phenomenon of Emotional Acculturation to Heritage Culture Fit." H. A. Elfenbein and N. Ambady ("Cultural Similarity's Consequences: A Distance Perspective on Cross-Cultural Differences in Emotion Recognition," *Journal of Cross-Cultural Psychology* 34, no. 1 [2003]: 32–110) similarly found that Chinese students in China showed an ingroup advantage for the Chinese pictures over the three other groups, *including* a group of international Chinese students temporarily residing in the United States. This finding might suggest that the cultural ways of face perception erode fairly soon, once one is not part of everyday cultural interactions. However, the sample size for international Chinese students was very small (n=12), and additional research is needed to confirm this conclusion.

182 **Many biculturals switch between their cultures on an everyday basis:** Using a day reconstruction method, Marina Doucerain, Jessica Dere, and Andrew G. Ryder ("Travels in Hyper-Diversity: Multiculturalism and the Contextual Assessment of Acculturation," *International Journal of Intercultural Relations* 37, no. 6 [November 2013]: 686–99) showed that immigrant students at a Canadian university—largely of Arab and Chinese heritage—in fact moved back and forth between contexts that highlighted their mainstream (e.g., Canadian), heritage (e.g., Arab, Chinese), or a hybrid identity (e.g. East Asian Canadians).

183 **prompt the associated ways of doing emotions:** E.g., W. Q. E. Perunovic, D. Heller, and E. Rafaeli, "Within-Person Changes in the of Emotion Structure the Role of Cultural Identification," *Psychological Science* 18, no. 7 (2007): 607–13; De Leersnyder, Kim, and Mesquita, "My Emotions Belong Here and There: Extending the Phenomenon of Emotional Acculturation to Heritage Culture Fit."

183 **happiness and unhappiness . . . in many East Asian cultures?:** Co-occurrence of positive and negative emotions has been referred to as "dialectical emotions." See e.g., Richard P. Bagozzi, Nancy Wong, and Youjae Yi, "The Role of Culture and Gender in the Relationship between Positive and Negative Affect," *Cognition and Emotion* 13, no. 6 (1999): 641–72; Ulrich Schimmack, Shigehiro Oishi, and Ed Diener, "Cultural Influences on the Relation between Pleasant Emotions and Unpleasant Emotions: Asian Dialectic Philosophies or Individualism-Collectivism?," *Cognition & Emotion* 16, no. 6 (2002): 705–19. For a summary of this research, see Mesquita and Leu, "The Cultural Psychology of Emotion."

183 **identified more with Western culture, or more with Asian culture:** Perunovic, Heller, and Rafaeli, "Within-Person Changes in the of Emotion Structure the Role of Cultural Identification."

183 **private space:** De Leersnyder, Kim, and Mesquita, "My Emotions Belong Here and There: Extending the Phenomenon of Emotional Acculturation to Heritage Culture Fit."

183 **Emotion profiles differed by cultural context:** The patterns were also slightly different between first and later generation immigrants. On the one hand, Korean Americans' and first-generation Turkish Belgians' ways of doing emotions were more similar to their Korean/Turkish heritage than to the European American/Belgian norms when they were at home (but not at work/school). On the other hand, second-generation Turkish Belgians were more similar to the Belgian than the Turkish way of doing emotions at work or school (but not at home).

184 **we designed a study to test this:** Jozefien De Leersnyder and Batja Mesquita, "Beyond Display Rules: An Experimental Study of Cultural Differences in Emotions" (Leuven, Belgium, 2021).

185 **differently in the Turkish and the Belgian context:** De Leersnyder and Mesquita, "Beyond Display Rules: An Experimental Study of Cultural Differences in Emotions." Turkish participants in a pilot study primarily perceived the insult as a betrayal to the relationship, whereas Belgian participants perceived it primarily as an attack on their individual integrity (denying their competence).

185 **contempt . . . anger:** P. Rozin et al. ("The CAD Triad Hypothesis: A Mapping between Three Moral Emotions [Contempt, Anger, Disgust] and Three Moral Codes [Community, Autonomy, Divinity]," *Journal of Personality and Social Psychology* 76, no. 4 [1999]: 574–86) find that anger is associated with ethics of autonomy, and that contempt is associated with the ethics of community.

185 **the same group of biculturals:** There is no reason to assume that the biculturals assigned to the Belgian condition or those assigned to the Turkish condition were different. The principle of random assignment plays a big role in psychological experiments. The underlying idea is that differences in outcomes (in this case, emotional behavior) can be attributed to the differences in the conditions, given that randomly assigned individuals come from the same population.

186 **"emotional" at the meeting:** There is actually some research suggesting that "being emotional" helps to remember core features of events: Willem A. Wagenaar, "My Memory: A Study of Autobiographical Memory over Six Years," *Cognitive Psychology* 50, no. 2 (1986): 225–52; Elizabeth A. Kensinger and Daniel L. Schacter, "Memory and Emotion," in *Handbook of Emotions*, ed. Michael Lewis, Jeannette M. Haviland-Jones, and Lisa F. Barrett, 3d ed. (New York: Guilford Press, 2008), 601–17.

186 **ceded some responsibility for my well-being to my colleagues:** These are some of the characteristics of a communal relationship, which Margaret Clark and her colleagues have extensively documented; see e.g., Margaret S. Clark et al., "Communal Relational Context (or Lack Thereof) Shapes Emotional Lives," *Current Opinion in Psychology* 17 (2017): 176–83. In a communal

relationship, partners assume non-contingent responsibility for each other's welfare; the relationship as such is valued by the partners.

187 **Margaret Clark gives the following example:** Clark et al., "Communal Relational Context (or Lack Thereof) Shapes Emotional Lives," 176. Reprinted with permission from Elsevier.

189 **constantly attuning our emotions:** Many examples can be found in Moors, Agnes. "Integration of two skeptical emotion theories: Dimensional appraisal theory and Russell's psychological construction theory." *Psychological Inquiry* 28, no. 1 (2017): 1–19.

189 **Emotional cultures are ever-changing:** E.g., Barbara H. Rosenwein, *Generations of Feeling: A History of Emotions, 600–1700* (Cambridge, UK: Cambridge Univeristy Press, 2016); Peter N. Stearns, "History of Emotions: Issues of Change and Impact," in *Handbook of Emotions*, ed. Michael Lewis, Jeannette M. Haviland-Jones, and Lisa F. Barrett, 3d ed. (New York: Guilford Press, 2008), 17–31.

Chapter 8 EMOTIONS IN A MULTICULTURAL WORLD

190 **Coates describes how . . . his ninth-grade teacher:** Terry Gross, "Ta-Nehisi Coates on Police Brutality, the Confederate Flag and Forgiveness," National Public Radio, December 29, 2015, https://www.npr.org/2015/12/29/46 1337958/ta-nehisi-coates-on-police-brutality-the-confederate-flag-and -forgiveness. Reprinted with the permission of WHYY.Inc.

191 **the Taiwanese toddler Didi:** Fung, "Becoming a Moral Child: The Socialization of Shame among Young Chinese Children."

192 **rather than a form of penance:** I thank my colleague Karen Phalet for this example (personal communication, December 2019).

193 **critical parents raise maladjusted children:** The idea that critical parents raise maladjusted children originally comes from Lewis, "Shame and Guilt in Neurosis." Criticism has been interpreted as "rejection" or "hostility." However, several studies show that parental criticism in interdependent cultures may be associated with adaptive parenting: See Ruth K. Chao, "Beyond Parental Control and Authoritarian Parenting Style: Understanding Chinese Parenting through the Cultural Notion of Training," *Child Development* 65, no. 4 (1994): 1111–19 for a critical discussion.

193 **not merely a matter of intellectual curiosity:** The philosopher Owen Flanagan, reflecting on diversity in morality, similarly suggests that mere tolerance for different moralities does not always suffice. Whether we can think "different strokes for different folks . . . depends on whether the confrontation is notional, in history books, anthropology books, table top in *National Geographic* magazine, or whether the confrontation of different values is real and occurs right here in River City, among neighbors, coinhabitants of a place, a village, a metropolis, or a nation state" (Owen J. Flanagan, *The Geography*

of Morals: Varieties of Moral Possibility [New York: Oxford University Press, 2017], 150).

193 **she should have been "justifiably angry":** Lutz, *Unnatural Emotions*, 167.

193 **The Inuit were mortified:** Briggs, *Never in Anger.*

194 **as a human species, we need kindness:** Jamil Zaki, *The War for Kindness: Building Empathy in a Fractured World* (New York: Penguin Random House, 2019).

194 **"Empathy is the mental superpower...":** Zaki, *The War for Kindness: Building Empathy in a Fractured World*, 4. Note that the notion that empathy as a force to keep societies together is contentious. In his book *Against Empathy*, psychologist Paul Bloom argues against relying on empathy, because empathy shines the spotlight on a limited number of people, and usually those who are close to us or like us; he argues for rational compassion instead.

195 **"...conjures an authentic inner world":** Zaki, *The War for Kindness: Building Empathy in a Fractured World*, 78.

195 **neither directly read ... nor simply "catch":** See, e.g., Gendron, Crivelli, and Barrett, "Universality Reconsidered: Diversity in Making Meaning of Facial Expressions"; A. Fischer and U. Hess, "Mimicking Emotions," *Current Opinion in Psychology* 17 (2017): 151–55, https://doi.org/10.1016/j.copsyc.2017.07.008; Parkinson, *Heart to Heart.*

195 **Projecting your own feelings:** Beatty (*Emotional Worlds*, 267, reprinted with permission by Cambridge University Press) makes a similar point: "If personal experience is useful in understanding others, its usefulness surely depends on relevance, closeness of fit; and relevance, in turn, depends on the historical particularities—in a word, the story. Yet, imagining or placing oneself in someone else's shoes may certainly provide a good start for empathy." Together with several colleagues, Zaki (*The War for Kindness: Building Empathy in a Fractured World*) used virtual reality to conjure up "an authentic inner world." Participants wearing goggles are literally transposed to the world of a person who becomes homeless. They experience being evicted from their home, then landing on a bus ride that accommodates other homeless people like themselves. Spending some time in the homeless person's shoes increased participants' enduring support for the homeless. It does not hurt to take the perspective of another person, but it is not enough.

196 **negative feelings would be more comforting:** Birgit Koopmann-Holm and Jeanne L. Tsai, "Focusing on the Negative: Cultural Differences in Expressions of Sympathy," *Journal of Personality and Social Psychology* 107, no. 6 (2014): 1092–1115. Birgit Koopmann-Holm et al., "What Constitutes a Compassionate Response? The Important Role of Culture," *Emotion*, n.d.; Birgit Koopmann-Holm et al., "Seeing the Whole Picture? Avoided Negative Affect and Processing of Others' Suffering," *Personality and Social Psychology Bulletin* 46, no. 9 (2020): 1363–77. Koopmann-Holm finds that differences in all these studies can be accounted for by how much Americans and Germans want to avoid negative feelings

196 **unpacking the emotional episode:** What I call "unpacking the emotional episode" has been called "narrative understanding" by anthropologist Andrew Beatty (*Emotional Worlds*).

197 **resonate with the maternal love of Simbo women:** Christine Dureau, "Translating Love," *Ethos* 40, no. 2 (2012): 142–63. The rhetorical question of the Simbo woman appears on p. 150, the conversation with Lisa on p. 142.

198 **not be too sure too soon:** Inga-Britt Krause, "Family Therapy and Anthropology: A Case for Emotions," *Journal of Family Therapy* 15, no. 1 (February 1, 1993): 35–56; Beatty, *Emotional Worlds*, chap. 8.

198 **"the problem with empathy . . .":** Leavitt, "Meaning and Feeling in the Anthropology of Emotions," 530.

198 **not the same as sharing:** Affective and cognitive empathy are commonly distinguished: affective empathy is "concerned with the experience of emotion," and cognitive empathy is "the ability to understand another's feelings related closely to theory of mind" (Benjamin M. P. Cuff et al., "Empathy: A Review of the Concept," *Emotion Review* 8, no. 2 [2016]: 147). Understanding emotions would be closer to what has been called "cognitive empathy."

198 **the *incongruence* of your emotions:** This point is made by Dureau ("Translating Love," 146).

198 **Empathy in a cross-cultural setting:** Andrew Beatty argues for "narrative empathy" (*Emotional Worlds*, 159, reprinted with permission by Cambridge University Press): "Approach to emotion through narrative recognizes the distinctiveness of emotional formation in other cultures and the possibility of sharply different kinds of experience. It offers a path to understanding specific episodes more empirically valid and more ethnographically interesting than a broad-brush static universalism. At the same time, it avoids mystification of out-and-out cultural relativism, the assumption that people who have different concepts of emotion and inhabit different lifeworlds must be opaque to us. For the narrativist, opacity lies not in alterity but in the observer's blinkered gaze, the shrinking of the emotion to an instant." See also Leavitt, "Meaning and Feeling in the Anthropology of Emotions."

199 **resonance:** The Norwegian anthropologist Unni Wikan provides a valuable reflection on the topic: "We need to refine our ways of attending, thus better grasp what people are up to, their multiple compelling concerns, and what is at stake for them, against a background of the social relations in which they are engaged and the resistance life offers them" (U. Wikan, *Resonance: Beyond the Words* [Chicago: University of Chicago Press, 2013], chap. 1).

199 **cross-cultural psychiatry and psychotherapy:** Batja Mesquita, "Emoties Vanuit Een Cultureel Perspectief," in *Handboek Transculturele Psychiatrie En Psychotherapie*, ed. Joop de Jong and Margo van den Berg (Amsterdam: Harcourt, 1996), 101–13.

199 **mental health disparities:** *Mental Health: Culture, Race and Ethnicity* (Rockville, MD: U.S. Office of the Surgeon General, 2001). Inadequacy of mental health provisions takes many shapes: racial and ethnic groups with

mental health problems seek less support from mental health providers, are more poorly diagnosed, and receive less-adequate or culturally-insensitive treatment.

199 **replaced by "cultural humility":** The *DSM-5* of the American Psychiatric Association has added the Cultural Formulation Interview, which provides structure to the assessment interview, allowing clinicians to collect information about the patients' (illness) experience, and social and cultural context (Neil Krishan Aggarwal et al., "The Cultural Formulation Interview since DSM-5: Prospects for Training, Research, and Clinical Practice," *Transcultural Psychiatry* 57, no. 4 (2020): 496–514). See also Patricia Arredondo et al., "Guidelines on Multicultural Education, Training, Research, Practice, and Organizational Change for Psychologists," *American Psychologist* 58, no. 5 (2003): 377–402.

200 **"embrace[d] uncertainty as a path to competence":** See Laurence J. Kirmayer, "Embracing Uncertainty as a Path to Competence: Cultural Safety, Empathy, and Alterity in Clinical Training," *Culture, Medicine & Psychiatry* 37 (2013): 365–72. Kirmayer points out that the term "cultural competence" also assumes that the clinician holds the expertise; in contrast, "cultural humility" emphasizes "the importance of clinicians' ability to acknowledge, tolerate and explore their own experiences of uncertainty, confusion and limitations in intercultural clinical work" (p. 369).

200 **all the more reason to want to find out:** My friend, clinical psychologist Sherry Johnson, helped me reach this conclusion, and validated it as useful to clinical practice.

200 **failure to fulfill her role:** Reported in Van Acker et al., "Hoe Emoties Verschillen Tussen Culturen."

200 **less respectable (in the eyes of others):** See chapter 4 for a discussion of honor-based shame. Shame is in the eyes of others. In this case, the result seems to be the urge to care for her mother.

201 **find common ground with their client:** Steven Regeser López et al., "Defining and Assessing Key Behavioral Indicators of the Shifting Cultural Lenses Model of Cultural Competence," *Transcultural Psychiatry* 57, no. 4 (2020): 594–609.

201 **your ethno-racial or national identity:** Wen-Shing Tseng ("Culture and Psychotherapy: Review and Practical Guidelines," *Transcultural Psychiatry* 36, no. 2 [1999]: 165) makes a similar observation: "Although cultural issues tend to be noticed only when cultural differences between patient and therapist are clearly evident, all psychotherapy is cross-cultural in that no two people have internalized identical constructions of their cultural worlds."

201 **Each of these junctures leads us:** Davis et al. ("The Multicultural Orientation Framework: A Narrative Review") note that *culturally humble* therapists take advantage of *cultural opportunities*—markers of the client's cultural beliefs, values and other aspects of the client's cultural identity that can be explored— and become *culturally comfortable*—at ease, open, calm, and relaxed with diverse others (p. 92). I propose that the culturally humble therapist can take

the junctures of cultural differences in emotion as *cultural opportunities*. Doing so will ultimately make them more culturally comfortable.

201 **"what people are up to, their multiple compelling concerns, and what is at stake for them":** Wikan, *Resonance: Beyond the Words*, chap. 1.

202 **shameful and offensive:** Patricia M. Rodriguez Mosquera, "Honor and Harmed Social-Image. Muslims' Anger and Shame about the Cartoon Controversy," *Cognition and Emotion* 32, no. 6 (2018): 1205–19. Psychologist Patricia Rodriguez Mosquera surveyed one hundred British Muslims about their "own opinions" on "the Danish illustrations of the Prophet Muhammad published in several European newspapers." The participants, who self-identified as Muslim and scored high on honor orientation, found the illustration harmful to their reputation as Muslims and very offensive.

202 **honor is a shared commodity:** E.g., Patricia M. Rodriguez Mosquera, Leslie X. Tan, and Faisal Saleem, "Shared Burdens, Personal Costs on the Emotional and Social Consequences of Family Honor," *Journal of Cross-Cultural Psychology* 45, no. 3 (2014): 400–16; Uskul et al., "Honor Bound: The Cultural Construction of Honor in Turkey and the Northern United States."

204 **adhered to the health recommendations:** Jeanne L. Tsai, L. Chim, and T. Sims, "Ideal Affect and Consumer Behavior," in *Handbook of Culture and Consumer Behavior*, ed. S. Ng and A. Y. Lee (New York: Oxford University Press, 2015). In fact, the best predictor of adherence to physician's recommendations was whether the size of a doctor's smile and activation of voice matched the activation the participant wanted to feel *that day*. Daily preferences fluctuated, even within the same person. Yet, on average, cultural groups differed with respect to the activation of positive affect they considered "right." Treatment adherence was higher in patients who found the doctor's affective behavior to be "right."

205 **to discuss a disagreement:** Michael Boiger, Alexander Kirchner-Häusler, Anna Schouten, Yukiko Uchida, and Batja Mesquita, "Different Bumps in the Road: The Emotional Dynamics of Couple Disagreements in Belgium and Japan," *Emotion*, 2020. Schouten, Anna, Michael Boiger, Yukiko Uchida, Katie Hoemann, Camille Paille, and Batja Mesquita, "Emotional Behaviors in Japanese and Belgian Disagreement Interactions," Leuven, Belgium.

206 **I agree with anthropologist Andrew Beatty:** The quote appears in Beatty, *Emotional Worlds*, 158. Reprinted with permission by Cambridge University Press.

207 **the futures of students:** Johanna Wald and Daniel J. Losen, "Defining and Redirecting a School-to-Prison Pipeline," *New Directions for Youth Development* 2003, no. 99 (2003): 9–15; Jason A. Okonofua and Jennifer L. Eberhardt, "Two Strikes: Race and the Disciplining of Young Students," *Psychological Science* 26, no. 5 (2015): 617–24.

207 **Breakdowns in compassion:** Making use of observational classroom data, Christopher A. Hafen et al. ("Teaching Through Interactions in Secondary School Classrooms: Revisiting the Factor Structure and Practical Application of the Classroom Assessment Scoring System–Secondary," *Journal of Early Adolescence*

35, no. 5–6 [2015]: 651–80). found that the level and intensity of expressed negativity among teachers and students ("negative climate") was higher as the teacher's management of class behavior ("behavior management") was at stake.

207 **"to understand and value students' experiences":** Jason A. Okonofua, David Paunesku, and Gregory M. Walton, "Brief Intervention to Encourage Empathic Discipline Cuts Suspension Rates in Half among Adolescents," *Proceedings of the National Academy of Sciences of the United States of America* 113, no. 19 (2016): 5221–26.

207 **it cut the number of suspensions . . . in half:** Okonofua, Paunesku, and Walton, "Brief Intervention to Encourage Empathic Discipline Cuts Suspension Rates in Half among Adolescents."

208 **add emotional and social skills:** Maurice J. Elias, *Academic and Social-Emotional Learning. Educational Practices Series* (Geneva: International Bureau of Education, 2003); James M. Wilce and Janina Fenigsen, "Emotion Pedagogies: What Are They, and Why Do They Matter?," *Ethos* 44, no. 2 (2016): 81–95.

208 **"emotional literacy":** Marc A. Brackett et al., "Enhancing Academic Performance and Social and Emotional Competence with the RULER Feeling Words Curriculum," *Learning and Individual Differences* 22, no. 2 (2012): 219.

208 **it does pay off:** Claire Blewitt et al., "Social and Emotional Learning Associated With Universal Curriculum-Based Interventions in Early Childhood Education and Care Centers: A Systematic Review and Meta-Analysis," *JAMA Network Open* 1, no. 8 (2018): e185727; Joseph A. Durlak et al., "The Impact of Enhancing Students' Social and Emotional Learning: A Meta-Analysis of School-Based Universal Interventions," *Child Development* 82, no. 1 (2011): 405–32. Emotional and social learning programs consist of an amalgam of nonacademic content and class processes that are implemented all at one. It is not clear, therefore, which part of the programs is responsible for their success.

208 **particularly clear for young children:** Blewitt et al., "Social and Emotional Learning Associated With Universal Curriculum-Based Interventions."

208 **"emotions" as the letters of the alphabet:** E.g., Neil Humphrey et al., "The PATHS Curriculum for Promoting Social and Emotional Well-Being among Children Aged 7–9 Years: A Cluster RCT," *Public Health Research* 6, no. 10 (2018): 1–116; Marc A. Brackett, *Permission to Feel: Unlocking the Power of Emotions to Help Our Kids, Ourselves, and Our Society Thrive* (New York: Celadon Books, 2019); Marc A. Brackett et al., "RULER: A Theory-Driven, Systemic Approach to Social, Emotional, and Academic Learning," *Educational Psychologist* 54, no. 3 (2019): 144–61. The idea in these programs is that children practice emotions until they are fluent—that is, identify them in themselves and others.

209 **unwittingly defined as literacy in the dominant culture:** A similar point has been made by Wilce and Fenigsen, "Emotion Pedagogies: What Are They, and Why Do They Matter?"; and Ilana Gershon, "Neoliberal Agency," *Current Anthropology* 52, no. 4 (2011): 537–55.

209 **create common ground within the school:** See for a similar analysis, Hoemann, Xu, and Barrett, "Emotion Words, Emotion Concepts, and Emotional Development in Children: A Constructionist Hypothesis." Hoemann makes the very important observation that there are no "correct" or "incorrect" emotion concepts because there are no single sets of physical features on which to make this determination (p. 1840). Therefore, any teaching of concepts will provide students with knowledge about a (dominant) social, but not physical, reality.

209 **"when home and school collaborate":** Elias, *Academic and Social-Emotional Learning*, 19. This is assuming that both are willing and motivated to implement the same type of emotional literacy.

210 **the growing call for "equity":** E.g., Robert J. Jagers, Deborah Rivas-Drake, and Brittney Williams, "Transformative Social and Emotional Learning (SEL): Toward SEL in Service of Educational Equity and Excellence," *Educational Psychologist* 54, no. 3 (2019): 162–84.

210 **not just by generally respecting others:** As is a goal in many of these programs: e.g., Elias, Academic and Social-Emotional Learning; Linda Dusenbury et al., "An Examination of Frameworks for Social and Emotional Learning (SEL) Reflected in State K-12 Learning Standards," CASEL Collaborating States Initiative, February 2019; Robert J. Jagers, Deborah Rivas-Drake, and Teresa Borowski, "Equity and Social Emotional Learning: A Cultural Analysis," *Frameworks*, November 2018: 17, http://nationalequityproject.org/.

210 **cultural fluency with a second culture:** This point was also made by Jagers, Rivas-Drake, and Williams, "Transformative Social and Emotional Learning (SEL)."

Afterword

213 **The brain wires itself:** E.g., Kirmayer, Laurence J., Carol M. Worthman, and Shinobu Kitayama, "Introduction: Co-Constructing Culture, Mind, and Brain," in *Culture, Mind, and Brain: Emerging Concepts, Models, and Applications*, edited by Lawrence J. Kirmayer, Carol M. Worthman, Shinobu Kitayama, Robert Lemelson, and Constance A. Cummings, 1–49 (Cambridge, UK: Cambridge University Press, 2020).

213 **emotions are not excepted:** Maria Gendron, Batja Mesquita, and Lisa Feldman Barrett, "The Brain as a Cultural Artifact: Concepts, Actions, and Experiences within the Human Affective Niche," in *Culture, Mind, and Brain: Emerging Concepts, Models, and Applications*, edited by Laurence J. Kirmayer, Carol M. Worthman, Shinobu Kitayama, Robert Lemelson, and Constance A. Cummings (Cambridge, UK: Cambridge University Press, 2020), 188–222.

INDEX

Page numbers after 220 refer to notes.